D0064632

Rites and Religions
of the
Anglo-Saxons

Rites and Religions
of the
Anglo-Saxons

Gale R. Owen

DORSET
PRESS

All rights reserved. No part of this publication may be
reproduced, stored in a retrieval system, or transmitted,
in any form or by any means, electronic, mechanical,
photocopying, recording or otherwise, without the prior
permission of the Publisher

This edition published by Dorset Press, a division of Marboro
Books Corporation, by arrangement with David and Charles
(Publishers) Limited
1985 Dorset Press

Library of Congress Cataloging in Publication Data

Owen, Gale R.
  Rites and religions of the Anglo-Saxons.
  Bibliography: p.
  Includes index.
  1. England—Church history—Anglo-Saxon period,
449-1006. 2. England—Religious life and customs. 3.
Funeral rites and ceremonies—England. I. Title.
BR749.095 1981   293'.0947   81-66333

ISBN 0-88029-046-3

Formerly ISBN 0-7153-7759-0

Printed in the United States of America

For
R. A. C.
and
F. G. O.

Contents

Acknowledgements

It is a pleasure to record my thanks to those who have contributed, directly and indirectly, to the completion of this book. My interest in the Anglo-Saxon period was first aroused by my teachers at Newcastle University, Professor Barbara Strang and Dr Richard Bailey. My colleagues at Manchester University have been a constant source of help and discussions with students, both undergraduate and extra-mural, have guided me in shaping the material which has gone into this book. I am particularly grateful to Mr John Allegro who encouraged me to write it; to Mr Dennis Bradley, Miss Celia J. Watkin and Dr Kenneth Stevenson for discussing with me the translations from Latin and Old English and the Christian history, respectively; to Mrs Gillian Williams who typed the manuscript and made several constructive suggestions; and to Mrs Frances G. Owen and Mr Richard Crocker for their help in assembling and checking the material.

Quotations appear by kind permission of the following: G. N. Garmonsway, J. Simpson and J. M. Dent and Sons Ltd (*Beowulf and its Analogues*), D. Whitelock and Eyre Methuen Ltd (*English Historical Documents, I*), Columbia University Press (*The Anglo-Saxon Poetic Records*), Penguin Books Ltd (Bede, Tacitus, *Gods and Myths of Northern Europe*), Oxford University Press (*The Regularis Concordia*) and Phillimore and Co Ltd (Gildas).

I owe a special debt of gratitude to Mrs Christine Wetherell who drew most of the figures.

Gale R. Owen
Manchester 1980

1

Gods and Legends

The Roman province of *Britannia* had seen many gods. The conquering Roman army had tolerated the Celtic gods worshipped by the native population and had been responsible for introducing more of them, of which the most important were the three Mother Goddesses. About forty of the Celtic gods, major and minor, worshipped in Britain are known to us by name. They are commemorated in stone inscriptions, their names Romanized into such forms as Conventina, Latis and Matunus.

The Romans suppressed druidism, but imported other cults. Among the official gods of Rome, Jupiter, Mars and Mercury were particularly acknowledged in Britain. The imperial cult—worship of the Roman Emperor himself—was also introduced. Other, foreign religions came to Britain under Roman influence, including Mithraism, the colourful cult of the young god Mithras who sacrificed the bull. Christianity had arrived in the second century AD. It first took root among the poorer sections of society but had become firmly established among the more prosperous classes by the fourth century.

The young Christian Church in Britain had produced martyrs and fathered a famous heretic. The most famous of the martyrs, St Alban, was executed at Verulamium in the early fourth century, probably during the persecutions of Diocletian. The heretic, the scholar Pelagius, flourished in Rome and Carthage in the first years of the fifth century, but had been born in Britain. The British branch of Christianity was sufficiently in touch with the continental Church to send three bishops to the Council of Arles in 314 and the Council of Ariminum in 360; and to receive visits in 429 and 447 from St Germanus, Bishop of Auxerre, who came to combat the Pelagian heresy.

Yet the flourishing Christian faith in Britain was to receive such a blow that in 597 missionaries had to reintroduce it. By the beginning of the fifth century the Roman army had withdrawn from its remote province of *Britannia* and the civilizing influence of the Mediterranean was gone. The subsequent invasion by barbaric Anglo-Saxon peoples plunged England into a century-and-a-half of heathenism. Christianity survived only in the western extremities of the British Isles, in Wales, Cornwall and Ireland, where the invaders did not penetrate. Cut off from Gaul and Rome by a belt of Germanic paganism, the Celtic Church developed in isolation, continuing practices which rapidly became out of date by Roman standards. In Ireland there was nurtured a Christian art uniquely Celtic.

In retrospect, the Germanic conquest of England is hardly surprising. Since the withdrawal of the Roman army the Romanized Britons had continued to govern themselves for half a century but, bedevilled by attacks from the Picts in Scotland, the Scots in Ireland and piratical Saxons in the Channel, and finally weakened by plague, the Celtic population of England succumbed. According to tradition, Germanic people were invited into Kent as a peace-keeping force against the existing enemies, but they rebelled against their hosts, opening the way to a major invasion. Romano-British culture gave way to Anglo-Saxon. Its language was replaced by English and its religions disappeared before northern paganism. We have a contemporary account of the conquest by Gildas, a Welsh monk, which shows that the British people were shaken not only by the violence of the assault, but also by the heathenism of the attackers. Gildas assumed that the pagan invaders were God's punishment for the backslidings of the British Christians:

> In just punishment for the crimes that had gone before, a fire heaped up and nurtured by the hand of the impious easterners spread from sea to sea. It devastated town and country round about, and, once it was alight, it did not die down until it had burned almost the whole surface of the island and was licking the western ocean with its fierce red tongue...
>
> All the major towns were laid low by the repeated battering of enemy rams; laid low, too, all the inhabitants—church leaders, priests and people alike, as the swords glinted all around and the flames crackled. It was a sad sight. In the middle of the squares the foundation-stones of high walls and towers that had been torn from their lofty base, holy altars, fragments of corpses, covered (as it were) with a purple crust of congealed blood, looked as though they had been mixed up in some dreadful wine-press.
>
> (*De Excidio*, 24, 1; 24, 3; p.27)

Modern scholars find social and economic reasons for the invasion. Land-hungry and over-populated, the Germanic tribes had been moving south-westwards through Europe for two centuries in what is now recognized as a Migration Age. In their movement the barriers between individual tribes were broken down to some extent, and the invaders of England probably consisted of a mixture of tribal groups, with the characteristics of one people or another predominating in different areas. The historian Bede, reconstructing the origin of the English people almost three centuries after the invasion, tells us that they consisted of Angles (from Denmark), Saxons (from North Germany) and Jutes (from Denmark). The resemblance between the Old English language and Old Frisian, together with archaeo-

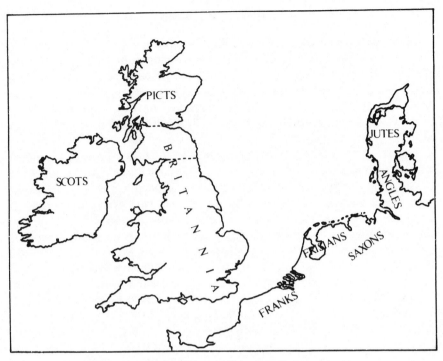

I   Britannia and her neighbours

logical evidence, demonstrates that among the invaders there was an element from Frisia (North Holland). Archaeologists are now also convinced that settlers from the Frankish Rhineland (Germany) contributed to the population of England, particularly in Kent.

The Anglo-Saxons, then, were kin to the continental German tribes, which had lived on the fringe of the Roman Empire, and to the Scandinavians, who, as the Vikings, were later to terrorize the civilized world. There were similarities between the languages and tribal traditions of all these peoples. In matters of religion groups might differ slightly from each other, but they shared a northern heathenism distinct from the heathenism of the Romano-Britons and anathema to Christians.

Gildas's view that the natives of Britain were either exterminated or expelled is perhaps extreme—probably there was some degree of co-existence and intermarriage—but Anglo-Saxon culture unmistakably predominated. In terms of civilization, the invasion was a retrograde step for Britain. The conquerors did not build or carve in stone, they did not write Roman script, they rarely produced naturalistic art, preferring abstract patterns. For those who wish to understand the minds and beliefs of their English ancestors, this is frustrating. No altars or idols, no inscribed names of gods or paintings of heathen rites guide us.

7

Fortunately Germanic paganism was sometimes recorded by observers from more advanced cultures. The Roman scholar Tacitus described heathen rites among the Rhineland tribes in *Germania*, which was written in the last decade of the first century AD. The Arab traveller Ibn Fadlan described in detail a pagan Viking funeral that he witnessed in the tenth century. Evidence like this is invaluable in building up a picture of Germanic rites.

The Anglo-Saxons themselves became literate and learned to depict human activities naturalistically in art only when, centuries after their arrival, they came under the influence of the Christian Church and its traditions of scholarship. Christian scholars, in mainland Germany as well as in England, were naturally more anxious to suppress than to record the pagan rites that their Church deplored, although in rare cases literary motifs rooted in paganism survive in Christian poetry simply because they had become part of a literary tradition (like the Beasts of Battle described on p.15). The nineteenth-century German scholar Jacob Grimm found in folk- and fairy-tales a wealth of material which he derived ultimately from heathen mythology.

In Scandinavia, where Christianity came late (variously in the tenth, eleventh and twelfth centuries), pagan mythology survived longest and was preserved in written form. The fullest source of information is the *Prose Edda* (*c*.1220) the work of an Icelandic scholar, Snorri Sturluson, who brought together stories of the northern gods as they survived in his time. The *Edda* gives an attractive account of gods and goddesses with distinctive characteristics who had adventures with giants, monsters and men. But, as a twentieth-century scholar warns: 'We must avoid the common error of supposing that the myths which we possess grew out of a fixed and permanent heathen faith possessed by the whole Germanic world' (H. R. Ellis Davidson, *Gods and Myths of Northern Europe*, p.14). Thirteenth-century tales of Scandinavian gods must be used with caution in interpreting the beliefs of Anglo-Saxon pagans in the fifth and sixth centuries.

The names of some heathen gods have survived in England, in place-names, in names of weekdays and thinly disguised as ancestors claimed by Anglo-Saxon kings.

Woden is the best documented of the pagan gods acknowledged by the Anglo-Saxons. His name is preserved in our word Wednesday (Old English *Wodenes-dæg*), and numerous English place-names, some obsolete, some still current, testify to his cult. They include Wednesfield (Staffs.), *Wodnesfeld* (Glos.), *Wodnesfeld* and *Wednysfeld* (both once field-names in Essex), which imply that areas of open land were named after Woden. A place that seems to have once been called *Wodnes beorg* (Adam's Grave, Alton Priors, Wilts.) together with Woodnesborough and Wormshill (also, significantly, called *Godeselle* [God's hill], Kent) record hills sacred to Woden, as perhaps

II   Early Anglo-Saxon England

does Wenslow Half Hundred (Beds.). Wensley (Beds. and Derbys.) records that woods or glades were dedicated to Woden. Wednesbury (Staffs.) may mark a fortified place dedicated to the god, perhaps part of the same sacred area as nearby Wednesfield. *Wodnes dene* (Wilts.) suggests that a valley was named after Woden, and, being close to *Wodnes beorg* and Wansdyke (see p.10), indicates that a large area may have been dedicated to the god. We must not assume too readily, however, that all these place-names commemorate heathen temples or sanctuaries. The settlers may have named pre-existing landmarks after their god without necessarily attributing sanctity to the places. They may have assumed that features which they could not have built themselves, lacking the skill, must be the work of gods, just as

9

they assumed Roman buildings to be the work of giants (see p.65). They certainly named existing earthworks after Woden, either in the forms Wansdyke (Hants., Som., Wilts.), Woden's Dyke (Hants.) or with names derived from Woden's nickname Grim, which apparently arose from the belief that the god habitually appeared in disguise (OE *grima*: a mask, visor or helmet). Thus we find Grim's Ditch (Herts., Middx., Oxon., Wilts.), Grims Dyke (Hants.), Gryme's Dyke (Essex) and the obsolete *Grimesdich*, a name for Woden's Dyke (Hants.) recorded in the thirteenth century. The nickname also survives in Grimsburyburh (Oxon.) where it again refers to an older earthwork. Perhaps this custom of attributing ancient features to Woden lies behind the statement, among gnomic sayings in the eleventh-century *Exeter Book*, that Woden made idols: *Woden worhte weos* (*ASPR*, III, p.161, line 132).

The large amount of place-name evidence demonstrates that the name of Woden came readily to the lips of Anglo-Saxon settlers, being found in the Jutish/Frankish kingdom of Kent, in the Saxon regions of Essex and Wessex and in the Anglian Mercia. According to surviving evidence the nickname Grim seems to have been confined to the Saxon kingdoms.

The scholar Bede, in his *Ecclesiastical History* which was completed in the year AD 731, tells us that Hengest and Horsa, the legendary brothers believed to be the first settlers of Kent and of Anglo-Saxon England, were descendants of Woden:

> They were the sons of Victgilsus, whose father was Vitta, whose father was Vecta, son of Woden, from whose stock sprang the royal house of many provinces.
>
> (*HE*, I, 15; p.56)

That Anglo-Saxon kings did indeed claim to be descendants of Woden is proved by the occurrence of his name in their genealogies. In the following list of Mercian kings (from Corpus Christi College, Cambridge MS 183) we may note the names of Penda, a famous pagan Anglo-Saxon king (632–54), of Offa the Angle, a legendary king mentioned in the Old English poems *Beowulf* and *Widsið*, an ancestor of whom the Mercians were extremely proud, and ultimately Woden, who is described as *Frealafing*. (The suffix *-ing* means 'son of'.) This genealogy, like other similar lists, does not mark a genuine tradition handed down from generation to generation. It was compiled after the eighth century, and arranges real and fictitious ancestors in rhythmic, alliterating groups of names.

> Æðelred Pending, Penda Pybbing, Pybba Creoding, Creoda Cynewalding, Cynewald Cnebbing, Cnebba Icling, Icel Eomæring, Eomær Angengeoting, Angengiot Offing, Offa Wærmunding, Wærmund Wihtlæging, Wihtlæg Wioþolgeoting, Weoþolgiot Wodning, Woden Frealafing.
>
> (Dumville (ed.), 'The Anglian collection of royal genealogies', p.33)

Seven Anglo-Saxon royal houses include Woden son of Frealaf among their ancestors: the Anglian dynasties of Bernicia, Deira, East Anglia, Lindsey and Mercia; Kent; and the Saxon kingdom of Wessex. Recent study of the genealogies suggests that Woden was originally adopted as forbear by an Anglian line, one of a group of pseudo-ancestors absorbed by Kent and Wessex during a period of Anglian supremacy, perhaps on the occasion of a dynastic marriage in each case. It is unlikely that the Christian scholars who created these pedigrees were interested in Woden's original paganism; but it is clear that the aura of his name persisted since most Anglo-Saxon dynasties felt that to have him as an ancestor was an important factor in legitimizing their rule.

The Anglo-Saxon Woden is essentially the same deity as the Odin of Scandinavian mythology, the Teutonic god who survives still as the Wotan of Wagner's operas in the *Ring* cycle. The Germanic peoples identified him with the Roman god Mercury (in a Latin-Old English glossary Woden renders *Mercurium*). This association is apparent still if we compare our 'Wednesday' with the equivalent words from Latin languages: French *mercredi*, Italian *mercoledi*. According to the Old Icelandic poem *Hávamál* Woden/Odin was hanged on a tree for nine days and nights, pierced with a spear, a voluntary sacrifice, as a result of which he learned wisdom, the secret of runes:

> ... I hung
> on the windswept Tree,
> through nine days and nights.
> I was stuck with a spear
> and given to Odin,
> myself given to myself ...
> I peered downward,
> I took up the runes,
> screaming, I took them—
> then I fell back.
>
> (Ellis Davidson (trans.), *Gods and Myths*, pp. 143–4)

The Anglo-Saxons probably knew this tradition that Woden was associated with the secrets of runic writing. There seems to be a reference to this belief in *Salamon and Saturn*, an Old English prose text in the form of a dialogue about the nature of creation and the world:

Tell me, who first set letters?
I tell thee, Mercurius the giant

> (Kemble (trans.), p.193 and p.197 note)

11

The identification made between Woden and Mercury already mentioned explains the Roman name, but the knowledge of letters mentioned in the text belongs to Woden's mythology.

Scandinavian mythology demonstrates that Woden/Odin was one of a family of gods, known as the Æsir. The Anglo-Saxons almost certainly knew this term. It may survive embedded in the place-name Easerfield Coppice (Worcs.), formerly *Eswaldfield* (although, as this is a late recording, from the seventeenth century, it is not certain that the name goes back to Anglo-Saxon times). Otherwise the Æsir may be traced in the Old English word *os* (god). *Os* is most often found as an element in personal names, such as Oswald, but it was also the name of the runic symbol ᚠ. The Old English *Rune Poem* tells us:

ᚠ (os) byþ ordfruma   ælcre spræce

(*ASPR*, VI, p.28, line 10)

'*os* is the origin of all speech'

which might be a further reference to Woden, called *os* as the most important of the Æsir, as the discoverer of runes.

In the Icelandic *Hávamál* the god boasts his knowledge of magical practices, and we find a reference to this tradition, again probably associated with runes, in the Old English metrical *Nine Herbs Charm*, one of a collection of charms in an eleventh-century manuscript. The poem has enumerated the names and properties of nine herbs to be used against snake-bite:

Wyrm com snican,   toslat he man;
ða genam Woden   VIIII wuldortanas,
sloh ða þa næddran,   þæt heo on VIIII tofleah.

(*ASPR*, VI, pp.119–20, lines 31–3)

A snake came creeping, it wounded someone. Then Woden took nine 'glory-twigs', then struck the snake so that it flew into nine pieces.

The 'glory-twigs' would be pieces of wood marked with runic symbols, representing the names of the herbs and providing a magic cure.

Although Woden had healing power through his knowledge of magic and runes, in northern legend he was a character noted for treachery. Snorri relates various anecdotes about him, but it is clear that essentially he was a god of battles and the slain. Traditionally he had brought about discord among the gods by throwing a spear. The practice of throwing a spear over the enemy before a battle evidently persisted in the North as part of the god's cult. Bede (*HE*, II, 13) tells the story of Coifi, a pagan priest associated with the court of King Edwin of Northumbria, who was converted to Christianity in 627. His gesture of repudiation was to fling a spear into the heathen temple before firing it. Bede saw this as a gesture of rebellion, explaining that priests had previously been forbidden to carry arms, but Hilda Ellis Davidson suggests that Coifi had been a follower of Woden and was, appropriately, using the god's own gesture to indicate that he was now an enemy of the old heathenism (*Gods and Myths*, pp.50–1). The same scholar has suggested that the cult of Woden may lie behind certain Anglo-Saxon burial rites (*The Battle God of the Vikings*, pp.4, 6): it was usual practice among the pagan Anglo-Saxons that when a man was buried his spear and shield were buried with him (see p.70). In a society where every man might be called upon to hunt for food and to defend his settlement against enemies, it was natural that each man would own a spear and shield; but to equip him for the grave as a warrior may be the act of Woden's followers, for Woden/Odin, according to Norse mythology, was a god of warriors. It was his role to select, from those fighting in a battle, who were to be victorious and who slain. The fallen warriors were taken to Valhalla where he presided. Valkyries (choosers of the slain) were the god's agents in this selection of warriors. We may have an illustration of this belief in one of the scenes decorating the Sutton Hoo helmet (plate 1), a Swedish piece owned by a seventh-century king of East Anglia. On a series of plaques which originally circled and mounted

Fig 1   'Battle scene' plaque from Sutton Hoo helmet

the helmet, there is stamped a battle scene: a fallen warrior is being trampled by a horse, which he stabs with his sword. The horse's rider is armed with a spear. A tiny figure, seated behind him, guides the spear. The wearer of the helmet hoped, no doubt, to be similarly favoured.

Hilda Ellis Davidson believes the cult of Woden/Odin is celebrated in the figures of men wearing horned helmets, dancing and carrying spears, who appear occasionally in Germanic art. A pair of such figures appears as ornament stamped on metal plaques decorating the cheek-pieces of the Sutton Hoo helmet. Another, naked except for a belt, appears on a sixth-century buckle (plate 2) from Finglesham, Kent. (According to Tacitus [*Germania*, 6], Germanic warriors traditionally fought naked, or wearing only cloaks. Helmets and breastplates were rare. A skilful dance in which naked youths dodged spears and swords was a traditional Germanic sport [*Germania*, 24].) Similar figures appear on a fragment of bronze from Caenby (Lincs.) and on the handle of an implement from Dover (Kent). The latter object was found in a woman's grave, and so was a similar implement from

Fig 2 'Dancing warriors' plaque from Sutton Hoo helmet

Breach Downs (Kent).[1] Although Woden was a god of battle, women were not excluded from his worship. Indeed in Scandinavian mythology women sometimes chose to die violently in company with their husband or lover in association with this god's cult. Anglo-Saxon women buried in the seventh century at Gilton and Kingston (Kent) carried miniature spears among the trinkets (plate 3) hanging by chains from their belts. They were probably amulets invoking Woden's protection.

Two wolves and two ravens were the familiars of Woden/Odin. These creatures are probably the source of the so-called Beasts of Battle, which appear as a stock literary motif in Anglo-Saxon poems as a prelude to battle, a warning of the carrion which will result.[2]

> Dynedan scildas,
> hlude hlummon.   Þæs se hlanca gefeah
> wulf in walde,   ond se wanna hrefn,
> wælgifre fugel.   Wistan begen
> þæt him ða þeodguman   þohton tilian
> fylle on fægum.

> (*ASPR*, IV, p.105, lines 204–9)

Shields clanged, resounded loudly. The lean wolf in the wood rejoiced at it, and the dark raven, bloodthirsty bird. They both knew that the warriors intended to provide for them their fill of doomed men.

The Beasts of Battle appear as a poetic convention in overtly Christian poems, having lost their pagan associations. The quotation is from *Judith*, a tenth-century narrative poem on a biblical subject.

In Scandinavian tradition, human sacrifices were offered to Odin, and because the god himself had endured stabbing and hanging, these methods of execution were employed. Corroborative evidence of sacrificial hanging comes from Iron Age Denmark, the most remarkable find being the well-preserved body of a hanged man from Tollund; but possibly this and other sacrifices from Danish peat bogs were directed towards a fertility god, such as Nerthus, rather than Woden (see pp. 40–1). There is no reliable evidence

---

1. I make the tentative suggestion that women's interest in weapons may have been connected with weaving, traditionally women's work at this time, and with the upright warp-weighted loom then in use. Weaving was a heavy task. The warp threads had to be beaten violently in an upward direction, with sword-shaped beaters made of wood or metal. There are cases of real swords and spears having been used for the task. The Anglo-Saxons themselves seem to have made the connection between weaving and warfare, as weaving is used figuratively in an Anglo-Saxon riddle about a mail-coat (*ASPR*, III, p.198, No.35) and battle imagery is used in a riddle which may be about a loom (*ASPR*, III, p.208, No.56). Perhaps the Dover and Breach Downs objects were textile implements such as stilettos for piercing cloth.
2. The full complement of 'Beasts' consisted of wolf, raven and eagle. Hilda Ellis Davidson suggests convincingly that Woden's creatures were joined here by the Roman eagle, a symbol that would have become familiar to the German people through contact with the Roman army (*The Battle God of the Vikings*, p.14).

Fig 3 Helmeted figure on implement from Dover, Kent. Adapted
from a drawing in *Antiquity*,
XXXIX (*by permission of the editor
and Professor Vera I. Evison*)

that humans were sacrificed to Woden in Anglo-Saxon England, but there
may have been a folk-memory of the tradition, which surfaces in poems
ostensibly Christian. There is an example of this in *The Fortunes of Men*,
which begins by stating that parents may bring up a child but that his fate,
prosperous or tragic, is in God's hands. Various destinies, unpleasant and
pleasant, are described:

Sumum þæt gegongeð   on geoguðfeore
þæt se endestæf   earfeðmæcgum
wealic weorþeð.   Sceal hine wulf etan,
har hæðstapa;   hinsiþ þonne
modor bimurneð.   Ne bið swylc monnes geweald! ...
Sum sceal on geapum   galgan ridan,
seomian æt swylte,   oþþæt sawlhord,
bancofa blodig,   abrocen weorþeð.
Þær him hrefn nimeþ   heafodsyne,
sliteð salwigpad   sawelleasne;

16

1 Reconstruction of the helmet found in the seventh-century ship burial at Sutton Hoo, Suffolk. The inside was probably padded. The outside was decorated with tinned plaques stamped with figural scenes or interlacing ornament (*Trustees of the British Museum*)

2 Gilded buckle found in a sixth- to seventh-century cemetery at Finglesham, Kent. The figure is naked apart from a belt and a helmet with horns terminating in the heads of birds of prey. He carries two spears and may represent the cult of Woden (*Institute of Archaeology, Oxford*)

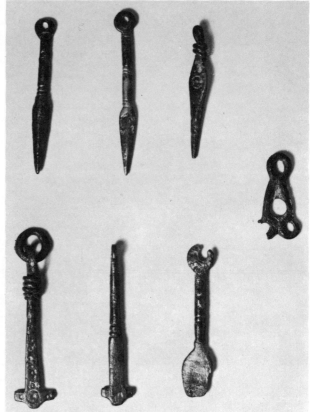

3 Amulets from a seventh-century grave at Gilton, Kent. The trinkets, designed to hang from a woman's belt, include miniatures of Thor's (Thunor's) hammer and spears (*Merseyside County Museum, Liverpool*)

noþer he þy facne mæg folmum biwergan,
laþum lyftsceaþan, biþ his lif scæcen,
ond he feleleas, feores orwena,
blac on beame bideð wyrde,
bewegen wælmiste. Bið him werig noma!

(*ASPR*, III, pp.154–5, lines 10–14, 33–42)

To one unfortunate man it happens that a miserable end comes in his youth. The wolf, grey wanderer of the heath, must eat him. Then his mother mourns his death. Such is not man's power ... One must ride on the crooked gallows, hang to death until the living body, bloody dwelling of bone, becomes broken. There the raven takes an eye from him, the dark-coated creature tears the lifeless one. Neither can he defend himself with his hands from the malice, from the hateful airborne robber. His life is fled, and he senseless, without hope of life. Pale on the beam he endures his fate, covered with the mist of death. Sad is his name.

Our knowledge that, traditionally, hanging was associated with the cult of Woden may be useful in explaining an obscure passage in the Old English poem *Beowulf*, which was probably first written down in the seventh century but contains a lot of older material. Towards the end of the poem we learn of the grief suffered by an aged king whose son has been killed, accidentally, by his brother. The father suffers doubly, for he cannot have revenge on the killer, also his son. The father's plight is compared to the suffering endured by an old man whose son has been hanged:

Swa bið geomorlic gomelum ceorle
to gebidanne, þæt his byre ride
giong on galgan, þonne he gyd wrece,
sarigne sang, þonne his sunu hangað
hrefne to hroðre, ond he him helpe ne mæg,
eald ond infrod, ænige gefremman.
Symble bið gemyndgad morna gehwylce
eaforan ellorsið; oðres ne gymeð
to gebidanne burgum in innan
yrfeweardas, þonne se an hafað
þurh deaðes nyd dæda gefondad.
Gesyhð sorhcearig on his suna bure
winsele westne, windge reste
reote berofene. Ridend swefað,
hæleð in hoðman; nis þær hearpan sweg,
gomen in geardum, swylce ðær iu wæron.
Gewiteð þonne on sealman, sorhleoð gæleð
an æfter anum; þuhte him eall to rum,
wongas ond wicstede.

(*ASPR*, IV, p.76, lines 2444–62)

19

So it is sad for an old man to endure that his son, as a young man, should ride on the gallows. Then he recites a tale, a sorrowful song, when his son hangs for the raven's pleasure and he, old and stricken in years, cannot do anything as a help to him. Always, each morning, his son's death is remembered. He does not care to wait for another heir in the dwelling, when one has experienced [evil] deeds through the necessity of death. He gazes, sorrowful, on his son's dwelling, the deserted wine-hall, the windswept resting-place deprived of joy. The riders sleep, warriors in darkness; there is not the noise of the harp there, entertainment in the enclosures such as were there before. Then he goes to his bed, sings a sorrowful song, one man for another. It all seemed to him too spacious, the fields and the homestead.

The deserted hall and its lost pleasures are standard themes in Christian poetry of the Anglo-Saxon age, but in this particular elegy the cause of the tragedy is obscure. Why can the father have no revenge? Was the son a criminal that he should be hanged? These questions can be answered if we accept that behind this passage lies a reminiscence of the sacrifice, by hanging, of a promising young nobleman to the hanged god.

The cult of Woden may lie behind the custom of cremating the dead, practised by some Anglo-Saxons before the conversion to Christianity, for Icelandic literature records that Odin established cremation and that those who were burned after death, with their possessions, went to be with Odin. Despite the antagonism of the Christian Church to cremation, references to burning the dead occur in several Old English poems written down in Christian times. In *The Seafarer*, in lines rendered obscure by damage to the manuscript (*ASPR*, III, p.146, lines 112–15), the Christian narrator seems to be warning that a pyre is not the means to salvation, and in *The Fortunes of Men* a cremation funeral follows the hanging among the list of unpleasant fates:

Sumne on bæle sceal   brond aswencan,
fretan frecne lig   fægne monnan;
þær him lifgedal   lungre weorðeð,
read reþe gled;   reoteð meowle,
seo hyre bearn gesihð   brondas þeccan.

(ASPR, III, p.155, lines 43–7)

A fire-brand must afflict one man on the pyre, greedy flame devour the doomed man. There his parting from life happens quickly; the red coal [is] fierce. The woman weeps. She sees the fire-brands consume her son.

The literary convention here makes it seem as if the fire is tearing a living body, rather than a senseless corpse, but there is no actual evidence for burning alive and the passage surely derives from the inherent belief that it was not death itself but the ritual burning that separated soul from body. The

Beowulf poet, who describes two cremation funerals (also gruesome), while non-committal about the creed dictating these rites, demonstrates that the rituals were enormously spectacular, sufficiently so to linger in the memory of witnesses and to inspire the imagination of poets long after. Burning was a suitable ritual for a god of war who could be mighty and cruel.

Numerous Anglo-Saxon cremation graves have been excavated in England, and it may be significant that this rite was generally preferred to inhumation in Anglian areas; it was the Anglian kings who remembered Woden and who first made him their ancestor.

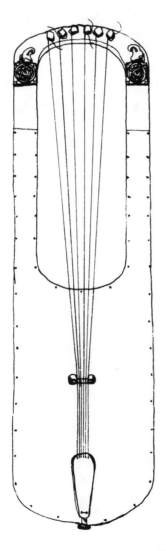

Fig 4   Reconstruction of lyre from Sutton Hoo with detail of plaque

Fig 5   Detail of 'bird of prey' plaque from Sutton Hoo purse lid

A cremation urn, now lost, from Newark (Notts.), had two birds forming a handle (J. N. L. Myres, *A Corpus of Anglo-Saxon Pottery*, II, fig. 286, No.3556), perhaps representing Woden's two ravens, but naturalistic designs are rare on Anglo-Saxon pottery and there are apparently no other motifs obviously associated with Woden. Cruel birds, however, are a frequent motif in the metalwork of the Sutton Hoo ship burial. They appear on peaceful objects such as the lyre, as well as on war-like objects like the shield (see fig. 23). Possibly birds first became popular with artists because they were the familiars of the most widely acknowledged god, but they seem sometimes to have escaped from this association to become natural birds— as on the Sutton Hoo purse lid (plate 4), where a gold and garnet bird of prey catches a duck of similar decoration.

The name of Woden's consort Friga or Frigg is perpetuated in the word Friday (OE *Frig-dæg*) and in certain English place-names: Frobury and Froyle (Hants.) may mean 'Friga's hill'; Fretherne (Glos.) links the goddess with a thorn-bush; Freefolk (Hants.) may refer to 'Friga's people'. Her name also occurs in Fridaythorpe (Yorks.) and in the obsolete place-names *Frigedæges tr[e]ow* and *Frigedæges east*. She was a goddess of childbirth and marriage, and was considered to some extent an equivalent of the Roman Venus, who is remembered in the French and Italian names for Friday, *vendredi* and *venerdì*. The Old English noun *frig* (meaning physical passion) may have derived from her name. The word is used twice in the Anglo-Saxon poem *Christ* to signify a man's sexual love, for example:

... sio weres friga   wiht ne cuþe

(*ASPR*, III, p.14, line 419)

'she [the Virgin] knew nothing of the passions of a man'

22

Once, possibly, the word is used in the sense of illicit passion. The context is a disputed stanza of the poem *Deor* referring to two obscure legendary characters:

We þæt Mæðhilde   monge gefrugnon
wurdon grundlease   Geates frige ...

(*ASPR*, III, p.178, lines 14–15)

Many of us have learned that Geat's passions for Mæðhild were boundless

The modern obscenity 'frig' is probably also a debased reminiscence of the goddess of married love. Icelandic literature has a few references to Friga's infidelity with her husband's brothers, but, on the whole, northern sources present her in a favourable light, certainly without the sensuality which became attached to the Roman Venus. Possibly the English settlers were less reverential towards her. Perhaps, though, since Christianity soon provided them with a pure Mother-figure, Mary, the pagan matriarch degenerated to become synonymous with lust.

Northern mythology attributed to Friga foreknowledge and skill in magic. Germanic peoples seem in general to have respected the prescience of women. Tacitus mentions it (*Germania*, 8), and in *Beowulf* women, usually mothers, prophesy disaster and strive to avoid it. Possibly some memory of a wise goddess or of foresighted priestesses lies behind this literary motif, but there is no overt connection.

Even in Scandinavian literature Friga is an obscure figure, although of undoubted stature among the gods. Her role may have overlapped to some extent with that of Freyja, who was also concerned with sexual love and fertility in general. As a matriarch Friga may have been identified with one of the Mother Goddesses mentioned by Bede and with Mother Earth. These fertility cults are discussed in more detail on pp.30–5.

Continuing our study of Woden's family, the Æsir, we come to the god Thunor, a son of Woden. He was called Thor in Scandinavia, and his name is preserved in our Thursday (OE *Þunres-dæg*). He was considered the Germanic equivalent of Jupiter or Jove. Thus in a Latin–Old English glossary we find *Joppiter: Þunor oððe Đur*, and we note that Thursday corresponds to *jeudi* and *giovedì* in Romance languages. English place-names, both current and obsolete, testify to a cult of Thunor, mostly in Saxon areas (and apparently not at all in Anglian areas). Thunor was probably worshipped in sacred groves or meadows, or was perhaps associated with such landscapes, since the majority of place-names containing his name link him with the Old English word *leah*. Thundersley and Thunderley Hall (Essex), Thursley (Surrey), two places once referred to as *on þunres lea* (Hants.) and one as *on þunorslege* (Sussex) testify to this, together with *Thunerleaw*, the only Kentish place-name associated with this god. Thunderfield (Surrey)

Fig 6 Sword with swastika from Bifrons, Kent. (Adapted from a drawing supplied by Maidstone Borough Council for Maidstone Museum)

and *to ðunresfelda* (Wilts.) show the same link, and Thundridge (Herts.) again relates Thunor to a natural feature. Rather differently Thurstable (an Essex Hundred) and the lost *Thunreslau* (also Essex) link Thunor's name to a pillar. Possibly the worship of this god involved a pole or pillar such as the one which archaeologists believe stood outside a pagan temple in Northumbria (see p. 43). Oak pillars were later associated with this god in Iceland, where they perhaps represented sacred trees (Ellis Davidson, *Gods and Myths*, p.88).

Unlike Woden, Thunor does not feature in Old English literature. There is only one doubtful reference to him, in one version of the *Anglo-Saxon Chronicle*. In the entry for the year AD 640, two Kentish princes are said to have been murdered by Thunor (see D. Whitelock (ed.), *English Historical Documents*, I, p.151, 'A' text, note). This reference might record revenge by the worshippers of Thunor against the royal family of Kent who were systematically destroying heathenism at that time (see the 'E' text of the *Chronicle* for 640: 'Eorcenberht ... demolished all the idols in his kingdom'), but it is equally possible that the princes were killed by someone who happened to be called Thunor.[3]

---

3. The *Chronicle* itself was a ninth-century compilation and this statement is an addition to it, so (although heathenism doubtless still persisted in 640) this reference to it is too retrospective to be relied upon.

Northern mythology provides us with the essential characteristics of Thunor/Thor, although Icelandic records sometimes make him into a comic character, a degeneration belonging to a late phase of his development, later than Anglo-Saxon times. He was a god of simple physical strength, associated with thunder, which still bears his name (OE *þunor*). He habitually carried a short-handled hammer, which he could use as a weapon either held in his hand or thrown; he used it to restore his goats to life, having eaten them, and to consecrate a bride. Amulets made in the characteristic shape of Thunor's hammer were carried by women buried in the seventh century at Gilton and Kingston in Kent. They were worn with other trinkets, including the little spears which were amulets of Woden (see p.15 and plate 3). They are rare in graves of this period, but became more popular in Viking times, probably in imitation of the Christian habit of wearing a small cross, for the hammer and cross are of similar shape.

The swastika symbol was also associated with Thunor, perhaps as a representation of the lightning he created. The swastika appears on a sword hilt found in a sixth-century grave at Bifrons and on a seventh-century cloisonné brooch from Faversham (both Kent). It is frequently found on cremation urns. It may be drawn freehand, either as a large single symbol or as a group of smaller symbols, a technique used more on earlier (fifth-century) urns than later, or it may be stamped, with a metal die. The stamped swastika sometimes occurs in conjunction with stamped animals and belongs to the seventh century. The animals may also have some mythological origin.

Thunor's signs—hammer and swastika—link him, therefore, with both cremation and inhumation graves in England. Although his name has not survived as a place-name in Anglian areas, the sign of the swastika on Anglian urns is evidence of his influence.

One of many anecdotes told about Thunor/Thor in Norse mythology involves a conflict between the god and a giant armed with a whetstone. A piece of the whetstone, shattered by the god's hammer, lodged in Thunor's head. The story no doubt reflects an association between whetstone, which sharpens and causes sparks, and the god with power over lightning and fire. It is an interesting association for us, since the sceptre of an East Anglian king found at Sutton Hoo consisted of a decorated whetstone (plate 6). An impressive object, it obviously symbolized the power of the king who owned it; possibly a pagan association lay behind the choice of whetstone for a sceptre.

It is appropriate at this point to mention Balder, since, according to late Norse sources he was, like Thunor, a son of Woden/Odin. Balder seems to have particular attraction for modern students, partly because he was traditionally beautiful and partly because the version of his story told by Snorri has a timeless appeal. Like the Greek Achilles, Balder was very nearly invulnerable, but not quite. The goddess Friga had extracted a promise from

Fig 7   The whetstone or sceptre
from Sutton Hoo

all things not to hurt Balder, but had omitted the mistletoe. The malicious god Loki brought about Balder's death by guiding the hand of the blind god Hoder, who shot Balder with a missile made of mistletoe. He was given a magnificent ship funeral and passed to the land of the dead. Since he was beloved, the gods requested the goddess Hel, who ruled that realm, to return him. She agreed, provided that all things wept for him, and we are told that they did so, men, animals, earth, stone and metal, as they do when thaw follows frost; but one old woman (the malicious Loki in disguise) would not weep and Balder was not redeemed. The stories of Loki's subsequent punishment and the final doom of the gods were certainly brought to England by the Viking settlers who came in later centuries, for they are depicted on the tenth-century cross which still stands at Gosforth (Cumb.; see p.170 and fig. 32); but it is doubtful whether the Anglo-Saxon heathens of the fifth and sixth centuries acknowledged Balder as a god. Attempts to prove his cult through place-name evidence lack conviction: Bolsterstone (Yorks.) probably signifies a stone resembling a bolster rather than a stone sacred to Balder. However, his name and some version of his story may have become known: there is a man named Baldæg mentioned as Woden's son in Bernician and West Saxon genealogies; Hilda Ellis Davidson revives the suggestion (*Gods and Myths*, p.189) that there is a reminiscence of Balder's story in *Beowulf*, where one brother accidentally shoots another, an event followed by the mysterious elegy about hanging already discussed (see pp.19–20); the ritual of the ship funeral was certainly carried out in England, but differed in several details from Balder's.

Perhaps the most interesting aspect of Balder is that his near-resurrection and the disaster which followed for the old gods may have led to the identification of Balder with Christ. The crucifixion and the pagan gods are depicted together on the cross at Gosforth. A male figure, stretched out in the position of crucifixion, is flanked by two figures at the foot of the cross; on the left the soldier with a spear, on the right (the position normally occupied in Christian art by the spongebearer) a woman wearing the hairstyle and the trailing dress of northern art. The iconography of this cross may be read as a narrative of the doom of the northern gods, ending with the death of Balder, who like Christ had the possibility of resurrection (see p.171). It is possible, but not proved, that the influence of Balder's story lies behind the treatment of the crucifixion in *The Dream of the Rood*, surely the most moving of all Anglo-Saxon poems.

The poem is carved in runes on the late seventh- or early eighth-century Ruthwell Cross (Dumfriesshire) and exists in a fuller, manuscript version in the tenth-century *Vercelli Book*. The poem relates the events of the crucifixion as if told by the Cross itself, and scholars recognize that the poet deliberately exploits the traditional Germanic vocabulary and concepts of heroism. The result is a moving paradox, for Christ, the hero of his people, is fighting a battle in which, ironically, he must die in order to save them. The critical question is whether the poet goes further than using traditions from Germanic heroic poetry and actually exploits pagan mythology. When the stricken Cross says:

eall ic wæs mid strælum forwundod

(*ASPR*, II, p.63, line 62)

'I was all wounded with darts'

it is making a poetic reference to the nails which pierced it by speaking of them as missiles. There is precedent for this in Christian tradition—the martyr St Sebastian was shot with arrows—but there could equally be an echo of Balder's fate. Similarly, at the climax of the poem the Cross says:

Weop eal gesceaft

(*ASPR*, II, p.62, line 55)

'All creation wept'

This may represent the cataclysm which the Gospels record, but is strongly reminiscent of Balder's story. Thus the memory of the pagan story may have been exploited to enrich the Christian one, for the Anglo-Saxon audience and for us.

Moving away from Woden's family, the Æsir, we must consider a god who was probably of greater antiquity than Woden and his sons. Tiw is the god for whom Tuesday (OE *Tiwes-dæg*) is named. A god of battle, to whom the continental Germans made human sacrifice, Tiw (or Tiwaz) was also a god of law and order and probably once the supreme deity, since his name is related to that of the Roman Jupiter and Greek Zeus. He was also equated with Mars, the Roman war-god (as seen in French *mardi*, Italian *martedi*). In the Norse legends his role has become taken over by Woden/Odin, although the older deity survives in the figure of the less important but valiant god Tyr. In England his cult is confirmed by several place-names. The obsolete *Tyesmere* (Worcs.) suggests a lake sacred to Tiw. He is associated with a grove or open space in the obsolete *Tislea* (Hunts.) and in Tuesley (Surrey), which is near to Thursley, a name associated with Thunor, in an area which may have been particularly devoted to pagan worship. Tysoe (Warwicks.) signifies a spur of land named for Tiw. The figure of a horse was cut on a hill there, from which the place-name 'Vale of the Red Horse' developed. Possibly Tiw was associated with horses in that place. We know that sacred horses played a part in northern religion: Tacitus speaks of white horses kept in sacred groves. They were believed to be confidants of the gods and were used for predictions (*Germania*, 10), which suggests that they were used to forecast the results of war and were probably linked with the war-god. (Scandinavian evidence, however, associated sacred horses with the fertility god Freyr.) Perhaps the sacred associations of the horse account for its use as a decorative motif on the boss of the shield found at Sutton Hoo (Suffolk). A similar design of interlacing horses, perhaps copied from the shield, is worked in garnet cloisons on the purse-lid.

The runic symbol ↑ represented the name of Tiw and was traditionally carved on weapons to ensure victory. The Icelandic poem *Sigrdrífomál* provides interesting, if late, evidence of this practice (the text is thirteenth century). A valkyrie instructs a hero about different kinds of runes. She tells him that 'victory runes' should be carved on the hilt of a sword, on the ridge along the blade, on some other (unidentifiable) part of the sword, and that

Fig 8   Horse motifs from the Sutton Hoo shield and purse

the name of the god 'Ty' should be carved twice (G. Neckel (ed.), *Edda*, I, pp.186–7). Isolated ↑ symbols on an Anglo-Saxon sword pommel from Faversham and a spear from Holborough (both Kent) as well as a rune-like symbol which might also be a ↑ on a pommel from Gilton (Kent) confirm that such carving took place. This sign is also the commonest of all the runes and rune-like symbols to appear on English cremation urns, on which it is either drawn freehand or stamped.

Fig 9   Urn with ↑ rune from Sancton, Yorkshire

Dr Ellis Davidson has suggested (*Gods and Myths*, p.60) that Tiw was identical with the god known as Seaxnet. The latter was worshipped (as 'Saxnot') together with Thor and Woden until the eighth and ninth centuries by Saxon peoples on the continent, and he was claimed as an ancestor by the Anglo-Saxon kings of Essex (the East Saxons). Theirs is the only surviving Anglo-Saxon royal genealogy to go back to Seaxnet rather than Woden:

Offa sighering, sighere sigberhting, sigberht s(aweard)ing, saweard saberhting, saberht sledding, sle(dd) æscwining, æscwine offing, offa bedcing, bedca (sigefugling), sigefugl swæpping, swæppa antsecging, ants(ecg) gesecging, gesecg seaxneting.

(Sweet (ed.), *The Oldest English Texts*, p.179, lines 13–16)

Since the pedigree of the West Saxon kings was a political 'borrowing' from their Anglian superiors and in the absence of a genealogy for the South Saxons (Sussex), Dr Dumville argues that originally Seaxnet may have been acknowledged by all the Saxon tribes (P. H. Sawyer and I. N. Wood (eds.), *Early Medieval Kingship*, p.78).

The name of a fertility god, Ing, is represented by the runic symbol ᛜ. The Old English *Rune Poem* gives us some cryptic information about him:

ᛜ (Ing) wæs ærest   mid Eastdenum
gesewen secgun,   oþ he siððan eft
ofer wæg gewat,   wæn æfter ran;
ðus heardingas   ðone hæle nemdun.

(*ASPR*, VI, pp.29–30, lines 67–70)

Ing was first seen by men among the East Danes until he afterwards went over the sea again. The wagon sped after. Warriors named the hero thus.

The wagon seems to have been a feature of fertility cults in northern religion. Tacitus records the rituals associated with the goddess Nerthus or Mother Earth, whose carriage was kept in a sacred grove or was drawn from place to place by oxen (see pp.40–1). In Sweden the god Freyr, unseen in a wagon, journeyed from place to place in the autumn.

The Anglo-Saxon Ing is an obscure figure. Germanic people may have believed him to be the hero of the Ingwine (the Danes). One of the ancestors listed in the royal genealogy of Bernicia is named Ingebrand; possibly he was the same character as Ing or was named after him. It seems probable that the little-known Ing may be identified with the better documented Freyr, for the titles 'Yngvi', 'Ingunar' were applied to Freyr and some of his Icelandic worshippers had names beginning with 'Ing-'.

The name of the god Freyr is not, apparently, recorded in England (although it is closely related to the Old English word *frea* (lord), which came to be applied to the Christian God); yet certain rituals associated with the fertility god in Scandinavian mythology are demonstrated by English archaeological finds.

Apart from the sacred horses already mentioned, which were linked with Freyr in Scandinavia, Freyr and his twin sister Freyja were both associated with boars. The boar appears often in Anglo-Saxon culture, usually as a protective symbol for warriors. In *Beowulf* decorative boar-figures are mentioned in relation to helmets, occurring both on the cheek-guards and on top (lines 303–4, 1286, *ASPR*, IV, pp.11, 40). This is no poetic fiction, since gilded boarheads surmount the cheek-pieces of the Sutton Hoo helmet (plate 1) and a realistic figure of a boar, bronze with garnet eyes, stands on the helmet (plate 7) from Benty Grange (Derbys.). Originally a crest ran down its back and its body was probably covered with iron plates into which gilded silver studs were sunk, in imitation of bristles. This may be seen as direct reference to Freyr's boar *Gullinbursti*, (golden-bristled; R. Bruce-Mitford, *Aspects of Anglo-Saxon Archaeology*, p. 238). Interlaced boars of gold and garnet decorate the shoulder-clasps of the royal regalia from Sutton Hoo (plate 8), and three boars appear on the blade of an East Anglian sword (H. R. Ellis Davidson, *The Sword in Anglo-Saxon England*, p.49 and fig. 21). It may seem strange that Freyr's symbol should be a protective one for, as far as we know, he was not a god of war (although the boar itself, as a fierce beast, is not inappropriate); but the association seems to be ancient. Tacitus (*Germania*, 45) mentions that the Germanic tribes called *Aestii* cultivated crops and worshipped the Mother of the gods (presumably a fertility symbol), in whose honour they wore boar masks instead of armour.

The boar symbol also appears out of military context and persisted long after paganism was officially eradicated. We find it on a seventh-century pendant from White Low (Derbys.), which probably belonged to a woman, on a (Christian) hanging bowl, found at Sutton Hoo, and on the Alfred Jewel, a ninth-century piece made when Christianity was firmly established.

Fig 10 Boar motif from the Sutton Hoo clasps

Freyr was believed to own a miraculous ship, and there is Icelandic evidence for the priests of Freyr being buried in ships (*Gods and Myths*, p.135). Freyr's father Njord was also closely associated with ships, so possibly this family of gods (the Vanir) were originally honoured by ship funerals (although there is some overlap with the Æsir, since Balder, a son of Woden, was himself given a ship funeral). The fertility god then, may be ultimately behind the ship funerals which took place in Anglo-Saxon Suffolk and the one described poetically in *Beowulf* (see chapter 4).

Scyld Scefing, the legendary king whose career and ship funeral form the unforgettable prologue to *Beowulf*, himself evolved from a fertility myth. He was evidently a composite figure, embodying in his name the two qualities essential for the successful survival of a people—military might (shield) and agricultural prosperity (sheaf). In *Beowulf* this character is the eponymous founder of the Danish dynasty, the 'Scyldings', but other evidence makes it clear that 'Scyld Scefing' ('shield with the sheaf' or 'shield son of sheaf') was a conflation of two myths. In *Beowulf* we are told that Scyld Scefing:

> ærest wearð
> feasceaft funden ...
> ... hine æt frumsceafte forð onsendon
> ænne ofer yðe umborwesende.
>
> (*ASPR*, IV, p.3, line 4, p.4, lines 45–6)

was first discovered destitute ... in the beginning [people] sent him forth as a child, alone over the ocean.

The story of a child who came over the ocean evidently belonged to the character named Sheaf, Sceaf or Scef, a fertility figure who was believed to have appeared from the unknown and brought prosperity. This tradition is preserved in the *Chronicle* of Æthelweard (*c*.1000) and in a twelfth-century account by William of Malmesbury:

> [Sceaf] so they say, as a small child, was driven ashore in a boat without oars on a certain island of Germany called Scandza ... He was asleep, and at his head was laid a sheaf of corn; for this reason he was given the name Sceaf, and was received as a miracle by the men of that region and carefully reared. As an adult he reigned in the town which was then called Sleswic, but is now in fact called Hedeby. That region is called 'Old Anglia'; from there the Angles came to Britain ...
>
> (Garmonsway and Simpson (trans.), *Beowulf and its Analogues*, p.119)

To Sceaf there was attributed a son named Beow, a word which means barley, supporting the possibility that a fertility myth lies behind the legend of Sceaf. Sceaf was remembered as a great king in the literature and history of England, Denmark and Iceland. Most writers (including the author of

Beowulf, our oldest source of information) acknowledged that he was King of Denmark but he is also variously said to have ruled the Langobards (in the poem *Widsið*), the *Scanii* (Æthelweard) and the Angles (William of Malmesbury, above). William of Malmesbury recorded that the Anglo-Saxons were supposed descendants of Sceaf's people. The genealogists of the West Saxon kings similarly transformed Scyld, Sceaf, Beow and other legendary characters into ancestors. As we have seen, the semi-fictional pedigrees of most Anglo-Saxon kings went back to Woden. In Christian times, when Woden no longer had the sanctity of a pagan god, the genealogists of the West Saxon kings treated him as a human ancestor and added generations beyond him, ultimately giving the Anglo-Saxon dynasty the authority of a biblical origin, as demonstrated by this excerpt from a genealogy in the *Anglo-Saxon Chronicle* for 855:

... Woden Frealafing, Frealaf Finning, Fin Godwulfing, God wulf Geating, Geat Tætwaing, Tætwa Beawing, Beaw Sceldwaing, Sceldwea Heremoding, Heremod Itermoning, Itermon Haðraing, Haþra Hwalaing, Hwala Bedwiging, Bedwig Sceafing. id est filius Noe se wæs geboren on þære earce Noes.

(Plummer and Earle (eds.), *Two of the Saxon Chronicles Parallel*, pp.66, 67 and note 6)

The list concludes with Bedwig, son of Sceaf, who, we are told, 'is the son of Noah; he was born in Noah's ark'. Sceaf, who traditionally arrived by boat, is neatly made the son of the ark-builder.

Thus Sceaf, a fertility figure, was, like Freyr and his father, associated with a ship. Possibly Nerthus, the fertility goddess whose rites Tacitus describes, was also linked with a ship, for the author mentions (*Germania,* 9) that some of the *Suebi* worshipped a goddess whom he identifies with the Egyptian Isis (see *Gods and Myths,* p.100). Nerthus, or Mother Earth, was, he mentions elsewhere (*Germania,* 40), worshipped by many Suebian peoples.

In Germanic mythology we find fertility cults associated with either gods or goddesses, sometimes with both, as in the case of the twins Freyr and Freyja, children of Njord and his sister. In England we have ample evidence for the cult of Freyr and it is clear that the names of Ing and Sceaf were long remembered in association with heroes. We do not have the names of any fertility goddess from Anglo-Saxon England but it is clear that, like their continental neighbours (and, indeed like most pagan peoples), the Anglo-Saxons acknowledged an Earth Mother whose favour was essential if they were to survive. Before the coming of Christianity she may have been worshipped with elaborate rituals such as Tacitus associates with Nerthus (see pp.40–1), but our only evidence is of a superstition that persisted long after the supposed suppression of heathenism; in the following charm for unfruitful land, from an eleventh-century manuscript, a series of ritual actions is punctuated by metrical chants, which both acknowledge the Christian God and make a timeless plea to the earth as fruitful Mother:

Erce, Erce, Erce,   eorþan modor,
geunne þe se alwalda,   ece drihten,
æcera wexendra   and wridendra,
eacniendra   and elniendra,
sceafta hehra,   scirra wæstma,
and þæra bradan   berewæstma,
and þæra hwitan   hwætewæstma,
and ealra   eorþan wæstma ...
... Hal wes þu, folde,   fira modor!
Beo þu growende   on godes fæþme,
fodre gefylled   firum to nytte.

(ASPR, VI, pp.117–18, lines 51–8, 69–71)

Erce, Erce, Erce, Mother of earth, may the All-ruler, eternal Lord, grant you fields growing and flourishing, bringing forth and strengthening; high blades, bright fruits and wide barley-crops, and splendid corn, and all the fruits of the earth ... hail to you, Earth, Mother of men, may you spring up, in God's bosom, filled with food for the use of men.

The Christian scholar, Bede, who was interested in the subject of chronology, tells us in his work *De Temporum Ratione* that in heathen times the year began on 25 December (*ab octavo kalendarum ianuariarum*) and that this night was called *modranect*, or in Latin *matrum noctem*—'Mothers' Night' (C. W. Jones (ed.), pp.211–12, lines 11–15). Probably this title indicates a pagan festival which was absorbed into the celebration of Christmas as was the name *Giuli* (Yule), which Bede tells us was the English name given to the period December–January (Jones, p.211, lines 6–7, 10–11). Since this was a mid-winter festival, Mothers' Night may have acknowledged the cult of Mother Earth to ensure fertility in the coming spring season. The Mother Goddess of the Æsir, was, as we have seen, Friga, who presided over matrimony. Possibly she, with a (named) fertility goddess and a third figure, made up a triumvirate of goddesses, such as are found in the mythologies of other civilizations, for example, the Greek. It is more likely though, that rather than three individually named goddesses, we have in Bede's 'Mothers' a group of figures like the Mother Goddesses who had already appeared in Roman Britain (see p.5) and who were widely acknowledged in the Germanic world as well as the Celtic. In the Roman-influenced provinces they appear on stone sculptures, often in groups of three, sometimes holding fruit. Fertility and childbirth were their province, and in Germany and Scandinavia they were long remembered for their power to determine a child's destiny. They are known as the Norns in northern literature. Three hooded figures appear

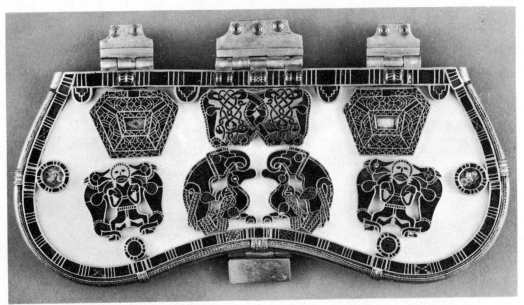

4 Purse-lid from Sutton Hoo, Suffolk. Gold plaques decorated with cloisonné garnets and millefiori glass were mounted upon a plate of some perishable material. The purse contained Merovingian gold coins which help to date the deposit to *c.* AD 625 (*Trustees of the British Museum*)

5 Hand-made cremation urn from North Elmham, Norfolk, decorated with swastikas (*Trustees of the British Museum*)

6 Whetstone or sceptre from Sutton Hoo, Suffolk. At each end of the sceptre are four human heads, then a red-painted knob. A bronze stag, apparently a royal emblem, mounted upon a ring, stands on the top of the sceptre (*Trustees of the British Museum*)

on the side panel of the Franks Casket (plate 9), a seventh-century Northumbrian box made of whalebone, which combines Christian scenes with northern and Roman mythology. The left-hand side of this obscure panel, with its armed warrior, horse and birds, may have something to do with Woden, while the group of three female figures could be Norns, or Mothers.

We have the names of a few lesser-known gods. Bede, in his treatise on Time, mentions two goddesses, Hreda and Eostre, equating *Hredmonath* with March and *Eosturmonath* with April (Jones, p.211, lines 7–8, p.212, lines 29–32). We know nothing about Hreda, except that her name may relate to Old English *hreða* (glory or fame). Bede adds that Eostre gave her name to Easter, and we may note that while French- and Italian-speaking Christians celebrate Easter under names deriving (through Latin and Greek) from the Hebrew word for Passover, thus French *Pâques*, and Italian *Pasqua*, the English word, like the German *Ostern*, is related to 'east'. If Bede is right and the name of a goddess lies behind the Germanic names, Eostre may have been a goddess of the east, that is, of the dawn.

We know a little about some of the characters named, with Sceaf and Scyld, in the generations beyond Woden in the West Saxon royal genealogy (see p.33). One at least was revered as a god. Asser, biographer of King Alfred, lists these ancestors and mentions that Geat was worshipped as a god long before by the heathens. Kenneth Sisam ('Anglo-Saxon royal genealogies', p.314) suggests that he was the tribal god of the Geat people, the race about to be conquered at the close of the partly fictional/partly historical poem *Beowulf*. Possibly, when this destruction took place, the name and role of the Geat god were taken over by the more celebrated Woden, who is called by the name *Gautr* in a Norse text. (No connection has been established between Geat the god and Geat the [?] lover mentioned in the poem *Deor*.)

Heremod, who occurs in the royal pedigree, was known as a northern god. He was a son of Woden/Odin, and it was he who rode to Hel to request the release of Balder. There is also a human hero of the same name in Norse literature and conversely, there is a Heremod in *Beowulf* who is the archetypal Bad King. Probably the Anglo-Saxon genealogies recall the hero or the god.

Finn and Hwala were not gods, but they were legendary kings of great power, mentioned in Old English poems. We know nothing of the other remote ancestors.

Finally we must consider a legendary figure who was not a god, nor was he celebrated as an ancestor, yet who has achieved that most Germanic of ambitions, lasting fame. He is Welund the Smith, whose legend is depicted on the front of the Franks Casket (plate 10). His story is mentioned in the first two stanzas of the poem *Deor*, so allusively that the poet must have known that his audience was familiar with the events:

Welund him be wurman   wræces cunnade,
anhydig eorl   earfoþa dreag,
hæfde him to gesiþþe   sorge ond longaþ,
wintercealde wræce;   wean oft onfond,
siþþan hine Niðhad on   nede legde,
swoncre seonobende   on syllan monn ...
Beadohilde ne wæs   hyre broþra deaþ
on sefan swa sar   swa hyre sylfre þing,
þæt heo gearolice   ongieten hæfde
þæt heo eacen wæs;   æfre ne meahte
þriste geþencan,   hu ymb þæt sceolde.

(ASPR, III, p.178, lines 1-6, 8-12)

Welund endured misery through serpents[?]. The steadfast man suffered hardships. He had for a companion sorrow and longing, wintry cold exile. He often found woes after Niðhad laid compulsion on him, supple sinew bonds on the better man ... Beaduhild was not so sore in her heart about the death of her brothers as about her own matter, in that she clearly saw that she was pregnant. She could never think with confidence about what must happen.

We have clearer versions of the story in Old Norse, from which we learn that Welund,[4] a smith of outstanding ability, had been captured by his enemy, King Niðhad, who crippled him by hamstringing him – cutting the tendons in his leg. Welund was set to work for the king, but got his revenge by killing the king's sons, making cups from their skulls, jewels from their eyes and brooches from their teeth. He raped the king's daughter Beaduhild, and escaped with the help of his brother Egil, who captured birds and made for Welund a feather coat, with which he flew away. In the scene on the Franks Casket, Welund is seen in his forge, holding a gruesome cup and facing Beaduhild. The smaller figure of his brother, outside, strangles birds.

So great was Welund's legendary skill, that the claim that a piece of metalwork had been forged by him was a device used by poets to indicate highest quality. Thus the *Beowulf* poet attributes a coat of mail to Welund's workmanship (*ASPR*, IV, p.16, line 455) and the *Waldere* poet a sword (*ASPR*, VI, p.4, lines 1–3). That classic work of the Middle Ages, Boethius's *Consolation of Philosophy*, contained, in its original Latin version, a reference to 'faithful Fabricius':

Ubi nunc fidelis ossa Fabricii manent?

(Book II, metre 7; Weinberger (ed.), p.43, line 15)

King Alfred of Wessex, translating Boethius for the benefit of an English

---

4.   I give the English forms of the characters' names.

audience in the ninth century, replaced Fabricius with Welund, better known in the Germanic world:

Hwæt synt nu þæs foremeran and þæs wisan goldsmiðes ban Welondes?
(Chap. XIX; Sedgefield (ed.), p.46)

What now are the bones of the illustrious and wise goldsmith Welund?

Welund's name was perpetuated by being given to a Bronze Age chambered tomb near the White Horse at Uffington (Berks.) which is still known as Wayland's Smithy. Welund's appeal has lasted into our own times—he appears in Kipling's historical fairy-story *Puck of Pook's Hill*.

2

Everyday Life in Pagan Times

It seems that in the days of Anglo-Saxon heathenism, the pagan gods meant more to the people than merely names invoked to explain massive earthworks and other mysteries, more than actors in the mythological tales handed down from one generation to another. They certainly occupied these roles, but in addition they had to be worshipped. Holy places were designated for the rituals that ensured the continued beneficence of the chosen god or gods.

Traditionally among the Germanic peoples a grove was often chosen as the sacred place, and, originally at least, the god was not represented by statues; rather his presence was *felt* by the worshippers as they visited the holy place:

> They do not ... deem it consistent with the divine majesty to imprison their gods within walls or represent them with anything like human features. Their holy places are the woods and groves, and they call by the name of god that hidden presence which is seen only by the eye of reverence.
>
> (*Germania*, 9; p.108)

More than once Tacitus refers to gruesome rituals associated with worship in the sacred grove. Describing a tribe he calls the *Semnones*, he writes:

> At a set time all the peoples of this blood gather, in their embassies, in a wood hallowed by the auguries of their ancestors and the awe of ages. The sacrifice in public of a human victim marks the grisly opening of their savage ritual. In another way, too, reverence is paid to the grove. No one may enter it unless he is bound with a cord. By this he acknowledges his own inferiority and the power of the deity. Should he chance to fall, he must not get up on his feet again. He must roll out over the ground. All this complex of superstition reflects the belief that in that grove the nation had its birth, and that there dwells the god who rules over all, while the rest of the world is subject to his sway.
>
> (*Germania*, 39; pp.132–3)

Many Germanic tribes acknowledged Nerthus, whose ritual Tacitus relates in detail:

40

In an island of Ocean stands a sacred grove, and in the grove stands a car draped with a cloth which none but the priest may touch. The priest can feel the presence of the goddess in this holy of holies, and attends her, in deepest reverence, as her car is drawn by kine. Then follow days of rejoicing and merry-making in every place that she honours with her advent and stay. No one goes to war, no one takes up arms; every object of iron is locked away; then, and then only, are peace and quiet known and prized, until the goddess is again restored to her temple by the priest, when she has had her fill of the society of men. After that, the car, the cloth and, believe it if you will, the goddess herself are washed clean in a secluded lake. This service is performed by slaves who are immediately afterwards drowned in the lake. Thus mystery begets terror and a pious reluctance to ask what that sight can be which is allowed only to dying eyes.

(*Germania*, 40; pp.133–4)

We have no evidence as to exactly what rites the Anglo-Saxons carried out, but they evidently remembered the wagon of the fertility god (see p.30) and may have used a symbolic replica. Human sacrifice was certainly carried out in Dark Age Scandinavia, but we have no evidence that it took place as a general practice in England—only a few unusual burials in Anglo-Saxon cemeteries suggest that it may have occurred in individual instances. Perhaps human life was too precious to be thrown away in the new and struggling immigrant communities.

The Anglo-Saxons evidently continued the ancient Germanic practice of worshipping in a grove, since so many of the place-names incorporating the name of a god link that god with a word meaning 'grove', as we have already seen. We might add (tentatively) Easewrithe (Sussex), possibly the 'copse of the gods', and Godley (Ches. and Surrey) with Godley Bridge (Surrey), possibly meaning 'grove of the gods' and (with more certainty) a number of place-names in which the OE *wig* or *wih* (idol) is linked with *leah* (open space): Weeley (Essex), Wheely Down and Wheeley Farm (Hants.), Weoley (Worcs.), Whiligh and Whyly (Sussex) and Willey (Surrey).

The original animistic beliefs associated with the sacred grove became superseded by more tangible aids to worship. By the time of the Christian mission the heathen religion in England had temples with idols in them. Bede mentions the destruction of a temple with altars dedicated to idols when Northumbria was first converted, under King Edwin in AD 627 (*HE*, II, 13), and that King Earconberht of Kent enforced the destruction of idols in his kingdom during his reign which lasted from 640 until 664 (*HE*, III, 8). The notorious temple of King Rædwald of East Anglia (see p.107) survived into the lifetime of King Aldwulf, a contemporary of Bede (*HE*, II, 15). According to Bede, sacrifices were carried out in this building; whether human or animal we do not know.

A Danish scholar, Professor Olaf Olsen, has made a study of sites where pagan worship was carried out in Denmark, and this is cited by Mr Rupert Bruce-Mitford in his study of Rendlesham, the East Anglian royal dwelling-place and the supposed site of Rædwald's temple (*Aspects of Anglo-Saxon Archaeology*, p.88). There were evidently two kinds of worshipping place. One, an ordinary building in a farm or home, used on special occasions for religious feasts. The other, away from the dwelling, 'need be no more than the idols or sacred features themselves, which might in the course of time come to be protected by a tent or other temporary cover'. It is this latter type of temple that developed from the sacred grove and is perpetuated in the place-names we have mentioned. When, in *Beowulf*, the poet describes the collapse of morale in a kingdom repeatedly attacked by a monster, he mentions that the population stooped to worshipping 'at heathen temples' (*æt hærgtrafum, ASPR*, IV, p.8, line 175); OE *træf* signifies 'tent', 'pavilion' or 'building'. The poet's choice of word shows that he was thinking of external structures of the kind described.

We can only speculate about the substance and appearance of pagan idols in Anglo-Saxon times. Bede mentions (*HE*, III, 22) that King Oswiu argued against the efficacy of making 'gods' out of stone, metal and wood but we have no way of knowing if the king was citing actual practice or merely speaking rhetorically (see p.147). The Sutton Hoo sceptre (plate 6, fig. 7) is our only evidence that the Anglo-Saxons attempted to carve stone in pagan times. They were skilled metalworkers, but nothing resembling a metal idol survives. It seems likely that they would make idols of wood, but if any escaped destruction by Christians, they would not have survived in English soil conditions. Whatever the medium, it is unlikely that the 'gods' were naturalistic carvings, for the human form is represented very rarely in the art which survives from the pagan period. It is more likely that the idols were pieces of wood on which carvers accentuated a natural resemblance to the essential feature of the 'god', as in a Danish example from an Iron Age site. In this case a side-branch on a length of oak made an obvious phallic symbol (plate 11). A little carving and the addition of a stylized face turned the whole into a fertility 'god'.

Although the notion of a temple may have grown from a simple protection for the holy objects in the sacred grove, it is evident that temples came to be built in areas other than groves. Place-name evidence suggests that hills were very often used for heathen temples. Gadshill (two places in Kent), Godsell Farm (Wilts.) and Godshill (Hants.), Harrow Hill (Sussex), Harrow-on-the-Hill (Middx.), Harrowden (Beds. and Northants.) and Harrowdown (Essex), Weedon (Bucks.), Weedon Beck and Weedon Lois (Northants.), Weyhill (Hants.) and Wyham (Lincs.) all indicate pagan sites on hills. (The Harrow- element derives from OE *hærg*, heathen.) The names Weeford (Staffs.) and Wyville (Lincs.) may indicate temples built by water, perhaps sacred streams or springs. In Alkham (Kent), the modern place-name commemorates a 'homestead by a heathen temple' (OE *ealh*, temple), and the lost name *ealhfleot* (Kent) also hints at the presence of a temple. Prosperous individuals built temples for themselves. Their names occasionally survive in place-names such as the now obsolete *Cusanweoh* (Surrey), 'Cusa's temple', the still current Peper Harrow (Surrey), formerly *Pipereherge*, 'Piper's temple', and Patchway (Sussex), formerly *Petteleswig*, perhaps 'Pettel's temple'. The obsolete place-name *Besinga hearh* (Surrey) referred to a temple of a people called the 'Besingas', while Harrow-on-the-Hill (Middx.), which is referred to in an eighth-century charter as *gumeninga hergae*, was once the site of a temple where the 'Gumeningas' worshipped.

At Yeavering[1] in Northumberland archaeologists have excavated what is believed to be a heathen temple. The site was in the Anglo-Saxon kingdom of Bernicia, an area where the majority of the population were Celtic. The Anglo-Saxons were acknowledged as rulers in Bernicia during the sixth century and Yeavering became a royal dwelling-place from the reign of Æthelfrith in the first years of the seventh century.

The site had long been a centre of ritual importance. A Bronze Age barrow, surmounted by a tall post (a later addition) was at the eastern end of the site. At the western end a knoll had been used for cremations *c*.2000–1000 BC. Beside it a stone monolith and a stone circle once stood, to be replaced by a wooden enclosure containing radially arranged inhumations. The Anglo-Saxons showed respect for these ancient features. They aligned their buildings with reference to the post on the barrow, which, ultimately, they were to enclose in a Christian churchyard. In the area of the western knoll, already sanctified by two eras of burials, they made their heathen temple.

The temple (Building D) was a rectangular wooden structure, orientated north–south. Its internal dimensions were roughly 35ft (10·5m) by 17ft (5·1m). It had doors in both the long sides, which became double entrances when the original building was elaborated by being enclosed by a massive outer shell of heavy vertical timbers with similar doorways. The outer walls were rendered and supported by buttresses. The inner walls were lined with wattle and daub. Posts at the middle of each end wall supported the roof. At the southern end of the building (and encroaching on the area which in ancient times had been used for cremation burials) there was a fenced enclosure which contained posts, presumably with some ritual function. This was probably a common arrangement since the temple Bede describes at Goodmanham, near York, also had enclosures (see p.51). The entrance to the Yeavering enclosure was from the east side, not from the building. Beyond this was an inhumation cemetery. Outside the temple building to the north-west there was erected a massive post, 22–3in (56–8cm) square,

---

1. See B. Hope-Taylor, *Yeavering*, London, 1977.

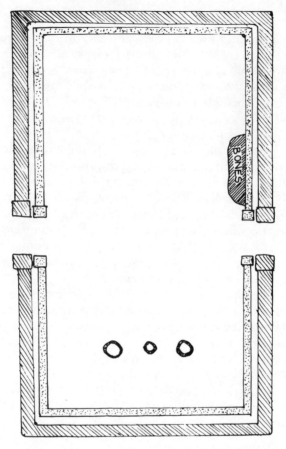

Fig 11   The 'temple' at Yeavering, Northumberland, probable plan. Adapted from B. Hope-Taylor, *Yeavering* (*DOE Archaeological Reports No 7*). Figs 43 and 44 (*by permission of Her Majesty's Stationery Office*)

which probably towered high since it was sunk 4ft (1·2m) into the ground. This almost certainly had ritual significance, perhaps symbolically representing the sacred tree of more primitive Germanic heathenism, while also continuing the tradition of sacred pillars already established on the site. The presence of stake-holes suggests that flimsy structures were erected close to the post.

The temple building contained none of the domestic rubbish associated with the dwelling houses and workshops on the site, so it was clearly reserved for special purposes. Its heathen nature was proved when archaeologists discovered that a pit had been dug inside the building against the east wall, north of the door. It was 6ft (1·8m) long, more than 1ft (30cm) wide and about 16in (41cm) deep. Within the pit were animal bones, mostly of oxen, a high proportion of which were skulls. There were so many of these pagan offerings that they had overflowed the pit and had been stacked against the wall. At the south of the building three post-holes marked the position of some structure or structures. As the posts were removed and the holes were packed with stones some time before the destruction of the building, we may speculate that the posts related to some specifically heathen custom and were removed when Yeavering first became Christian following the visit of Paulinus in 627. Possibly a pagan altar occupied the southern end of the temple and was demolished when the building became a church.

Outside the building, on the west side, and possibly on the north, a succession of sunk-floored huts had been erected. These were flimsy, temporary structures probably erected for some specific purpose and demolished when the occasion had passed.

To the north of the temple, and exactly in a line with it, there was a wooden hall of similar dimensions to the temple, but separated from the sacred area by a screen. To the west there was a building probably used as a kitchen for cooking the ceremonial feasts. Associated with this structure was an area apparently reserved for butchering the sacrificial beasts. It contained many remains of the long bones of oxen, but, significantly, not skulls—they ended up in the temple.

This whole temple complex at Yeavering was destroyed by fire, almost certainly as the result of arson. This probably occurred in 633 when Edwin of Northumbria was defeated by Cadwalla, King of Gwynedd.

In Scandinavian paganism animals, particularly oxen, were offered to Freyr on his annual journey, and it seems likely that the English also honoured the fertility god in this way. The ritual sacrifice of oxen is a feature of Anglo-Saxon paganism evidenced repeatedly by archaeology and confirmed by a historical document. Apart from the ox-skulls found in the temple at Yeavering, in Bernicia, there are examples from the Anglo-Saxon kingdoms of Sussex, Essex and East Anglia. At Harrow Hill (Sussex) where, to judge from its name, a heathen temple once stood, over one thousand ox-skulls were buried (G. Copley, *An Archaeology of South-East England*, p.162). In the early fourteenth century ox-heads were found at the south side of St Paul's Cathedral in London (A. W. Smith, 'The luck in the head: a problem in English folklore', *Folklore*, LXXIII, 1962, p.23). A single ox-head was buried among human inhumations and cremations in a pagan cemetery at Soham (Cambs.), and a cremation urn at Caistor-by-Norwich (Norfolk) rested on the front of an ox- or horse-skull. At Sutton Courtenay (Berks.) part of an ox-skull, including the horns, was found at the centre of the floor of an Anglo-Saxon building. The sacrifice of oxen was one of the details of Anglo-Saxon paganism which came to the notice of Pope Gregory after he sent Augustine as a missionary to Kent. In 601 Gregory wrote to Mellitus, who was about to follow Augustine to England (where he became the first bishop of the East Saxons). Gregory instructed the missionaries about rededicating pagan temples as Christian churches and that, where possible, they should absorb heathen rituals into Christianity. Bede quotes the letter:

> ... since they [the heathen English] have a custom of sacrificing many oxen to devils, let some other solemnity be substituted in its place, such as a day of Dedication or the Festivals of the holy martyrs whose relics are enshrined there. On such occasions they might well construct shelters of boughs for themselves around the churches that were once temples, and celebrate the solemnity with devout feasting. They are no longer to sacrifice beasts to the Devil, but they may kill them for food to the praise of God, and give thanks to the Giver of all gifts for His bounty.

> > (*HE*, I, 30; pp.86–7)

Perhaps the 'shelters of boughs' were to continue a heathen tradition in which huts were erected against the temple walls, as at Yeavering. Probably it was no innovation to kill the oxen for food. Copley suggests (*loc. cit.*) that Harrow Hill was the site where the autumn slaughter of cattle took place 'and that the heads of the animals were offered at the shrine', pointing out that Bede (*De Temporum Ratione*, XV) gave the English word *blodmonath* as the equivalent of November, explaining it: '*Blodmonath* [was] the month of sacrifices because in it they dedicated to their gods the cattle which they were on the point of slaughtering' (Jones (ed.), pp.211, 213). In England in Anglo-Saxon days, and indeed until the agrarian revolution of modern times, the majority of cattle were slaughtered in the autumn and the carcasses salted as a winter food supply for the population since there was not sufficient fodder to keep the beasts alive through the winter. No doubt the slaughter, with its sudden excess of food, was an occasion for feasting. This probably was made a religious occasion in pagan times, when the ox-head was dedicated to the gods. We can only guess at the precise reasons behind the ritual gesture of the severed head: perhaps this part of the beast, least useful for food, was given back to the god whose beneficence had provided the feast; perhaps the gift was to ensure that the food supply would last the winter and that the surviving beasts would breed well in the coming year; perhaps the magnificent head of the beast, with the brain which had controlled the powerful shoulders and strong limbs, was an awesome object containing heathen magic. The Anglo-Saxon place-name *Faresheued*, now Farcet (Hunts.), may mark another place where the ritual slaughter of ox or bull took place (OE *fearr*, bull, *heafod*, head).

The association of magic with the head of an animal is a not uncommon feature of heathenism. The Celts hung the heads of sacrificial animals on trees (J. Grimm, *Teutonic Mythology*, trans. J. S. Stallybrass, I, p.77). Animals'-head ritual is well documented among Germanic peoples. The goat in particular features in more than one account. In the sixth century, for example, the Lombards had a custom of singing and dancing around a goat's head. In later Scandinavian tradition goats were associated with Thunor/ Thor; they drew his chariot. In one account the flesh of Thor's goats was eaten but the bones and the skin were kept by the god, who revitalized them with his hammer. This myth may have led to the bones, including the skull, of the goat being considered sacred to the god.

The skull of a goat was laid at the foot of a ritually significant grave at Yeavering. The burial was at the entrance of Hall A4, and contained, as well as a body, a staff-like implement which might have been a standard or a measuring rod, surmounted by a device perhaps intended to represent a goat's head. The goat-skull at Yeavering may be a relic of Celtic rather than Anglo-Saxon paganism, since the place-name Yeavering probably derives from a British title meaning 'The Hill of the Goats', but the place-name Gateshead (Durham), which Bede called *ad caprae caput*, provides corroborative evidence for Anglo-Saxon interest in the head of the goat.

A pig's head was buried in a cemetery at Frilford (Berks.; see p.73) so it seems that the head of a pig or boar may also have carried some magical significance. Dickins finds a number of place-names suggestive of this ('Place-names formed from animal-head names', *Place-Names of Surrey*, *EPNS*, XI, 1934, p.405), and although consultation of Ekwall's *Concise Oxford Dictionary of English Place-Names* (1936) could lead us to dismiss from the list Swineshead (Beds.) as 'Pig Hill', Swineshead (Lincs.) as 'the source of the creek' and Grizehead (Lancs.) as a later, Scandinavian development, we are still left with Eversheds Farm (Surrey; OE *eofor*, boar), Swineshead Hundred (Glos.), Swinesherd (Worcs.) and Swynset in Oxnam (Roxburghshire) as possible places where the boar's head was worshipped. The boar, it will be recalled, was associated with Freyr in Scandinavia, and was a striking motif in Anglo-Saxon jewellery. The boar's head, of course, persisted as a ritual object into modern times as a feature of banquets, particularly those held at Christmas.

The evidence for rites connected with a sheep's head is more dubious. Dickins offers the place-names Shepshed (Leics.), Rampside and Ramshead (Lancs.) as evidence, but Ekwall suggests instead the meanings 'a hill where sheep grazed' and 'a promontory which may well have been thought to resemble a ram's head' for the first two. Ramshead might similarly signify a hill where rams grazed or a hill where wild garlic (OE *hramsa*) grew. There does not seem, in general, to be much evidence from literature or folklore of rites involving sheep-sacrifice among Germanic peoples. Grimm suggests the sheep was a sacrifice of small value. As sheep bones have been found in cremation urns the beast must not be dismissed as a sacrificial animal, but there does not seem to be any evidence for rites connected with the sheep's head to support the doubtful place-name evidence.

Evidence for places where the stag's head was worshipped is similarly dubious. Ekwall interprets Hartshead (Lancs. and Yorks.) as 'stag's hill' and similarly innocuous etymologies may lie behind Hartside (Cumb.) and the obsolete *Byssheye Hertesheved* (Herts.). We may, however, set against this the continued practice of displaying the severed head of a stag as a trophy of the hunt. The stag was certainly of significance to the Anglo-Saxons, since in *Beowulf* the King of Denmark gave the name *Heorot* (hart) to his royal hall, a magnificent building which was to be the scene of tragedies and triumphs in the poem. Furthermore the stag appears on the sceptre of the East Anglian kings (plate 6 and fig. 7) and on a cremation urn (see p.91). One would suppose, however, that the stag, associated with royalty, had rather a different significance from the ox, goat and other sacrificial beasts.

Dickins produces place-name evidence of rites connected with the heads of other animals and birds: the badger in Broxhead (Hants.) and Broxted (Essex), the wild cat in Cats Head Lodge (Northants.) and the snake in Worms Heath (Surrey). Ravenshead (Notts.) may refer to the raven or to a personal name (*Hrafn*), while Heronshead (Surrey) is interpreted by Dickins as a reference to the head of the eagle (OE *earn*).

We do not know if animal-head ceremonies took place as regular, perhaps annual, events or if they were occasional festivals, celebrated only when an animal was caught. We have a little evidence that an important occasion like the inauguration of a new building might involve sacrifice and the burial of the victim as a kind of 'guardian spirit': beneath the two posts which supported the roof of a hut in the Anglo-Saxon village of Sutton Courtenay (Berks.) were placed the feet of a dog—forefeet under one post, hind under the other. Under the entrance to King Edwin's hall at Yeavering rested the body of a man (see p.47).

It seems that the regular practice of the pagan religion of England involved seasonal festivals, since these are hinted at in the pagan names for the months of the year which Bede gives us, and since such events are documented in relation to Germanic peoples on the continent. The festival which marked the beginning of winter (*Blodmonath*) was, as we have seen, an occasion for the dedication of slaughtered oxen. It was almost certainly marked by bonfires, which the Church failed to suppress. An illustration in a late Anglo-Saxon calendar (plate 12) shows the tending of a fire as the occupation typical for November. It was no doubt a desirable activity from a farmer's point of view as well as being a pagan festivity. It is interesting to find that fires were lit at this time of year long before the life and death of Guy Fawkes, now celebrated on 5 November in England as 'Bonfire Night'.

The winter festival which Bede called Mothers' Night marked the pagan New Year and was held on 25 December. It is likely that this Yule festival (the pagan name for December and January, we may remember, was *giuli*) involved the bringing in of evergreens, the burning of a Yule log and a feast centred round a boar's head, since these non-Christian features became associated with the Christmas festival celebrated at that time.

February, Bede tells us, was called *Solmonath* in heathen times, but 'it is possible to call *Solmonath* the month of cakes which, in it, they used to offer to their gods' (*De Temporum Ratione*, XV, Jones, p.212). The cakes baked on this occasion were almost certainly special in some way, perhaps not so much in their ingredients as in their shape. There is Scandinavian evidence for the baking of cakes in the images of the gods and in the shape of Freyr's boar (Grimm, *Teutonic Mythology*, I, p.63 and note). It is quite possible that the pagan Anglo-Saxons baked birds, boars or horses in honour of their gods, but if so, this is a form of sculpture unfortunately lost to us. The name *Solmonath* does not itself seem to have a religious meaning unless *Sol* relates to the sun. Bosworth and Toller's *Dictionary* suggests that *sol* meant 'mire'. Such a name would refer to the bad weather of this month, which was later to be called 'February Fill-dyke'.

Bede tells us that sacrifices were made to the goddess Hreda in March and that the festival of Eostre fell in April. At this time of year the associated rites would almost certainly be concerned with the celebration of spring. The rituals might have involved flowers and perhaps the dancing and processing we associate today with May Day and Whitsuntide, plus the feast which became assimilated into the Christian Easter. Almost certainly bonfires were lit on hills during spring festivals, for in Christian times 'Easter fires' of this kind were lit throughout the territory of the more northerly of the Germanic peoples (Grimm, *Teutonic Mythology*, II, p.615).

Bede gives us no hint of a midsummer festival, but this celebration was so common throughout Europe that it almost certainly took place in England too. The festival was appropriated by the Christian Church as St John's Day (24 June). Again bonfires were lit, sometimes in the hills, but often in the streets. Grimm cites numerous instances (pp.617–27) from medieval to modern times, showing that it was traditional to dance round or jump over the midsummer fire, to cast herbs in it and so to gain immunity from ill-health and misfortune.

September was known as *Halegmonath* (Holy month) in pagan times, no doubt because a festival was celebrated at that time. A religious occasion at this time of year would almost certainly involve feasting in celebration of the crop, as perpetuated by the Christian Harvest Festival. Probably the shadowy mythical figures of Sheaf and his son Beow (barley) were once associated with these rites. Decoration and veneration of the last sheaf brought in (from which the craft of making corn dollies derives) may have been part of the 'Holy month' celebrations.

From this brief survey of the pagan year, we can see that the people in general would have been closely involved in these festivals, raising crops and animals, baking cakes, collecting fuel for bonfires, flocking to see images or wagons carrying the gods and joining them in procession. Above all they feasted, enjoying the fruits of their own labour while propitiating the deities.

There must, however, have been some professional priests to explain the symbolism of their actions to the people, to make the proper consecrations, to keep the mysteries which the populace were not allowed to share and to carry out any necessary sacrifices without fear of reprisal from offended parties. Priests may have worn special insignia when carrying out their duties and they were certainly required to keep to certain 'taboos' during everyday life. Germanic paganism on the continent employed both priests and priestesses. We have no literary evidence of priestesses in England, although it is possible that the small number of Kentish ladies who were buried in gold-brocaded fillets and who carried perforated spoons and crystal spheres pp.69–70) performed some magical rite with these mysterious objects. Priests are well attested from literature, however. Bede tells us that the East Saxons rejected Christianity and Bishop Mellitus in 616, the people of London preferring 'their own idolatrous priests' (*HE*, II, 6; p.109). Bishop Wilfrid, according to his biographer Eddius, was opposed by a priest who cursed the Christians and tried to put spells upon them from the vantage point of a high mound (perhaps a barrow). He was killed by one of the Christians, who, David-like, slung a stone at him (*Vita Wilfridi*, ed. and trans. B. Colgrave, p.28). The outstanding pagan priest of Anglo-Saxon literature is not, however, a villain but a man who saw the light. Coifi, High Priest to King Edwin of Northumbria, was among the King's trusted councillors at the time of Paulinus's mission in 627. As Bede tells his story, Coifi put forward a reasoned argument against paganism, before making the dramatic gesture of destroying his own temple which ensured him literary immortality and, no doubt, the royal favour he apparently craved:

[King Edwin] summoned a council of the wise men, and asked each in turn his opinion of this new faith and new God being proclaimed.

Coifi, the High Priest, replied without hesitation: 'Your Majesty, let us give careful consideration to this new teaching, for I frankly admit that, in my experience, the religion that we have hitherto professed seems valueless and powerless. None of your subjects has been more devoted to the service of the gods than myself, yet there are many to whom you show greater favour, who receive greater honours, and who are more successful in all their undertakings. Now, if the gods had any power, they would surely have favoured myself, who have been more zealous in their service. Therefore, if on examination these new teachings are found to be better and more effectual, let us not hesitate to accept them.' ...

... Coifi then added that he wished to hear Paulinus' teaching about God in greater detail; and when, at the king's bidding, this had been given, the High Priest said: 'I have long realized that there is nothing in what we worshipped, for the more diligently I sought after truth in our religion, the less I found. I now publicly confess that this teaching clearly reveals truths that will afford us the blessings of life, salvation, and eternal happiness. Therefore, Your Majesty, I submit that the temples and altars that we have dedicated to no

50

advantage be immediately desecrated and burned.' In short, the king granted blessed Paulinus full permission to preach, renounced idolatry, and professed his acceptance of the Faith of Christ. And when he asked the High Priest who should be the first to profane the altars and shrines of the idols, together with the enclosures that surrounded them, Coifi replied: 'I will do this myself, for now that the true God has granted me knowledge, who more suitably than I can set a public example, and destroy the idols that I worshipped in ignorance?' So he formally renounced his empty superstitions, and asked the king to give him arms and a stallion—for hitherto it had not been lawful for the High Priest to carry arms, or to ride anything but a mare—and, thus equipped, he set out to destroy the idols. Girded with a sword and with a spear in his hand, he mounted the king's stallion and rode up to the idols. When the crowd saw him, they thought he had gone mad, but without hesitation, as soon as he reached the temple, he cast a spear into it and profaned it. Then, full of joy at his knowledge of the worship of the true God, he told his companions to set fire to the temple and its enclosures and destroy them. The site where these idols once stood is still shown, not far east of York, beyond the river Derwent, and is known as Goodmanham. Here it was that the High Priest, inspired by the true God, desecrated and destroyed the altars that he had himself dedicated.

(*HE*, II, 13; pp.124–6)

Although Coifi may have been a conspicuous actor in this drama, it was clearly the king who was the spiritual leader of his people. Edwin had already promised tolerance of Christianity and hinted that he would become a convert when he made a politically important marriage with Æthelberg of Kent in 625, and received her chaplain, Paulinus, into his kingdom. The debate in which Coifi and another councillor spoke movingly was the vehicle for a democratic decision to convert, but clearly Edwin guided his people to that decision, just as his wife's father, Æthelberht of Kent, led his court to tolerate Augustine's mission in 597. This leadership of the king in religious matters must go back to heathen times. Kings and tribal chiefs no doubt figured in sacrificial and other pagan ceremonies. They habitually surrounded themselves with councillors who fulfilled (variously or collectively) both the ritual function of priests and the advisory capacity of cabinet ministers.

A king of ancient times had two main responsibilities—to keep his people fed and to ensure military victory (cf. the dual symbolism in the name of King Scyld Scefing; see p.32). The first of these needs, which concerned the cyclic planting and harvesting of crops and the breeding and killing of beasts, was presumably satisfied by the seasonal sacrifices and feasts. Warfare, less regular in its occurrence, was prefaced by divination.

When the young prince Beowulf, as the poet tells us, proposed going to Denmark to fight the man-eating monster which held sway there, the wise men of his own land 'examined the omens' (*hæl sceawedon*; line 204, *ASPR*, IV, p.9). Tacitus gives us a description of the kind of ritual such a custom

51

involved in his account of religious rites among the continental Germans:

> For auspices and the casting of lots they have the highest possible regard. Their procedure in casting lots is uniform. They break off a branch of a fruit-tree and slice it into strips; they distinguish these by certain runes and throw them, as random chance will have it, on to a white cloth. Then the priest of the State if the consultation is a public one, the father of the family if it is private, after a prayer to the gods and an intent gaze heavenward, picks up three, one at a time, and reads their meaning from the runes scored on them. If the lots forbid an enterprise, there can be no further consultation that day; if they allow it, further confirmation by auspices is required....
>
> (*Germania*, 10; pp.108–9)

Tacitus's word *notis* clearly indicates magical symbols which could be carved on to wood and has here been translated 'by ... runes'. Runic writing was widely known among the Germanic peoples. Runic 'letters' are angular symbols suitably shaped for carving. Some of the letters, such as the ↑, which represented the name of the god Tir, were prehistoric devices, religious or magical symbols in use from ancient times. Others, like ß, were probably adopted from an alphabet already in use in the alpine region. About the second century BC these were brought together to form a runic alphabet of twenty-four 'letters'. Runes probably first reached England via migrants from Anglian regions of the continent, who settled in what was to become East Anglia. A second import of runes, from Frisia, was first effective in the south-east of England, especially Kent. The twenty-four symbols common to all the Germanic areas had now evolved into twenty-eight.

Each of the original runic symbols had a name, the name of the object or concept which the symbol represented. Each rune also had a phonetic value, which was the initial sound of its name, hence ↑ (Tir) represented the name of the war god and also the sound *t*. There exist runic poems in Old English, Norwegian and Icelandic which give the name of each rune and a brief description of what it represents. The Old English poem was preserved in a tenth-century manuscript and was certainly not composed before Christian times. The Scandinavian texts are similarly late. All, therefore, are liable to have been influenced by changing conditions which made old words obsolete, and the English version specifically by the religious change, which made overtly pagan ideas distasteful. Nevertheless the runic poems are invaluable in helping us to interpret the single symbols and the longer inscriptions which survive. We have two complete alphabets of English runes, one in a manuscript now in Vienna, the other on a scramasax (a fighting-knife or one-edged sword) which was found in the River Thames (plate 13). Both alphabets are similar, with twenty-eight runic letters. The runes inlaid into the scramasax blade are:

ᚠ ᚢ ᚦ ᚨ ᚱ ᚳ ᚷ ᚹ ᚻ ᚾ ᛁ ᛂ ᛚ ᛤ ᛣ ᛘ ᛏ ᛒ ᛗ ᛉ ᚻ ᚽ ᛈ ᛞ ᛗ ᚠ ᚠ ᚪ ᛏ

7 Seventh-century helmet from a grave at Benty Grange, Derbyshire. The helmet was probably padded with fabric or leather and the iron ribs were covered by plates of horn. The pagan figure of a boar stands on the top, a small silver cross is fixed to the nose-piece (*Sheffield City Museum*)

8 One of a pair of gold shoulder-clasps from Sutton Hoo, Suffolk. These were probably meant to be stitched to a protective leather garment and were fastened together by a gold pin. The decoration consists of a chequer-pattern of millefiori glass framed by interlacing beasts in gold and garnet. Intertwined boars ornament the ends (*Trustees of the British Museum*)

9 The Franks Casket, cast of the right end. It is a whalebone box of Northumbrian workmanship, probably seventh-century. When the casket was recognized as Anglo-Saxon in the nineteenth century this end was missing. It was recovered later and is now exhibited in Florence, Italy (*Trustees of the British Museum*)

10 The Franks Casket, front. Framed by a border of runes, on the left Welund wreaks vengeance in his smithy, on the right the three Kings approach the Virgin and Child in the stable (*Trustees of the British Museum*)

This alphabet is followed by ᛒ ᛏ ᛉ ᛁ ᛗ ᚦ, which probably spelled out the name of the maker or the owner of the weapon.

ᚠ (*f*) signified *feoh* (wealth). (The word *feoh* essentially means 'cattle', but since stock was a measure of wealth the word came to have the more general meaning 'property', 'money'.)

ᚢ (*u*) represented *ur* (aurochs, a wild ox). Since oxen were a favourite form of sacrifice to Freyr, it is possible that this rune was originally used in connection with pagan rites. Since killing the aurochs was a test of a young man's strength in ancient Germany (see p.107), the meaning 'achievement', 'strength' may have become attached to the runic symbol.

ᚦ (*th*, thorn) is almost certainly an innocuous substitution made under Christian influence, for an unacceptable rune-name. This earlier name was probably *þyrs* (giant or demon), since this is the name given to the equivalent runic symbol in Scandinavian languages. The inoffensive 'thorn' was perhaps suggested by the shape of the letter.

ᚩ (*o*) represented *os*. This word probably related to the Æsir, and so meant 'a god', in particular Woden, who was the father of the Æsir (see p.12). This is confirmed by the fact that the equivalent symbol in Icelandic signified 'heathen god'. In Norwegian, however, the meaning was 'river mouth' and the late Old English *Rune Poem* gives an ambiguous definition:

ᚩ (*os*) byþ ordfruma ælcre spræce
(ASPR, VI, p.28, line 10)

'*os* is the origin of all speech'

This may refer to Woden as the legendary discoverer of runes, as already suggested (see p.12), or may be interpreting ᚩ as if it were the Latin word *os* (mouth). It seems probable that the 'mouth' interpretations were the substitutions of Christian scholars learned in Latin who either did not understand, or did not wish to perpetuate, references to heathenism.

ᚱ (*r, rad*) meant 'riding', 'a journey'. R. W. V. Elliott (*Runes*, p.57) points out that although in the runic poems of England and Scandinavia the symbol is interpreted literally as riding (on horseback) there may have been some belief in the journey after death, such as the journey taken by the body in a funeral ship, implicit in this rune.

ᚳ (*c*) stood for *cen* (torch) in the Old English runic poem, and in Christian times may sometimes have been used for *cene* (bold). The symbol is given other meanings in other languages. It might be tempting to speculate on pagan rituals, but the discrepancies in the use of the symbol are so great that it would be unwise to assume that any one was the original meaning.

ᚷ (*g, gyfu*) signified 'a gift' or 'generosity'. The giving of gifts was an essential part of Germanic life as we learn of it from heroic literature. Chiefs gave generously to incite and reward loyal warriors whose support was necessary in the traditionally war-conscious Germanic world. Elliott suggests tentatively (*Runes*, p.58) that the word may have originally signified sacrifices given to the gods, or gifts awarded by them, but there is no evidence in support of this idea.

ᚹ (*w*, *wyn*) signified 'joy'. This concept, as far as we can tell from heroic poetry, normally involved the enjoyment of a stable position under a generous chief, and life in a hall where there was music and companionship. There is no evidence for any religious meaning.

ᚻ (*h*, *hægl*) meant 'hail'. Anglo-Saxon poems such as *The Wanderer* and *The Seafarer* depict for us the miseries of winter experienced by northern peoples in ancient times. Hail is one of the unpleasant features mentioned in both poems. The ᚻ rune apparently formed a group with the next two.

ᚾ (*n*, *nyd*) meant 'affliction'.

ᛁ (*i*, *is*) meant 'ice', another uncomfortable aspect of winter.

+ was usually written ✳ or ⌽. It had the sound-value *j* and the meaning *ger* (year), with the particular application 'fruitful year', 'abundant harvest'. Agricultural prosperity, the most important thing in life to a self-sufficient people, was a primary reason to invoke divine aid and a major cause of celebratory banquets. The northern god most concerned with fertility was of course Freyr, so this rune may have played a part in his cult.

ᛇ or ⟨, (ȝ) meant *eoh* (yew-tree). The Old English *Rune Poem* (lines 35–7) simply describes a yew-tree in explanation of this runic symbol, but it is likely that the yew-tree was included among the runes for some superstitious reason. One could make various suggestions: for example it is known that yew-wood, being hard, was used to make bows in the Middle Ages, so perhaps the yew rune was a protection in battle. Yew does not, however, feature in Anglo-Saxon poetry as ash-wood does. (Spears were traditionally made of ash.) The Germanic people venerated sacred groves and trees in general. They did not, as far as we know, single out the yew-tree, but Elliott believes that they may have learned superstitions about yews from their neighbours the Celts, who cut ogham characters into wands made of yew-wood. (See R. W. V. Elliott, 'Runes, yews, and magic', *Speculum*, XXXII, 1957, pp.250–61.) Possibly yew-wood came to have a particular association with runes, since archaeological excavation in the Frisian area has revealed four objects of yew-wood with runic inscriptions, two of them apparently amulets.

The yew-tree can be either an optimistic or a pessimistic symbol; as an evergreen its branches might be used in winter fertility ceremonies as a reminder of rebirth. Yet its leaves are very dark, and to walk in a wood composed of such dark trees can be an eerie experience. To the Romans the yew was associated with poison and death, and in England yews were often found in churchyards (an association which modern poets have exploited). Elliott argues that yews were found in churchyards because the churches were built on sites sacred from pre-Christian times—sites chosen for their yew-trees.

ᛈ (*p*) is a rune of uncertain meaning. The *Rune Poem* tells us that it meant *peorð*, but the word is otherwise unknown.

ᛉ (*x*, *eolh*) is another rune of uncertain meaning. In Norway this rune was used of 'yew-tree' (cf. ᛇ above). OE *eolh* signified 'elk'. The *Rune Poem* (line 41) explains the symbol as *eolhx* (the name plus the sound or perhaps a genitive of *eolh*).

ᛊ (*s*), normally written ᛋ, signified *sigel* (sun). Julius Caesar (*De Bello Gallico*, VI, 21; H. J. Edwards (trans.), p.344) mentioned that the Germans worshipped the sun and the moon, but we do not know whether the latter were generally personified into gods in the Germanic world. They must, however, have been of great importance to daily life, governing the seasons and tides.

ᛏ (*t*, *Tir*) was the name of the pagan god of war (Tiw or Tyr; see p.28), although the *Rune Poem* takes it to be a stellar constellation; but the rune was certainly used in England in pagan times in ways which suggest the invocation of the heathen god.

ᛒ (*b*) represented *beorc* (birch-tree). This was probably, originally, a symbol of fertility and rebirth in the spring, as there is evidence for the use of birch twigs and saplings in this role from many European countries (Elliott, *Runes*, p.47).

ᛖ (*e*) represented *e(o)h* (horse). Not only were horses valuable possessions, they were also sometimes sacred (see p.28) and occasionally sacrificed with their owners. This rune, then, might have related to religious beliefs.

ᛝ, *ŋ* (that is, the sound *ng*) represented *Ing*, remembered in the *Rune Poem* (lines 67–70) as one who travelled in a wagon and probably identical with the fertility god Freyr (see p.30).

ᛞ, also represented as ⋈, expressed the sound *d* and the meaning *dæg* (day). Like the 'sun' and 'year' runes, this symbol represented one of the essential features of the cycle of life.

ᛚ (*l*) represented *lagu* (water) and expressed a terrifying yet fascinating feature of existence to the seafaring northern peoples. There may possibly have been an earlier meaning for the symbol associated with pagan practices (R. I. Page, *An Introduction to English Runes*, pp.82–3).

ᛗ (*m*) represented *man*. It meant, or came to mean, 'mankind'. Tacitus mentions a god, Mannus, acknowledged by the Germans as the author of mankind (*Germania*, 2), and it is possible that the rune originally referred to this god, but Tacitus emphasizes that rather than Mannus himself it was his father Tuisto who was celebrated, so the identification is perhaps unlikely.

ᛟ, more often found as ᛟ, represented the sound *oe* and the concept *eþel* (native land, home).

The last four symbols are additions to the common Germanic runes but still date to the pagan era.

ᚪ (a) represented *ac* (oak-tree). The *Rune Poem* (lines 77–80) refers to the oak's functions in providing acorns for pigs to feed on and timbers for ships, but let us not forget the Germanic predilection for sacred trees and groves. Grimm (*Teutonic Mythology*, I, pp.72–4; II, p.651) finds that oaks were considered sacred more commonly than any other trees. Indeed, the tradition of 'holy oaks' survived in several German areas until modern times.

ᚫ (*æ*) expressed the concept *æsc* (ash-tree). Like the oak, the ash-tree was useful for its wood, but also was often sacred in pagan times. The ash is very significant in northern mythology since, according to Snorri Sturluson's account, the centre of the world was a great ash-tree, called *Yggdrasill*. Its three great roots stretched into the three realms of the Æsir (the gods), the frost giants and the dead, and its branches stretched over heaven and earth.

ᚣ or ᚤ (*y, yr*) is a rune of uncertain meaning.

ᛠ (*ea*) is a rune of which the date and meaning have been much disputed. (See R. I. Page, 'The Old English rune *ear*', *Medium Ævum*, XXX, 1961, pp.65–79.) It was probably in use before the conversion, and represented the word *ear*. Old English has two known words spelt *ear*, one of which means 'ocean' the other 'ear of corn', but clearly the rune did not mean either of these things to the author of the *Rune Poem*:

> ᛠ (ear) byþ egle   eorla gehwylcun,
> ðonn fæstlice   flæsc onginneþ,
> hraw colian,   hrusan ceosan
> blac to gebeddan;   bleda gedreosaþ,
> wynna gewitaþ,   wera geswicaþ.

(ASPR, VI, p.30, lines 90–4)

Ear is hateful to every man, when the flesh, the pale corpse, surely begins to cool, to choose the earth as a bed-fellow; flowers disappear, joys depart, pledges fail.

Page supports the opinions that the name of the rune here was 'death' or 'the grave'.

Since each rune had a phonetic value, the runic symbols could be used to spell out words, such as the ᛒ ᛠ ᚷ ᚾ ᚪ ᚦ or *beagnoþ* on the Thames scramasax. They were not used for lengthy inscriptions in England until after the conversion had made the written word common. Indeed, in its earliest manifestations, runic writing was not intended to be comprehensible to the majority. The Old English word *run* meant 'a runic letter' (which could also be called a *run-stæf*), but it also signified 'secret', 'mystery' or 'whisper'. The word is, in fact, related to the modern German verb *raunen* (to whisper). The concept *run* essentially referred to confidential matters, hence in *Beowulf* the King of Denmark refers to his dead friend and advisor as a *runwita*, a 'confidential councillor' (line 1325, *ASPR*, IV, p.41) and the author of the Old English poem *The Wanderer* speaks of a man being *æt rune*, meaning either 'in council' or 'in secret meditation' (line 111, *ASPR*, III, p.137).

Those who knew how to cut runes, and those able to interpret them were, in earliest times, an élite few. If runes were originally associated with the supernatural through relation to paganism and use in divination, the esoteric nature of runic writing added to the superstition. The very act of inscribing a secret sign on to an object seems to have given that object a talismanic quality. Thus, according to a story narrated by Bede, a young Englishman taken prisoner in 679 could not be chained (since his brother, assuming that he was dead, was offering masses for his soul). His captors enquired whether he possessed any 'written charms' (*HE*, IV, 22, p.239). Bede used the Latin words *litteras solutorias*. The ninth-century scholar who translated Bede's *History* into English paraphrased the passage into an enquiry *hwæþer he þa alysendlican rune cuþe, and þa stafas mid hine awritene hæfde* (J. Schipper (ed.), p.457, lines 2857–9), 'whether he knew releasing runes and had the written letters with him'.

The Eddic poem *Sigrdrífomál* shows that, in the Scandinavian tradition, there were runes that could save one from all sorts of perilous situations, such as battle, a dangerous sea-voyage, malice, sickness and childbirth. We cannot be certain that such an elaborately detailed system of rune-magic was practised by the Anglo-Saxons, but it is clear that they invoked the protection of runes in warfare, in sickness and in death.

That the Anglo-Saxons, like the Scandinavians, traditionally placed runes on their weapons is proved by a few surviving examples. A spearhead from Holborough and a sword pommel from Faversham (Kent) appropriately bear the ↑ symbol of the pagan war-god (see pp.28–9). Another sword pommel from Kent (found at Ash or Gilton) has an obscure inscription, which may include some meaningless patterns among the genuine symbols which probably represented a name. (Apparently meaningless rune-like forms are not uncommon and suggest that unskilled craftsmen sometimes fobbed off their uninitiated clients with something that 'looked magic'.) A sword found in a grave at Chessell Down (Isle of Wight) had had a runic inscription added to its scabbard mount, probably not long before it was buried in the sixth century. The runes on the Thames scramasax may have been decorative rather than magical, but its owner, who may have commissioned it as late as the ninth century, invoked an ancient tradition when he chose a runic ornament for his weapon.

The use of runes at times of sickness is indicated by their survival in charms. These texts were not written down until centuries after the conversion and we find that the pagan superstitions in them mingle with garbled

Fig 12   Runic sword hilt from Chessell Down, Isle of Wight

Christian lore. Nevertheless, in the *Nine Herbs Charm* already quoted (see p.12) the god Woden and nine 'glory-twigs' (which were probably rune-engraved slips of wood) are invoked against snake-bite. In a charm *wiþ lenc-tenadle* ('against typhoid fever'; G. Storms, *Anglo-Saxon Magic*, pp.270–1) a person is advised to recite certain words in Latin and Hebrew including the names of the Evangelists, and some words given in runes. Then, in silence, he is to write down the runic inscription and lay it on his right breast. He is not to take it indoors. Clearly the written symbols in themselves contained curative magic.

Runes were associated with death in that they have sometimes been found decorating the earthenware pots in which the ashes of the dead were deposited (see p.92). There may be further evidence of this association in that runic objects were sometimes buried with the dead.[2] They include the weapons already mentioned, a bone, probably used as a gaming piece, found in an urn at Caistor-by-Norwich (Norfolk) and a cruciform brooch with a crudely-scratched symbol, which may be ⋈, a variation on ᚻ (*d*), from a cemetery at Sleaford (Lincs.).

We have seen that the Germanic people were constantly alert to the possibility of warfare, and that they needed to practise divination and to ensure the support of the gods in their enterprises. According to Tacitus even the ceremony of marriage was focused upon the militaristic:

> ... there is no question of sexual passion. The dowry is brought by husband to wife, not by wife to husband. Parents and kinsmen attend and approve of the gifts, gifts not chosen to please a woman's whim or gaily deck a young bride, but oxen, horse with reins, shield, spear and sword. For such gifts a man gets

---

2.   Admittedly most objects from the Anglo-Saxon pagan period which survive come from burials; but I think it possible that some few objects may have been chosen to accompany their owner because of their rune-magic (which may have been added for the occasion) just as in the conversion period jewellery may have been tolerated in burials if it included a cross.

his wife, and she in her turn brings some present of arms to her husband. In this interchange of gifts they recognize the supreme bond, the holy mysteries, the presiding deities of marriage. A woman ... is reminded, in the very ceremonies which bless her marriage at its outset, that she is coming to share a man's toils and dangers, that she is to be his partner in all his sufferings and adventures, whether in peace or war. That is the meaning of the team of oxen, of the horse ready for its rider, of the gift of arms.

(*Germania*, 18; pp.115–16)

There is evidence from late medieval Germany of marriage ceremonies involving the ritual use of a sword. Man and woman might both lay their hands upon the sword in token of their heroic duty. (It might also serve as a fertility symbol. See H. R. Ellis Davidson, 'The sword at the wedding', *Folklore*, LXXI, 1960, pp. 1–18.) Despite this traditional emphasis on war, a woman was, nevertheless, thought of by the Anglo-Saxons as a *freoðuwebbe* (weaver of peace), and as such was sometimes given in marriage as part of a peace treaty. In *Beowulf* several such marriages are mentioned, more than once ending tragically for the bride when the pull of hereditary blood feud proved stronger than the newer bond of matrimony. In England royal women travelled as brides from one kingdom to another. Traditionally Germanic women were respected for their prophetic powers (*Germania*, 8), and Anglo-Saxon queens evidently influenced their husbands: the wife of King Rædwald of East Anglia twice dissuaded him from taking steps she considered unwise (killing Edwin of Northumbria and converting to Christianity, *HE*, II, 12 and 15). Æthelberg, wife of King Edwin, was expected by the Pope to use her influence to further her husband's conversion (*HE*, II, 11).

We see from *Beowulf* that women played a ceremonial role in the male-orientated life depicted in heroic literature. The royal women, bejewelled, would enter the hall where the banquet was taking place and would carry the drinking vessel to the king, his guests and to the retainers in the hall. This ritual gave the women a chance to praise and placate. In *Beowulf* the Queen of Denmark is depicted making a public speech in which she openly advises her husband on political and family alliances. She also gives gifts to the hero Beowulf, who has saved her home from a monster. Beowulf in his turn shares his spoils with the queen of his own country as well as with his king.

It was the king, or chieftain, however, who played the most important role in secular life. From the *gif-stol* (gift-seat) he bestowed largesse upon valiant warriors who had deserved reward and upon promising young men. The latter would receive the gift of weapons which they would be expected to use in defence of the chief who had presented them. Traditionally the equipping of a young warrior with shield and spear was a public, ceremonial occasion (*Germania*, 13). Tacitus (*Germania*, 14) writes of the loyalty which warriors were expected to feel for their chief, and this bond is often mentioned in Old English literature. Probably the mutual pledge—the chief offering protection, the retainer loyalty—was the occasion for a public ritual, for in the poem *The Wanderer*, the protagonist, who, tragically, has outlived his chieftain, nostalgically recollects:

Þinceð him on mode   þæt he his mondryhten
clyppe ond cysse,   ond on cneo lecge
honda ond heafod,   swa he hwilum ær
in geardagum   giefstolas breac.

(*ASPR*, III, p.135, lines 41–4)

It seems to him in his mind that he embraces and kisses his liege lord, and lays hands and head on his knee, just as for a time, in former days, he enjoyed the gift-thrones.

In laying his hands and head on his lord's knee, the retainer perhaps touched the sword, symbolically laid there, or the royal sceptre (see p.113).

In heroic poems from the Old English period, formal speeches made by various characters occupy a good deal of space. While this is no doubt a poet's rhetorical device, it seems that speech-making and debating did play an important role in Anglo-Saxon life, at least in royal circles: Bede gives an account of the debate that preceded the acceptance of Christianity by Northumbria (see pp.50–1 and p.64) and at Yeavering archaeologists have recovered traces of a building especially constructed for the presentation of such speeches. It was a wedge-shaped structure, like a section of a Roman theatre, in which the audience sat or stood in tiers above and around a central stage.

The more usual theatre for speeches, as for other ceremonies, was the hall. This was a rectangular, wooden building around which the workshops and humbler dwellings of the community were grouped. In literature it is often called the 'mead-hall' or 'beer-hall' since it was the refectory for banquets which traditionally played a major part in Germanic life (*Germania*, 22). Here, presumably, there took place the celebratory feasts for religious occasions, about which we know little (see pp.42 and 45), and the secular feasts which are commemorated in Old English poetry. Women carried the ceremonial drinking vessels from warrior to warrior—a necessary action since the vessels, whether horns or beakers, did not have flat bottoms and could not be laid down while they still contained liquid. The feasters might be entertained by a *scop* (minstrel) who recited tales of legendary or ancestral heroes. His chant was composed of formulaic phrases from the poetic stock, varied suitably for the occasion and bound together by recurrent alliteration. He strummed on a lyre as an accompaniment to the song. Sometimes a warrior might make a *beot* (boast or vow) of the great deeds he hoped to achieve in battle. It was considered honourable to speak in this way, unless of course a man (perhaps influenced by liquor) over-estimated his own courage. In the Old English poem *The Battle of Maldon* warriors faced with an insuperable enemy are rallied by a young man named Ælfwine:

'Gumunan þa mæle   þe we oft æt meodo spræcon,
þonne we on bence   beot ahofon,
hæleð on healle,   ymbe heard gewinn;
nu mæg cunnian   hwa cene sy ....'

(*ASPR*, VI, p.13, lines 212–15)

'Let us remember the speeches which we often uttered at the mead, when we, on the bench, heroes in the hall, raised up vows about harsh battle; now it will be possible to prove who is brave ...'

There is an ironical ring about the phrase *hæleþ on healle*; it was easy to appear a hero in the security of the hall.

The king and women slept in chambers separate from the hall, but the chieftain's band of warriors slept in it at night, pulling out bedding from under the benches. These benches, 'mead-benches' as they were often called, seem to have been fixed to the floor. (We know this because of Beowulf's fight with the monster Grendel which uprooted the fixed benches in the hall where it took place; *Beowulf*, lines 775–6; *ASPR*, IV, p.25.) It was apparently a feature of Germanic dining arrangements that each person had his own place at a particular table (*Germania*, 22). Almost certainly this place was fixed by the man's position in the hierarchy of the community, as illustrated by an amusing incident in the Icelandic *Hrolfs Saga Kraka*. A man named Bǫðvarr, who is to emerge as a hero later in the story, arrives at the court of King Hrolfr and kills a retainer of the king who has tormented a weakling. The king offers him the place which the dead retainer used to occupy, but Bǫðvarr, who has befriended the weakling, Hǫttr, is dissatisfied with the offer:

Bǫðvarr said: 'I am not refusing to become your man, but as things are at present the two of us, Hǫttr and I, are not to be parted, but should both of us remain near you—nearer than that man used to sit—or else both of us will be gone from here.'

The king said: 'I can't see that he will be an honour to us, but I won't grudge him food.'

So now Bǫðvarr walked over to the seat which pleased him best, and would not occupy the one which the other man had had. He lifted three men bodily off a certain bench, and then he and Hǫttr sat themselves down on it, farther up the hall than the place assigned to them. The men thought it would be rather a difficult matter to tackle Bǫðvarr, and they felt great anger against him.

(*Beowulf and its Analogues*, pp.104–5)

Perhaps because the benches were a permanent fixture in the hall and because, when seated, a man knew his place in relation to his lord and his fellows, the mead-benches became symbolic of security. Thus, when the *Beowulf* poet wished to express the idea that a powerful Danish king had made all his neighbouring peoples subject to him, he wrote that he 'deprived them of their mead-benches' (*meodosetla ofteah;* line 5; *ASPR*, IV, p.3). The hall, too, brightly lit and filled with laughter and music, seemed a secure place while the world outside was mysterious and often menacing. This was expressed by one of King Edwin's nobles when the Northumbrian court was debating whether to convert to Christianity. The (unnamed) speaker was expressing the idea that man's lifetime is short, and that he himself and his fellow pagans knew nothing of man's existence before or after that brief lifespan on earth:

> Your Majesty, when we compare the present life of man with that time of which we have no knowledge, it seems to me like the swift flight of a lone sparrow through the banqueting-hall where you sit in the winter months to dine with your thanes and counsellors. Inside there is a comforting fire to warm the room; outside, the wintry storms of snow and rain are raging. This sparrow flies swiftly in through one door of the hall, and out through another. While he is inside, he is safe from the winter storms; but after a few moments of comfort, he vanishes from sight into the darkness from whence he came.'
>
> (*HE*, II, 13; pp.124–5)

To the superstitious Anglo-Saxons the dark world outside was populated by supernatural creatures, potentially harmful to man. The *Beowulf* poet enumerates:

> eotenas ond ylfe ond orcneas,
> swylce gigantas ...
>
> (*ASPR*, IV, p.6, lines 112–13)

monsters and elves and spectres, also giants ...

Grendel, the first monster killed by Beowulf on his visit to Denmark, is a man-eating giant. Beowulf himself refers to the monster as a *þyrs* (giant or demon; *ASPR*, IV, p.15; line 426). This monster was commemorated in the (now obsolete) place-names *Grendles mere* (Wilts.) and *Grendeles pytt* (Devon), while many other place-names testify to belief in giants: the obsolete *eotanford* (Shrops.) may commemorate an *eoten* (if it does not relate to the name of a person, Eota), and Edinshall (Berwickshire) may also derive from this word. The *þyrs* gave its name to several places, such as Thursden (Lancs.), Thursford (Norfolk), Thyrspittes (Lincs.) and *þyrs pyt* (Warwicks.), *Thirsqueche* ('*þyrs*-thicket', Northants.) and Tusmore ('*þyrs*-mere',

Oxon.), plus a number of others in areas settled by the Vikings which were probably named from *þurs*, the Scandinavian word for this kind of monster.

The Anglo-Saxons were also in awe of *entas* (giants) to whom they attributed the creation of the great stone buildings which the Romans had left in Britain. The Anglo-Saxons, who in the first centuries after their immigration built only in wood, viewed these crumbling monuments of a superior civilization as *eald enta geweorc* (ancient works of giants). The *ent* is commemorated in the place-names Indescombe (*'ent'*'s valley', Devon) and the (now obsolete) *to ænta dic* and *on enta hlewe*. Both are in Hampshire. They refer to a dyke and a (funeral) mound of *entas*.

The Germanic *ælf* (plural *ylfe*) was a hostile creature quite unlike the whimsical being of modern fairy-stories. Elves brought disease, *ælf-adl* and *ælf-sogoða*, as well as nightmare, *ælf-siden*. There are several Anglo-Saxon herbal remedies against elves, and one Old English charm against 'elf-shot' in a horse describes a series of ritual actions to be performed on the unfortunate beast (see p.197). Alveden (Lancs.) and Elveden (Suffolk) commemorate elf-valleys, Elva Hill (Cumb.) and Ilfracombe (Devon) hills of elves and the obsolete *Elvenfen* (Lincs.) an elves' fen.

The *dweorg* (dwarf) was also an unfriendly creature against which ritual actions and a metrical charm were employed (*ASPR*, VI, pp.121–2). The name of this creature was preserved in Dwarfholes (Warwicks.) and Dwarriden (Yorks.), both associating the dwarf with a valley, as well as in Dwerryhouse (Lancs.).

A kind of demon, *scucca*, is remembered in several place-names. It is associated with a hill or mound in Scoughall (E. Lothian), Shacklow (Derbys.), Shuckburgh (Warwicks.), Shucklow Warren (Bucks.) and Shucknall (Heref.). The creature is linked with a town in Shuckborough and Shugborough (both Staffs.), with a thorn in Shuckton Manor (Derbys.) and with ' a trap' or 'a water channel' in Shocklach (Ches.).

Lakes might be haunted by water-monsters, as Beowulf discovered when he tracked Grendel and his mother to their lair. These monsters, *niceras*, were tusked and harmful. They are remembered in the Sussex place-name *Nickerpoll*, now obsolete.

Beowulf's final monster fight was against a dragon, called *wyrm* and *draca* in the poem. This dragon was a coiled, scaly creature which could fly. Its weapons were fiery breath and a poisonous bite, although in the poem the dragon did not take any hostile action against mankind until a human being offended it by pillaging the hoard of treasure it guarded. Guarding burial mounds was apparently a normal occupation for dragons, as one of the Old English gnomic maxims indicates (see p.90), which may account for such place-names as Dragley (Lancs.), Drakedale (Yorks.), Drakeholes (Notts.), *dracenhorde* (Yorks.), Drakelow (Derbys. and Worcs.), Drakenage Farm (Warwicks.), Drake North (Wilts.) and Drake Pits (Yorks.). The appearance of dragons was considered an evil portent: the *Anglo-Saxon Chronicle* records that dragons were seen flying over Northumbria in 793, an event soon followed by famine and the destruction of the famous church at Lindisfarne by heathen Vikings.

Thus the Anglo-Saxons lived their lives, cosy in their brightly lit halls, cheered by feasting and music. They placated their gods with sacrifice and strove to keep out the hostile creatures who lurked in the outer darkness. They enjoyed formal ceremonies—pledging of oaths and speechmaking— and superstitious rituals, like the casting of lots, decided the major issues of their lives. The ritual which was perhaps most important of all came, however, at the end of life. The pagan funeral ceremony, which honoured the achievements of a lifetime and, it was hoped, equipped the dead one for the afterlife, will be considered in the following chapters.

3

Pagan Inhumation and Cremation Rites

We are in a position to learn more about funeral customs than about any of the other pagan rituals the Anglo-Saxons may have practised, for we have both literary and archaeological evidence of them. Not only were the funerals of legendary heroes celebrated in poetry, but also thousands of real Anglo-Saxon burial sites have been discovered and explored by archaeologists in our own era.

Faced with the mystery of death, the Anglo-Saxons, like modern man, resorted to well-established ritual, which no doubt provided some cathartic effect for the bereaved and also assumed the continued existence of the dead one. Some of the ritual may have been demanded by the religious cult of the tribe: that certain gods demanded appropriate sacrifices from their worshippers. Many of the mourners' actions, however, were obviously dictated by belief in an afterlife much like the life here, where men and women would require their material possessions, as appropriate to their rank. Often, it seems, both motives were present: the burial of a man with his spear may reflect the cult of Woden, as suggested earlier (see p.13), but we must not forget that in everyday life a man needed his spear for protection and to kill for food, and that he would need that weapon in the next life, just as a woman would need her jewellery and her spinning equipment.

For what, then, may be a variety of reasons, the Anglo-Saxons habitually provided their dead with grave-goods before disposing of the body. Many of these objects survive and, cleaned and preserved, are exhibited in museums throughout England. Experts can easily distinguish these Germanic-style objects from the artefacts of other peoples who have lived in England (Bronze Age and Roman, for example). They vividly illustrate life and death in Anglo-Saxon England fifteen hundred years ago.

Organic matter (flesh, textile, leather and wood) of course normally decays in the earth after a short time. Unless soil is extremely acid, bones and teeth usually survive, and cremated bone is even more resistive. Pottery is preserved, also metal. Gold and silver can be removed from the earth after a thousand years without having suffered damage. Bronze objects turn green with verdigris and iron rusts, but articles made of these metals are very often recovered in such a state that their shape and decoration is recognizable.

Even organic matter may survive in unusual conditions. We have numerous scraps of textile and leather, preserved only because the iron to which they were attached rusted, surrounding and protecting tiny areas of fabric. Leather sometimes survives in soil as the result of the action of tannins, and in rare cases wood may be preserved, for example in extremely wet ground.

The Anglo-Saxons practised both inhumation and cremation in pagan times. Both rites ended with burial in the earth, the former consisting of the burial of a corpse with grave-goods in a grave, the latter ending with the burial of the ashes, usually in a container. Broadly speaking, cremation was more popular in Anglian areas, inhumation in Saxon areas and in Kent. The two rites did coexist in some places, and we find mixed cemeteries in which urns containing cremated bone were deposited among apparently contemporary inhumation graves. Possibly the mixture arose when a community was made up of different family groups who coexisted to the extent of sharing a cemetery but followed their individual beliefs in the disposal of the bodies. Some settlers may have been influenced to abandon cremation by the example of their Romano-British neighbours, who inhumed. Only in Anglian areas do we find cemeteries exclusively devoted to cremation.

Inhumation was no doubt easier than cremation. It is likely that when a death occurred among barely established settlers or small groups of warriors, whatever their beliefs, the body had to be buried, since isolated burials have been found, but not isolated cremations. Cremation required skill and facilities, but inhumation was a simpler task. There must have been many people, however, among whom inhumation was the more desirable funeral. We find inhumation cemeteries ranging in size from small (perhaps family) sites, like the ten-grave cemetery at Winterbourne Gunner (Wilts.), to burial sites which must have served large communities, like the one at Sarre (Kent) with over two hundred and seventy burials. Burial practice was remarkably similar throughout Anglo-Saxon England. The corpse was evidently laid out with care and dressed in its clothes, in some cases in its most elaborate costume. A woman dying in the fifth or sixth century (plate 14) would be dressed in a gown which was clasped on the shoulders by a pair of bronze

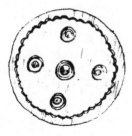  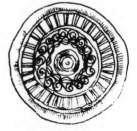

Fig 13   Typical circular brooches

Fig 14 Typical long brooches

or gilded brooches, either circular or long. Circular brooches might be flat and shiny, decorated in a simple way with ring and dot ornament, or they might be saucer-shaped with cast ornament in the shape of a star or in a scroll pattern. Long brooches had square or radiate heads, or were cruciform, with three projecting knobs at the head, often with a stylized horse's head at the foot. Attached to these brooches there would be a festoon of beads, of multi-coloured glass, of amber and sometimes of crystal, the last two types perhaps cherished for prophylactic reasons as well as for their appearance. The woman's gown or cloak might be fixed with a third brooch, unlike the pair at her shoulders, or with a pin. If she owned other brooches her kin might pin or stitch them to her clothes. If she were rich, she might wear bracelets and a ring or two. At her wrists, if she were an Anglian woman, she might wear metal clasps, to fasten her sleeves. Her headdress might be secured by a pin. The belt which fastened her gown would be of leather or braided textile, secured by a buckle, a toggle or a knot. In life it had provided a convenient attachment point for the tools and personal articles the woman carried about with her. They would be carefully arranged about her hips and thighs as she lay ready for her grave. An iron knife with a bone handle was thrust through the belt, to which a toilet set—implements for cleaning the nails and the ears—might be attached by a suspension ring. Also hanging from it could be keys, latch-lifters for unlocking the chests in which her household goods were kept, and in themselves symbolic of her role as housekeeper. A woman sometimes carried tweezers, a 'strike-a-light' or a purse. She might have a large bead to act as a flywheel for her spinning. She may have carried a wooden spindle, too, but that would decay before any archaeologist could find it. If she were Anglian she might have a pair of girdle hangers—iron objects from which small articles could be suspended. If she were a rich Kentish woman, she might carry a silver spoon,

69

decorated with garnet and perforated in the bowl (plate 15), together with a crystal ball, mounted in a silver sling. We do not know the purpose of these last-mentioned luxuries, but possibly the few women who owned them (who were elaborately dressed with gold headdresses) performed some magical rite with the objects. Ordinary women carried amulets—an animal's tooth, pierced and suspended, an eagle's claw in one case or, not uncommonly, a cowrie shell, perhaps for fertility. All the woman's treasures were arranged at the front of her body, perhaps because that is how she wore them habitually—even the beads being festooned at her chest, rather than passing round her neck—or perhaps because her body was displayed and carried uncovered on a bier to the grave.

Of course, not every woman possessed the jewellery deemed necessary for her life in the next world. Thus, a young girl buried at Holywell Row (Suffolk) was decked out in old brooches and strings of beads too long for her by relatives wishing to provide lavish grave-goods, over-lavish indeed, by the standards of the seventh century, when she was buried. Many women were buried wearing incomplete or badly matched sets of wrist clasps.

Men were not decked out with jewellery as women were. Belt buckles were common, however, and some men wore more elaborate metal belt fittings. Men also went to the grave with personal and useful items attached to their belts. Almost all had a knife, sometimes carried in a sheath. Some had 'strike-a-lights' or purses (which may in some cases have contained fire-making materials), tweezers and shears. Like women they carried amulets—such as an animal's tooth or a shell. In other cases a man's tool, his axe or whetstone, was attached to his belt or laid beside him. His shield was placed over his body, the circular wooden board surrounding the metal boss, which is all that survives for the archaeologist to find. His spear, taller than he was, was placed by his side. The iron spearhead was attached to a wooden shaft, which was sometimes tipped with a metal ferrule. If he was wealthy, a man might own a sword which could accompany him to the grave. It would be laid at his side, perhaps suspended by a sword belt or a baldric. A ring or a bead attached to the sword hilt would indicate particularly high rank.

The bodies of children were often equipped as if they had been adults. A child might be provided with a knife it was too young to use, and a girl with jewellery damaged by more wear than she could have given it in her short lifetime. Young boys were not provided with weapons, however. Many children's corpses were buried with two or three tiny beads at the neck.

Graves were long enough to accommodate a supine body. Corpses were not normally flexed or crouched. Graves were quite shallow, and it was not normally the practice to place one corpse above another. Double and triple graves are sometimes found, with bodies lying side by side, but there is no indication that human sacrifice preceded these multiple burials. Probably

70

11 Fertility 'god' from Broddenbjerg Fen, Denmark. The natural phallic shape of
an oak branch was augmented by carving. Associated objects date the 'god' to the
Early Iron Age (from *c.* 400 BC to the birth of Christ). The object is now in the
National Museum of Antiquities, Copenhagen (*Dr P. V. Glob*)

12 November bonfire from BL MS Cotton Tiberius Bv, fol. 8, detail. This early eleventh-century calendar carries on each page an illustration of the occupation for the month (*British Museum, British Library*)

13 Scramasax from Battersea, London. Found in the River Thames, this late Anglo-Saxon fighting knife is decorated with the runic alphabet and a man's name in runes (*Trustees of the British Museum*)

members of the community or of a family who died at about the same time of disease were buried side by side. Children are sometimes found buried together, and with adults of both sexes. No doubt infant mortality was high and bodies may have been buried for convenience with any adult who was being interred.

Inhumation cemeteries were often situated well away from settlements. *Cemeteries* Graves were often orientated north–south, but archaeologists always find deviations from this arrangement in cemeteries of any size, and the graves are never arranged systematically in rows. There are a few instances of burials being arranged radially, at Blewburton Hill (Berks.), for example, where the line followed an earlier (Iron Age) feature, and at Newport Pagnell (Bucks.) where, it was thought, there had been a central burial of an important person. Possibly some cemeteries contained family groups, and graves at some sites, for example at Lyminge (Kent), may have been laid out in relation to buildings. At Yeavering an inhumation cemetery was sited beside the heathen temple. There may have been temples, undetected by excavators, at other burial sites.

Bodies were apparently buried in coffins only rarely. They were sometimes wrapped in linen shrouds and probably laid in the graves on biers. In some cases the graves were elaborate: Roman tiles were used to line one at Frilford (Berks.) and other skeletons at this site had their heads resting on stone 'pillows', but such refinements were uncommon.

Articles for the use of the dead person were placed on or around the corpse. Women might have a pouch decorated with an ivory ring, and both sexes were often provided with a comb. Pottery vessels were placed in many graves, and also wooden containers. Probably these held food or drink, for eggs, nuts, oysters and the bones from joints of poultry and meat have been found at various sites. Glass beakers, bowls and cups were sometimes placed in graves to provide luxury drinking vessels for their owners.

Sacrifice of animals or human beings may have taken place occasionally, but was certainly not the general rule. It has been suggested that skeletons found in positions consistent with being bound, arranged in a circle round a (presumed) barrow burial at Cuddesdon (Oxon.) were sacrifices, but the evidence is not firm. Archaeologists have occasionally found the remains of bodies buried unceremoniously, usually face down, on top of carefully laid-out corpses of men and in one case, on top of a woman. These may be wives or servants who died violently and were pushed into the graves of their spouses or masters. A pig's head buried in a grave without a human corpse (at Frilford, Berks.) may be evidence of some other pagan rite (see p.47).

In some cases superstitious practices may have been performed to prevent the dead person from troubling the living. These included decapitation of the corpse, the strewing of flints or placing of stones over the body and the burning of corn. Evidence of all these customs is rare, but has been found more than once.

When the grave was filled in, some kind of marker may have indicated its position since grave-diggers mostly avoided cutting into earlier interments. Archaeologists have found no evidence of marker stones and burial mounds were rare before the seventh century, so if there were any above-ground markers they must have been of perishable material, probably wood.

In the course of the seventh century, Anglo-Saxon England was converted to Christianity. The Church exerted its influence against pagan burial and the deposition of grave-goods, as a result of which many communities abandoned their old burial grounds in favour of new cemeteries nearby. It is evident that the old, established practices were not readily abandoned, however. These 'new' cemeteries contain a higher proportion of unfurnished graves, or graves furnished only with a knife, than the fifth- and sixth-century burial grounds, but it seems that some people, misunderstanding or defying the Church's teaching, still deposited grave-goods with their dead. We find that fashions in clothing and weapons were changing. Women no longer wore the traditional pairs of brooches, but instead used single annular brooches or more elaborate jewelled ones. The barbaric necklaces gave way to amethyst beads, gold jewelled pendants or imitations of these made by stringing beads on rings. A necklace sometimes carried a cross (plate 16), which perhaps justified its owner in wearing it to the grave. The cross also appeared on some buckles. Women now hung chatelaine chains and tiny thread boxes from their belts and secured the necks of their garments with neat pairs of pins, linked by chain. Men were buried with new-style shields, which had tall bosses, and with scramasaxes, long knife-like weapons. Sometimes corpses were buried with boxes or pouches, which no doubt contained precious possessions, a kind of compromise between placing grave-goods on the body and eschewing grave-goods altogether.

Even while the Anglo-Saxons were burying their dead in new cemeteries with graves orientated east–west in the Christian manner, some anxiety about the efficacy of Christian burial was obviously felt. These seventh-century burial grounds often display signs of superstitious precautions in greater variety and concentration than in earlier cemeteries belonging to a totally heathen era. At Winnall (Hants.) both decapitation and the casting of flints on head or body took place. At Leighton Buzzard (Beds.) charcoal and pieces of pottery were among the soil filling the graves. At Driffield (Yorks.) a spear had been deliberately broken, ritually 'killed'. At Totternhoe (Beds.), round the necks of two skeletons were small satchels containing human teeth, a feature unparalleled in other cemeteries, earlier or contemporary. At Winnall many bodies were placed in the ground carelessly or hastily, inexplicable unless we suppose that some of the old skills and traditions had been lost with the token acceptance of Christianity. Surprisingly, it was in the seventh century, when Christianity was influencing people both physically and spiritually, that the Anglo-Saxons revived the custom of burial under barrows. We may use the term 'revived' because Bronze Age and Iron Age barrows already existed in England, but among the Anglo-Saxons themselves the practice seems to have begun only in the seventh century.

Barrow burial plays a part in northern mythology and in Icelandic literature is associated with Woden and with Freyr, who was himself believed to have been laid in a mound; but if the Anglo-Saxons practised barrow burial with this in mind it is strange that they did not do so immediately after their immigration. The raising of a burial mound also has a purpose which, while not directly linked with any heathen deity, is undeniably pagan: the ensuring of posthumous fame for the dead man. In *Beowulf*, which was first written down in the same century that these barrows were made, the dying hero gives intructions about the tumulus that is to ensure his immortality:

'Hatað heaðomære hlæw gewyrcean
beorhtne æfter bæle æt brimes nosan;
se scel to gemyndum minum leodum
heah hlifian on Hronesnæsse,
þæt hit sæliðend syððan hatan
Biowulfes biorh, ða ðe brentingas
ofer floda genipu feorran drifað.'

(ASPR, IV, pp.86–7, lines 2802–8)

'Command the veterans to make a bright barrow after the funeral fire at the promontory by the sea. It must tower high on *Hronesnæss* [Whale-cliff] as a remembrance to my people, so that afterwards seafarers, who urge ships far over the oceans' mists, will call it Beowulf's barrow.'

Another Anglo-Saxon poet refers to the posthumous fame which was the pagan ideal:

... bið eorla gehwam æftercweþendra
lof lifgendra lastworda betst ...

(The Seafarer, lines 72–3; ASPR, III, p.145)

... for each man, praise of the living, speaking in afterdays, is the best of epitaphs ...

(but he goes on to make it clear that the Christian should strive to deserve another kind of immortality).

The Anglo-Saxons who had barrows constructed over their bodies were often clearly the rich and royal persons whose lives may have led them to expect posthumous fame. At Taplow (Bucks.) a barrow 15ft (4·6m) high and 240ft (73·1m) in circumference made a lasting memorial to the chief buried under it. Assuming that the place took its name from this landmark, the man may have been called Tæppa (*Tæppa-hlæw*; OE *hlæw*: barrow). He had been buried in an unusually large grave, dug below ground level, with a floor of gravel. His barrow was excavated in the nineteenth century when archaeologists were not always as precise as they are today, and interpretation of the find was handicapped by the fact that very little skeletal material survived. It seems, however, that 'Tæppa' was buried wearing a magnificent belt which was secured at the waist by a pair of triangular gold clasps. A triangular gold buckle decorated with garnet lay at his left shoulder, and leading away from it were found threads of gold which had been brocaded into the material fastened by the buckle. (It was at first thought that the gold had edged a cloak, but it now seems most likely that it had decorated a baldric.) The body was laid on planks. Over and around it were arranged the possessions of a wealthy man. His weapons included a sword, a throwing-spear, two other spears and two shields. There were containers—two buckets, each 1ft (30cm) across, a twelve-sided bronze bowl, 1ft (30cm) high, of Coptic (Christian Egyptian) type, and a bronze vessel 2ft (61cm) across, which contained two large drinking horns (plate 17) with metal rims and tips and two glass beakers. There were two smaller drinking horns and two other glass vessels. The dead man was also provided with the means of amusing himself: a set of bone gaming pieces and a stringed musical instrument were placed in his grave. Planks covered the grave and the mound, of loose gravel, was built over it. This obviously pagan burial was apparently made in a nominally Christian cemetery, for when excavated it stood within the churchyard. At that time it was the richest Anglo-Saxon burial to have been discovered.

Barrow burial was particularly popular in the Peak District in the seventh century. This area has produced several interesting examples of tumuli raised over primary Anglo-Saxon interments. Among them is the Benty Grange (Derbys.) barrow, a small (2ft; 61cm) but wide mound which contained the remains of the boar-helmet discussed on p.31. There may have been also a shaggy woollen cloak. There were the silver edging and ornaments of a leather cup, which like the helmet included a cross, the Christian symbol, in its decoration. Fragments of chain work (not sufficient for a set of chain-mail armour) and a mysterious six-pronged instrument, now lost, were among the finds, but the skeleton had not survived. At Brushfield (Derbys.) a man's barrow was excavated, like the Benty Grange tumulus, by the nineteenth-century archaeologist Bateman. The body lay in a shallow grave. It may have rested on a hide and had been buried in a wooden coffin, the bolts of which were found by the excavator. A sheathed sword, a knife and two javelins accompanied this body and a tumulus 4ft (1·2m) high and 51ft (15·5m) across was raised over it.

In Kent, Sussex and the Isle of Wight (Jutish/Frankish areas) whole cemeteries of barrow burials have been discovered. In several ways the culture of the 'Kentish' regions differs from the rest of Anglo-Saxon England, and archaeological finds suggest a materially richer civilization there than in any other region (except the royal court of East Anglia as exemplified by the Sutton Hoo ship burial). 'Kentish' graves have more swords, more gold, more glassware than the graves of other regions. It seems that the custom of raising a mound over a single grave, which elsewhere tended to be a tribute confined to a few outstanding men, was much more generally practised in 'Kentish' regions, and came into use rather earlier. Most of the mounds in the 'Kentish' barrow cemeteries were apparently quite small, about 3ft (91cm) for example, and, contrary to what one might have expected, the largest mounds did not necessarily contain the richest grave-goods.

A few of these barrow burials were lavishly equipped with grave-goods. At Chessell Down (Isle of Wight) for example, a woman buried in an unusually large grave wore a headdress adorned with gold, five brooches, a necklace of beads, a belt buckle and two finger-rings. From her waist hung a crystal ball and a silver spoon, a knife and a key. Buried with her were a bronze vessel, a wooden vessel edged with silver and a metal weaving sword.

Such elaborate grave-goods seem to belong to the earlier (sixth-century) 'Kentish' barrow burials. Many other graves under tumuli are unfurnished, or sparsely furnished, probably reflecting the Christian influence which was spreading in the seventh century. The barrow cemetery at Kingston (Kent) for example, contained over two hundred and sixty graves, but only four of the corpses there had been buried with brooches. Each of the four women had worn a circular brooch, decorated with garnets, at her neck, in two cases placed near the right shoulder. One of the women had a second brooch, of simpler design, in a box at her feet. Another had two functional safety-pin brooches to secure her skirt (or shroud) at her left thigh; but paradoxically this woman, who was not equipped with great quantities of grave-goods and who wore what are probably the most primitive-looking brooches yet found in Anglo-Saxon context, also wore the most splendid brooch to have survived from that era.

The so-called 'Kingston Brooch' (plate 18) consists of two circular gold plates 'sandwiched' together with a filling material. It measures $3\frac{1}{4}$in (8·2cm) across and is unique among polychrome brooches in that its backplate is elaborately decorated in filigree. The front of the brooch is built up into gold cloisons, which are lined with gold foil and filled with red garnets and blue glass. The cloisons, designed in step-shapes and semicircles, are arranged in concentric bands, alternating with zones of interlacing animals executed in filigree. A central boss, its jewels mounted on white shell, and four subsidiary bosses dominate the design. Four diamond-shaped cells set in transverse lines of cloisons alternate with the bosses, and give the whole brooch a cruciform theme. Many seventh-century polychrome brooches have such cross-shaped designs, perhaps reflecting Christian influence, perhaps just a natural evolution of the jewellers' art.

Many of the 'Kentish' bodies in barrow cemeteries had been buried in coffins, another difference between this region and others, where coffin-burial was unusual. Some of the coffins showed signs of having been in contact with fire. Perhaps the seventh-century inhabitants had some belief in the efficacy of burning, shared by those other peoples who cremated their dead. If so, with these inhumations, which had been touched by fire, buried under tumuli with few grave-goods, some of which had crosses upon them, we find an accumulation of beliefs and superstitions such as we have noted in seventh-century burials elsewhere (see p.74) and that we will see again in the Sutton Hoo ship burial (see pp.121, 125).

reuse of mounds

In what was probably the same urge to bury their dead under visible tumuli, certain sixth- and seventh-century inhabitants of England began using older barrows for their interments. Thus, mounds originally raised over Neolithic or Bronze Age graves came to be used, secondarily, by the Anglo-Saxons. We find this custom among the Anglians of the Derbyshire–Staffordshire Peak District, who as we have already seen (see p.76) also constructed barrows over their own, primary, interments at this time. A woman buried in an older barrow at Cowe Lowe was equipped with a pair of gold pins, set with garnet, and a wooden box which had contained her necklace of metal pendants, a glass pendant and an animal's tooth, a glass vessel, a comb and (perhaps) a needle. At nearby Galley Lowe, male and female burials evidently took place. Arrowheads and a whetstone were typically male grave-goods, while beads of gold, glass and enamel and gold pendants, some set with garnets, were relics of a woman.

The Anglian people of the Yorkshire Wolds used pre-existing barrows for large numbers of their own dead. Fifty Anglo-Saxon skeletons have been found in a barrow at Driffield and seventy-one at Uncleby, where the skeleton of a dog, charcoal and burnt earth indicated rituals of a complexity comparable to Kentish practice.

Among the West Saxon people, too, secondary barrow burial was practised. In the area of modern Wiltshire archaeologists have found many instances. In this region, however, the Anglo-Saxon graves occur singly or in very small numbers. Few are rich, although swords accompanied male interments at Kings Barrow and Sherrington, and there was a rich female grave at Roundway Down. The woman had been buried in an iron-bound wooden coffin, and the bones of cat, dog, boar and horse were scattered about her. The woman's head was to the north, the pre-Christian, pagan orientation. She wore jewellery typical of the seventh century, comparable with that found at Cowe Lowe and Galley Lowe (Derbys.). A pair of dainty gold pins, garnet headed, were at her neck, linked by a chain, with a central roundel decorated with a cruciform pattern, suggesting that she had come into contact with Christianity. Her necklace consisted of gold beads and chunky pendants of garnets and paste set into gold frames. A bronze-bound wooden bucket was at her feet.

By the end of the seventh century the Church seems to have exerted enough influence to prevent people from burying their dead in the pagan manner. Instead they were interred in a churchyard with Christian rites. A few possessions were at first buried with their owners, but the custom soon died out as the Anglo-Saxons forsook the idea of an afterlife not unlike life on earth in favour of the Christian conceptions of heaven and hell. Pope Gregory, the moving spirit behind the conversion of the English, had advised his missionaries to treat Anglo-Saxon heathenism with tact and compromise (Bede, *HE*, I, 30). We see this compromise working as the pagan burial sites were replaced in the seventh century, yet the old customs were not entirely lost. Then, gradually, the custom of depositing grave-goods was abandoned.

Compromise must have been almost impossible for those who practised cremation, for this method of disposing of the body, and the associated rituals were even further removed from Christianity than heathen burial.

Cremation, like inhumation, had ancient associations with gods (Woden and Thunor; see pp.20–2, 25), but those who cremated seem to have had a rather different conception of the afterlife from those who inhumed. People who buried their kinsman in the ground with his possessions about him evidently believed or hoped that those possessions would be used in some life like their own by the dead man in the form in which they knew him. Those who cremated the dead and burned his possession with him evidently believed that the fire worked some metamorphosis; the spirit of the dead one (and his possessions?) was apotheosized to some other plane by the act of cremating. In the *Ynglinga Saga*, Snorri alludes to this transformation:

> It was a belief that the higher the smoke rose in the air, the higher would rise the man whose pyre it was; and the more goods that were destroyed with him, the richer he would be.
>
> (*Beowulf and its Analogues*, p.348)

The same phenomenon was explained by an onlooker to the Arab traveller Ibn Fadlan when he witnessed a Viking cremation (see pp.100–1). In the following passage from *Beowulf*, the poet alludes to the smoke when describing the cremation of his hero, but (being a Christian) refrains from expounding the pagan belief associated with it. Beowulf has been killed fighting a dragon, but he dies a hero, having also killed the dragon and won the treasure it guarded:

Him ða gegiredan   Geata leode
ad on eorðan   unwaclicne,
helmum behongen,   hildebordum,
beorhtum byrnum,   swa he bena wæs;
alegdon ða tomiddes   mærne þeoden
hæleð hiofende,   hlaford leofne.
Ongunnon þa on beorge   bælfyra mæst
wigend weccan;   wudurec astah,
sweart ofer swioðole,   swogende leg
wope bewunden   (windblond gelæg),
oðþæt he ða banhus   gebrocen hæfde,
hat on hreðre.   Higum unrote
modceare mændon,   mondryhtnes cwealm;
swylce giomorgyd   Geatisc meowle
. . . .   bundenheorde
song sorgcearig   swiðe geneahhe
þæt hio hyre heofungdagas   hearde ondrede,
wælfylla worn,   werudes egesan,
hynðo ond hæftnyd.   Heofon rece swealg.
Geworhton ða   Wedra leode
hleo on hoe,   se wæs heah ond brad,
wægliðendum   wide gesyne,
ond betimbredon   on tyn dagum
beadurofes becn,   bronda lafe
wealle beworhton,   swa hyt weorðlicost
foresnotre men   findan mihton.
Hi on beorg dydon   beg ond sigiu,
eall swylce hyrsta,   swylce on horde ær
niðhedige men   genumen hæfdon,
forleton eorla gestreon   eorðan healdan,
gold on greote,   þær hit nu gen lifað
eldum swa unnyt   swa hit æror wæs.
Þa ymbe hlæw riodan   hildediore,
æþelinga bearn,   ealra twelfe,
woldon ceare cwiðan   ond kyning mænan,
wordgyd wrecan   ond ymb wer sprecan;
eahtodan eorlscipe   ond his ellenweorc
duguðum demdon,   swa hit gedefe bið
þæt mon his winedryhten   wordum herge,
ferhðum freoge,   þonne he forð scile
of lichaman   læded weorðan.

                                   (*ASPR*, IV, pp.96–8, lines 3137–77)

Then the people of the Geats made for him a firmly-built pyre on the earth, hung about with helmets, with battle shields, with bright coats of mail, as he was desirous. Lamenting warriors then laid the famous prince, the dear lord, in the midst. Then warriors kindled the greatest of pyres on the hill. The wood-

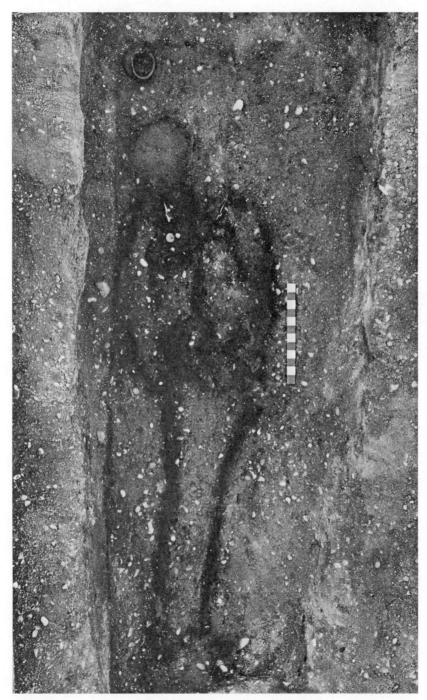

14 Grave-goods *in situ* at Mucking, Essex. The woman's skeleton is reduced to a mere silhouette in the soil but her possessions remain – a vessel at her head, a pair of brooches at her shoulders, beads and a pin at her chest. Fifth- or sixth-century (*W. T. Jones*)

15 A silver spoon with cruciform perforations in the bowl and a crystal ball in a silver mount from Chessell Down, Isle of Wight. Both objects were suspended at the waist of a richly equipped woman in a sixth-century grave (*Trustees of the British Museum*)

16 Necklace from Desborough, Northamptonshire. Gold beads and garnet pendants flank a small gold cross. Found in a woman's grave of the seventh century (*Trustees of the British Museum*)

17 Silver-gilt mount from Taplow, Buckinghamshire. Set round the wide end of an animal's horn, with a matching terminal at the narrow end of the horn, this mount formed part of an elaborate drinking vessel, one of a pair. The mount is decorated with stylized beasts. From a very rich male burial of the seventh century (*Trustees of the British Museum*)

18 Cloisonné brooch from Kingston, Kent. Found in the seventh-century grave of a woman, this gold brooch is decorated with filigree animals and inlaid with garnets and blue glass (*Merseyside County Museum, Liverpool*)

(*left*) 19 Cremation urn with 'wyrm' device from Kettering, Northamptonshire (*Terry Rice, Kettering Museum*). (*right*) 20 Cremation urn with stamped 'wyrm' from West Keal, Lincolnshire (*Lincoln Museum*)

21 Cremation urn with S-curve from Baston, Lincolnshire (*Lincoln Museum*)

smoke ascended, dark over the flame, the roaring blaze mingled with weeping—
the raging wind ceased—until it had destroyed the body, hot at the heart.
Depressed in spirits they lamented their care, the death of their liege-lord. Like-
wise a Geatish woman with bound-up hair sorrowfully sang a mournful song
[for Beowulf], said often that she feared harsh days of trouble for herself, much
humiliation, fear of the foe, injury and captivity. Heaven swallowed the smoke.

Then the people of the Weder-Geats made a barrow on the cliff. It was high
and broad, widely visible to seafarers; and in ten days they built a sign for the
man bold in battle. They surrounded the remains of the burning with a wall,
in the most splendid way that skilled men might devise. They placed circlets
and clasps in the barrow, all such ornaments as hostile men had taken previously
from the hoard. They let the earth keep the wealth of men, gold in the sand.
It is still there now, as unprofitable to men as it was before. Then men brave
in battle, the sons of nobles, twelve in all, rode round the tumulus. They wished
to lament their grief and tell of the king, to recite an elegy, and speak about
the man. They praised his heroic deeds and extolled his work of valour to the
host. Thus is it suitable, that a man should praise his friend and lord in words,
cherish him in his heart, when he has to be taken from the body.

Two cremation funerals are described in *Beowulf*. This, the second (and
the third funeral of the poem) ends the career of the great hero Beowulf.
The mood is elegiac, for the glorious days are over for the Geats, his people;
without their powerful protector they are all doomed to defeat and captivity.
The disappearance of Beowulf's body into smoke and ashes fittingly terminates the golden era. The magnificent funeral mound leaves a dual impression: that Beowulf has achieved posthumous fame, the wish of every Germanic pagan warrior, and that all his glory has ended in a heap of earth.

The earlier cremation in the poem is also exploited by the poet for moral
purposes. Like the poet of *The Fortunes of Men* (see p.20), the author seems
to be dwelling upon the gruesomeness of the ritual burning. He uses the
practice, which Christians would condemn as barbaric, to point out the
awfulness of disloyalty among kindred and of the perversion of the heroic
ideal, and the wastefulness of war. The poet is digressing from his main
narrative to discuss a battle fought at Finnsburg, in Frisia, evidently a
famous event since it was the subject of another (fragmentary) Old English
poem. The events preceding the funeral are that King Finn has ambushed
his brother-in-law Hnæf, who is visiting him at Finnsburg. After days of
fierce fighting a stalemate situation has arisen and there is a temporary lull
while the funeral is held. The heartbroken queen, Hildeburh, sees her
brother and her son, killed fighting on opposite sides, laid on the funeral
pyre together, shoulder to shoulder in death when they were not so in life.
The poet ironically focuses on the boar figure (the protective symbol which
decorated a helmet) demonstrating, without needing to expand the point,
that this pagan talisman had proved useless:

Ad wæs geæfned   ond icge gold
ahæfen of horde.   Herescyldinga
betst beadorinca   wæs on bæl gearu.
Æt þæm ade wæs   eþgesyne
swatfah syrce,   swyn ealgylden,
eofer irenheard,   æþeling manig
wundum awyrded;   sume on wæle crungon.
Het ða Hildeburh   æt Hnæfes ade
hire selfre sunu   sweoloðe befæstan,
banfatu bærnan   ond on bæl don
eame on eaxle.   Ides gnornode,
geomrode giddum.   Guðrinc astah.
Wand to wolcnum   wælfyra mæst,
hlynode for hlawe;   hafelan multon,
bengeato burston,   ðonne blod ætspranc,
laðbite lices.   Lig ealle forswealg,
gæsta gifrost,   þara ðe þær guð fornam
bega folces;   wæs hira blæd scacen.

(*ASPR*, IV, p.35, lines 1107–24)

A pyre was prepared and gleaming(?) gold brought up from the hoard. The best of battle-heroes of the war-like Scyldings was ready on the pyre. On the pyre was easily seen the blood-stained mail-shirt, the golden swine, iron-hard boar, many a prince fatally injured with wounds. Many fell dead in the carnage. Then Hildeburh commanded her own son to be committed to the heat on Hnæf's pyre, and to be placed on the pyre at his uncle's shoulder, his body to be burned. The woman mourned, lamented with dirges. The battle warrior was lifted up. The greatest of funeral-fires wound to the clouds, roared in front of the barrow. Heads melted, gashes sprang open, then blood flowed out of the body's wound. Flame, greediest of spirits, swallowed up all of those whom battle took there, from both nations. Their glory had passed.

The cremations of Beowulf and Hnæf were royal funerals described in the context of a heroic poem. While the poet drew upon the memory of actual funeral rites, we must allow for some poetic exaggeration with regard to the splendour of pyres and the richness of treasure sacrificed. Archaeological evidence suggests that real Anglo-Saxon cremations were more modest. Nevertheless they were complex ceremonies and probably costly for early Anglo-Saxon families.

Before the settlers could cremate their dead they needed a stable community where there was an established funeral site, and with the time and resources to supply sufficient kindling and a suitable vessel to receive the ashes. Burning a human body is not an easy task and the cremation must have required expertise. Possibly it was a 'family business', as undertaking often is today. Animal sacrifice seems to have played a part in some crema-

86

tions, but a village would need to be prosperous before it could afford to sacrifice animals reared for meat or labour.

Women seem to have been important in the cremation ceremony: indirectly, in that mostly ashes were placed in earthenware pots and in the less sophisticated communities these were probably made by women; and directly, in that a woman figured in the ritual. Literary evidence repeatedly focuses on female figures in association with cremation. In the first cremation described in *Beowulf*, it is Hildeburh, the bereaved mother and sister, who gives orders for the disposal of the bodies, not her husband the king. At Beowulf's own funeral an unnamed Geatish woman, like Hildeburh, utters a lament. As far as we know, Beowulf had no wife or surviving female relatives. The Geatish woman is perhaps a ritual mourner, a supervisor of funeral rites, like the woman called the Angel of Death who played a leading role in Viking Age cremation (see pp.99, 100).

Cremation, by its very nature, destroys evidence, but it is possible for us to reconstruct from the excavated remains something of the rite as performed in Anglo-Saxon times. The corpse was apparently taken to the place of burning dressed in its clothes. In the upper Thames valley many cremation sites were on the river, according to a study by Joan Kirk, so in that area at least, bodies may have been transported by water. Dr Calvin Wells has studied the cremated remains from a cemetery at Illington (Norfolk) and has recognized that certain parts of the corpses were regularly less exposed to the fire than others. He concludes that, rather than being laid upon a pyre as in the literary tradition, the corpses were normally laid on the ground, or in a shallow trench, and the pyre heaped over them. The pyre, which must have been large, was then set on fire and possibly stoked at intervals. It reached a very high temperature—about 900°C to judge from the effect on glass beads which were among the grave-goods. A minority of the cremation urns examined by Dr Wells contained burnt animal bone as well as human bones. It is possible that the animal remains derived sometimes from joints of meat placed with the corpse for food in the next world, but comparative evidence of cremation in the Viking Age (see p.99) would suggest that the animals were ritually killed as part of the funeral ceremony, and burnt on the pyre with their owner. At Illington only one child's bones were accompanied by animal's bones. In this case the animal was a dog, the only dog evidenced from the site. In this instance the animal had perhaps been a pet and personally associated with the child. In other cases the bones were of animals useful for food, clothing or labour. Sheep bones were found in some urns. The animals may have been selected for sacrifices according to the status of the dead person; pigs were found with the bones of adolescents, but the really valuable beasts, oxen and horses, were found with adults, oxen probably with both sexes. The sex of the corpses with horses was not clear except in one case: this corpse was male.

Horse burial is quite well known on the continent, where it is associated with richly furnished graves. The remains of a cremated horse were found under Mound 3 at Sutton Hoo, which was a royal burial site. It is likely, then, that the sacrifice of a horse was appropriate only for men of high rank.

Once the funeral fire had been allowed to die down, the remains of the body, sacrifices (if any) and grave-goods were collected, often incompletely burned. The burnt bone would be broken by the collapse of the pyre, but pieces sometimes had to be deliberately broken so that they would fit into a container. Practice here seems to have been irregular, sometimes careless. Modern experts have sometimes found the remains of more than one person in a cremation urn, or, conversely, fewer skeletal remains than one might expect from a body, suggesting that the ashes of one person could have been spread among more than one container. However, we do not have to postulate double cremation, human sacrifice or deliberate distribution of the remains between urns to explain these irregularities. J. N. L. Myres has drawn attention to an Anglo-Saxon pottery vessel from Lackford (Suffolk), a sixth-century piece, which contained the remains of two cruciform brooches, one earlier than the pot by about a generation, the other earlier still. This illustrates that the burning-place of a large cemetery may have been in use for years and a burnt object may have remained there for a long time after the associated burnt bone was removed, eventually being placed in another urn following a later burning (Myres, *Corpus*, I, pp.xx, 32). We may suppose therefore, that people other than the kinsmen (who knew their relative's jewellery) were responsible for gathering up the ashes. In the same way as Myres describes the mixing-up of grave-goods, the bones of one individual could have easily been confused with another's.

The majority of cremation remains were placed in pottery vessels and buried in the ground. A minority of wealthy families used other vessels (see pp.92–3) and some cremated remains were buried in the ground without vessels, perhaps being placed in containers which have since decayed and left no trace, or having been simply tipped into a hole in the ground. Archaeologists have found a few of these cases while excavating urn-fields, but there may have been more, destroyed because without the distinctive pots their significance would not be realized except by experienced archaeologists.

The earthenware pots in which these remains were placed were often domestic vessels such as cooking pots or storage urns. Other cremation urns were deliberately made for funeral purposes. Many had a hole made in them before burial. A few, so-called window urns, were set with pieces of glass, following some pagan belief: perhaps that the soul of the cremated person was in the pot and wished to see out, or to leave and enter the pot by this means. (Yet this belief would seem to conflict with the release of the spirit by fire which cremation was supposed to achieve.)

All the pots, whether originally domestic or purpose-made for funerals, are the hand-made, poorly fired vessels typical of the early Anglo-Saxon period. Without benefit of the potter's wheel, the makers produced vessels which were clumsy and irregular in shape and decoration. In the earliest communities, pots were made and decorated as they had been in the continental homeland. They were probably manufactured by women who made only enough to supply the needs of their own families. This domestic production continued, but alongside it there soon began organized manufacture on a larger scale. By the late fifth century pottery workshops were operating, producing vessels which could be acquired by barter, made in the distinctive styles of particular houses. By the sixth century stylistic ties with the continent had loosened and pots were made according to changing fashions in England.

Various shapes were popular. Myres (*Corpus*, I, pp.2–8) identifies bi-conical and shouldered urns, early pots of Scandinavian and Baltic ancestry which often lost their sharply distinctive shape as the type evolved in England; globular vessels, originating in Schleswig; low bulbous types, in use in the late sixth and seventh centuries; and wide-mouthed vessels, in use from the sixth century. Some urns were made with pedestals or foot-rings, others were without bases. Some pots were plain, but many were decorated. In the ornament the potter could reflect the fashion of the workshop or tribe he or she worked for, but could also express individual taste, sometimes decorating funerary ware in a way which shows some of the superstition associated with cremation.

Pots could be decorated by modifying their shape: the clay, when still soft, could be dimpled with the fingers, or by putting a hand inside the pot the craftsman could push out the clay into projecting bosses. Alternatively the potter might decorate the outside of a vessel by incising lines or dots on to it with a sharp tool, by stamping it with a die cut out of bone, horn or wood, or cast in metal; more rarely he might draw freehand upon the pot. Often a potter used a combination of techniques and patterns. The simplest decoration perhaps consisted of incising lines around the neck or body of a pot, a design known from earliest times and which persisted into the late sixth century. On other pots, linear ornament might be vertical or diagonal, and was sometimes used to divide the area of the pot into fields to be filled with other ornament, such as stamps. Curved lines were also popular, particularly arches. These, which were of Saxon origin, together with their 'opposites', swags, could be effectively combined with dots, chevrons, stamps or bosses to make elaborate pots. These curves were popular for many generations.

Stamps came into use in the sixth century. It is the repeated use of a particular die that, more than anything else, makes it possible for us to assign various pots to one particular craftsman or workshop. Stamped ornament was originally quite disciplined, being used in horizontal bands round vessels and then to fill fields of ornament, such as pendant triangles. This discipline was eventually lost as stamps were used at random. Stamps were used on various-shaped pots including those with bosses and on window urns.

Foremost among the pots with bosses are the so-called *Buckelurnen*. Clustered with bosses of at least two types, and elaborately decorated with arches, rectangular designs and diagonal whirling patterns, the *Buckelurnen* are surely the ugliest of all the unlovely pots the Anglo-Saxons produced.

It is of particular interest when we find that craftsmen have adapted or developed their normal techniques of decoration in order to make a vessel particularly appropriate for cremation. One of the most popular habits was to decorate a vessel with stylized dragons. We know that, traditionally, dragons were believed to live in barrows, guarding hoards of treasure. An Anglo-Saxon poetic maxim states this clearly: *Draca sceal on hlǣwe, frod, frǣtwum wlanc* (*ASPR*, VI, p.56, lines 26–7) ('A dragon must inhabit a barrow, ancient, splendid with ornaments'). Beowulf himself fought a dragon, a *wyrm*, which guarded such a place. Stylized *wyrmas* appear on many Anglo-Saxon cremation urns. Myres sees this device as a reflection of pagan belief: 'There can be little doubt that the "wyrm" motif owed its popularity in the first place to its ritual significance as a protective device. It was used on pottery to ensure the safety of the urn's contents' (Myres, *Corpus*, I, p.66). Long bosses arranged vertically or diagonally round an urn, with the addition of dots could easily become *wyrmas* with eyes (plate 19), as on an urn from Kettering (Northants.). Extra dots or incised lines could give the beast a crested spine. Both devices appear on a pot from St John's, Cambridge (Myres, *Corpus*, fig. 231, no.266). Curved shapes, which may be seen as stylized versions of this serpentine creature, were very often stamped on to pots. We may see such a stamp (plate 20), together with a sunburst and an X on an urn from West Keal (Lincs.) In particular *wyrm* stamps were used by potters operating from workshops, or possibly a single workshop, which specialized in animal stamps. Probably working from a centre near

Fig 15   Typical cremation urns

Caistor-by-Norwich (Norfolk) at the end of the sixth and beginning of the seventh centuries, these potters used two devices which Myres identifies as *wyrmas*. One is an S-shaped motif (plate 21) of three lines, the other is a simple curve. Other potters, who decorated their work with freehand drawings, often used curves or S-shapes which similarly derived from the *wyrm* motif. By linking together two serpentine creatures the craftsman was able to produce a device similar to the swastika, itself a popular motif among potters. One artist, in a linear design on a pot from Caistor-by-Norwich, may have intended to portray *wyrmas* guarding a mound inside a fence, or perhaps a doorway (Myres, *Corpus*, I, p.66).

Other animals and birds were sometimes stamped or drawn on pots. They were never a majority fashion, but survive in sufficient numbers on extant pottery to show that they enjoyed some popularity. They may have had mythical or magical significance; or they might have represented the sacrifices traditionally made at elaborate funerals; possibly some were meaningless decorations reflecting the delight in zoomorphic art which Anglo-Saxon craftsmen exhibit elsewhere.

The only 'illustration' yet to be found on an urn is a freehand drawing described by Myres as 'a wolf apparently barking at a retreating ship' (plate 22). If this identification is correct the picture may show Fenrir the wolf and the boat Naglfar at the Doom of the Gods. This would be unique evidence of a pagan myth in Anglo-Saxon England. The myth is recorded in Snorri's *Gylfaginning*. The urn, which is probably seventh century, was found at Caistor-by-Norwich. (See J. N. L. Myres and B. Green, *The Anglo-Saxon Cemeteries of Caistor-by-Norwich and Markshall, Norfolk*, p.118.)

There is a frieze of animals on a pot of unknown provenance (Myres, *Corpus*, fig. 364, no.1966), which may be of ritual significance since it includes the boar, Freyr's creature, and the deer, which was associated with royalty; but perhaps it was made specially for someone who loved hunting.

The horse-like creatures on a few East Anglian urns (eg Myres, *Corpus*, fig. 365, no. 883) may reflect the cult of Freyr and may be associated with

Fig 16   Typical cremation urns

Fig 17 Urn with motif of '*wyrm* guarding a mound' from Caistor-by-Norwich, Norfolk

the practice of burying or burning a horse with a dead man. Other quadrupeds of unidentifiable species appear on a number of cremation urns and stylized birds are stamped on a few East Anglian urns (Myers, *Corpus*, Fig. 359). As we have seen, birds were the familiars of Woden. Possibly these bird-decorations were associated with the god.

The swastika, a sign associated with Thunor, often appears stamped or drawn on pottery (plate 23). It was a particular favourite of the 'animal-stamp' potters of the conversion period, who specialized in *wyrmas* and backward-facing quadruped decorations. They used the swastika in its simple form and also elaborated it into intricate fret patterns. These professional potters of the late sixth and early seventh centuries, who almost certainly worked for Christian patrons as well as pagan, managed to achieve a barbaric, magical quality in their urn-decoration. One wonders how far decoration reflected beliefs in this late pagan period. Did people really believe that a few curves and dots represented a dragon which would guard the ashes of their kinsman, that a swastika would invoke the protection of the thunder god? Or did a potter with a commercial eye for the heathen cremation market dispassionately copy and develop traditional shapes and add animals because they were aesthetically pleasing?

When dealing with runes as pottery decoration, potter and client seem to have been satisfied with something which *looked* magical rather than demanding authenticity. Runes were often drawn upside down or incorrectly. A runic inscription on an urn from Loveden Hill (Lincs.) begins with genuine runes but tails off into scribbles, while a rune-like inscription on a Lackford (Suffolk) pot is in fact meaningless (plate 24). The only rune to appear consistently is the ↑ -symbol, the name of the ancient god Tiw and a traditional protective device (see fig. 9) ᛉ, The name of Ing, who was perhaps the equivalent of Freyr, ✕ , *gyfu* (gift), ✳ ,*ger* (year), ᛟ, *eþel* (native land) and ⸠ (a variant of ⸡), *sigel* (the sun) all appear on more than one surviving piece of pottery.

The ashes of wealthy or important people might be laid, not in a pot, but in some other, rarer kind of vessel. At Coombe (Kent) a person, or perhaps a man and his wife, was cremated, and the ashes laid in a bronze bowl which was covered by a fine cloak or blanket of wool in a luxurious weave. A sword, brooches and beads accompanied this deposit and a mound was raised over it.

At the royal burial ground of Sutton Hoo (Suffolk) two cremation graves have been found. Under Mound 3, a barrow 85ft (25·9m) in diameter and 5ft (1·5m) high, archaeologists found human and animal bones, cremated and placed on an oak tray. A pottery fragment, the remains of a limestone plaque decorated with a winged figure, the lid of a bronze vessel, pieces of engraved bone (perhaps from a casket and a comb) and a throwing-axe accompanied the ashes. Mound 4, which measured 70ft (21·3m) by 60ft (18·2m) had been disturbed before scientific exploration took place, but archaeologists were able to establish that a man, woman and horse had been burned and their remains placed in a bronze vessel. The horse, and possibly the woman too, represent sacrifices. Fragments of three different types of textile and feathers were probably the remains of bedding including a pillow. A gaming piece and the metal binding strip from a tub were the only other surviving grave-goods from what must have been a very elaborate funeral.

From the burnt remains of possessions which have been found in crema-tion vessels it seems that weapons were not committed to the pyre with their owner. The spear, ubiquitous in male unhumation graves, does not seem to have accompanied the dead who were cremated. The Coombe sword and the Sutton Hoo francisca (throwing axe), placed unburnt by the cremations, were costly objects, the francisca a rare one, which indicated the rank of their dead owners.

It is quite common to find unburnt objects in more modest cremations. While in the elaborate cremations under barrows the unburnt objects were arranged around the ashes in their container, in the case of commoner urn-burials, the additional grave-goods were simply placed in the pot with the cremated remains. Tweezers and combs are the items most often found un-burnt in cremation urns. Presumably these were tools for personal grooming (although the Anglo-Saxons may also have used combs in preparing wool for spinning). The exact purpose of the tweezers is unknown. They may have been for removing splinters and thorns from the skin. One would doubt that the pagan Anglo-Saxons were fastidious enough to pluck facial hair, particularly as they do not seem to have used mirrors, either metal or glass. To judge from the inhumation burials, it would seem that tweezers were used by both the sexes, although when they accompanied women, the women were in the upper age-range. At Caistor-by-Norwich (Norfolk) manicure 'sets' of shears, knife and tweezers seem to have been associated with men, although women had tweezers alone. It is strange that tweezers and combs appear more regularly in cremation urns than they do in inhuma-tion graves, and that some of the tweezers are apparently miniatures, dummies made especially for the funeral. It seems that these personal items played a significant role in the cremation ritual. Some combs were broken and incomplete when placed in the urn. Perhaps the combs and tweezers were used in preparing the body for lying in state and burning, and they were disposed of with the ashes, sometimes broken, so that they would not be used again by the living.

Funerary urns were generally disposed of in areas designated for that purpose. They were buried, not very deep, arranged (roughly) in rows and perhaps in family groups. There must originally have been some above-ground indication of the extent of the burials. Meaney has noted that cremations were more carefully deposited in the Anglian cemeteries exclusively devoted to this rite than in the mixed inhumation/cremation sites of Saxon and Jutish areas, where urns and graves seem to be scattered at random. In the cemeteries solely used for cremation the urns were often placed on gravel, or a flat stone, and covered by a stone or stones (A. L. Meaney, *A Gazetteer of Early Anglo-Saxon Burial Sites*, p.16). The largest of these urn-fields eventually contained hundreds of cremations.

At South Elkington (Lincs.) the population apparently imported flints to the area and spread them to make a burial mound which was subsequently used for over two hundred cremations. This is a unique burial site, which probably belonged to a poor community in an early phase of the Anglo-Saxon era. Such burial mounds, deliberately constructed for a number of cremations, are not to be found elsewhere, but the Anglo-Saxons in other areas did make use of pre-existing barrows to deposit cremations. In these cases cremations were laid with inhumations, as, for example, in the large tumulus called Cheesecake Hill, at Driffield (Yorks.). There inhumations accompanied by grave-goods (probably sixth century) were buried with cremated remains in urns.

Tumuli were occasionally raised over individual cremations. This practice was mostly confined to the more southern part of England—East Anglia, Kent, the Isle of Wight, Sussex, Surrey and Oxfordshire—and, like the raising of tumuli over single inhumations, seems to have been a seventh-century custom. Our richest cremation graves are under individual barrows like this, and include the Coombe and Sutton Hoo cremations already discussed as well as other notable instances, such as Brightwell (Suffolk) and Asthall (Oxon.). Possibly these mounds were circled by mounted warriors praising the dead, as the *Beowulf* poet describes.

Although Anglo-Saxon poets might keep alive the memory of cremation, they forgot, or glossed-over, the sacrifices and other rituals which accompanied the burning; for by the eighth century this heathen custom had been replaced by Christian burial. Ironically the splendid cremation funerals of the seventh century must have been among the last of their kind.

Some Anglo-Saxon peoples seem to have practised a combination of cremation and inhumation. They appear to have dug a grave and then made a fire in it. In at least two sites (Kempston, Beds., and Woodstone, Hunts.)

bodies had been laid in their graves and partly burnt, before the graves were filled in in the usual way. Meaney, noting that cemeteries containing such half-cremated burials tend not to be in the open country as other inhumation sites are, but 'close to rivers, and therefore presumably close to settlements', has suggested that the fire served to ensure that the spirit did not trouble the living (*Gazetteer*, p.17). This confirms, if proof were needed, that Anglo-Saxon cremation and inhumation involved far more than disposing of a body. They ensured the continued spiritual welfare of the dead and safety of the living.

4

Pagan Ship Funeral Rites

The ship funeral of Scyld Scefing, legendary King of the Danes, is one of the most memorable passages in Old English poetry:

Þær æt hyðe stod   hringedstefna,
isig ond utfus,   æþelinges fær.
Aledon þa   leofne þeoden,
beaga bryttan,   on bearm scipes,
mærne be mæste.   Þær wæs madma fela
of feorwegum,   frætwa, gelæded;
ne hyrde ic cymlicor   ceol gegyrwan
hildewæpnum   ond heaðowædum,
billum ond byrnum;   him on bearme læg
madma mænigo,   þa him mid scoldon
on flodes æht   feor gewitan.
Nalæs hi hine læssan   lacum teodan,
þeodgestreonum,   þon þa dydon
þe hine æt frumsceafte   forð onsendon
ænne ofer yðe   umborwesende.
Þa gyt hie him asetton   segen geldenne
heah ofer heafod,   leton holm beran,
geafon on garsecg;   him wæs geomor sefa,
murnende mod.   Men ne cunnon
secgan to soðe,   selerædende,
hæleð under heofenum,   hwa þæm hlæste onfeng.

(ASPR, IV, p.4, lines 32–52)

There at the harbour stood the ship with curving prow, the prince's vessel, icy and eager to depart. Then they laid the dear chief, distributor of rings, in the bosom of the ship, the famous one by the mast. A quantity of treasures, precious things from far away places, was brought there. I have never heard of a ship more splendidly equipped with battle-weapons and war garments, with swords and mailcoats. In his lap lay a multitude of treasures which must accompany him, go far into the possession of the flood. They did not furnish him at all with lesser gifts from the people's treasure than did those who, in the beginning, sent him forth alone over the waves, as a child. Then yet, they set a golden standard high over his head, let the sea bear him, gave him to the ocean. Sad heart, mourning mind was theirs. Nobody knows, truth to tell, councillors in the hall [or] heroes under the heavens, who received the cargo.

The splendour of the funeral rites given to this ancestor at the beginning of *Beowulf* prepares the audience for the glorious exploits of the heroic age which are to be celebrated in the poem. We might expect such a magnificent ritual, such elaborate provision of grave-goods, to be a poetic fiction. Yet the ship funeral is a rite which certainly took place in the Germanic world, as archaeological evidence proves. It was a ritual associated with the death of kings or chiefs and involved the provision of grave-goods just as elaborate as the poem suggests. The funeral of Scyld seems to be fictional only in the detail that the ship laden with treasure is set adrift at sea; if this was actual practice we have no concrete evidence of it. It is, in any case, unlikely, for the mourners might face the anti-climax of finding the funeral ship coming back on the next tide, or worse, the humiliation of losing their nation's treasure to an enemy if the funeral ship drifted to foreign shores. Scyld Scefing, eponymous founder of the Scylding dynasty, was, as we have seen (pp.32–3), a fictional character; the mysterious departure by ship was appropriate to him since the fertility myth of Sceaf involved the mysterious arrival by ship of a child who brought prosperity, and this mythical arrival is, in the poem, attributed to Scyld Scefing.

From other literature and from archaeology, we can see that in practice the role of the ship was more symbolic than in Scyld Scefing's special case. Since the soul had departed (or was, in some cases of imminent death, about to depart) the body was prepared for a journey. It was laid in a ship with the elaborate equipment the dead man would need for life in the next world appropriate to his rank; but the whole was not set aimlessly adrift. If it *was* towed out to sea it was set on fire. Alternatively, it could remain on land where it was burnt on a pyre or buried in the earth.

Snorri Sturluson, in the *Ynglinga Saga*, gives us an account of a ship which was launched then burnt:

> King Haki had received so great a wound that he knew his days would not be long. Then he ordered that a warship he owned should be fetched, and had it laden with dead men and weapons; then he ordered it to be launched, the rudder shipped and the sail raised, and that pine timber should be set alight and a pyre built on board ship. The wind was blowing from the land. Haki was at the point of death, or dead already, when he was laid on the pyre. Then the ship sailed blazing out to sea, and for a long while after this deed remained famous.
>
> (*Beowulf and its Analogues*, pp.348–9)

More common in literature is the burning of the corpse, grave-goods, other sacrifices and the ship which contained them, upon a pyre built on land. This was the type of funeral given to Balder, son of Woden/Odin:

> The gods took the body of Balder and took it down to the sea. Balder's ship was named Hringhorni, and it was the greatest of all ships. The gods wished to launch it and to build Balder's pyre on it, but the ship would not move. So then a message was sent to Jǫtunheimr for the giantess named Hyrrokkin. And when she came, she was riding a wolf and had vipers as reins; she leapt from her steed and Odin called four berserks to see to her steed, but they could not manage to hold it unless they stunned it. Then Hyrrokkin went up to the prow, and thrust it forward so violently at her first thrust that fire sprang from the rollers and the earth shook. Then Thor grew angry and grasped his hammer and threatened to crush her head, until all the gods promised her safety.
>
> Then the body of Balder was carried out on to the ship. And when his wife Nanna, the daughter of Nepr, saw this, her heart broke with grief and she died; she was carried to the pyre and laid in the flames. Thor stood beside the pyre and hallowed it with Mjǫllnir [his hammer]. Now a certain dwarf whose name was Litr ran in front of his feet, and Thor gave him a kick and sent him flying into the fire, and he burned to death.
>
> People of many kinds came to this burning ... Odin laid the gold ring called Draupnir upon the pyre; it had such power that every night there dropped from it eight gold rings as heavy as itself. Balder's horse was led to the pyre in all its trappings.
>
> (*Beowulf and its Analogues*, pp.347–8)

This funeral rite among the gods obviously contains some supernatural material, but it also reflects certain rituals which were actually carried out by Germanic peoples, such as the sacrifice of a horse in its trappings and the burning of a woman with her husband.

A detailed account of actual funeral practice was made by the Arab travel-ler Ibn Fadlan in the early tenth century. He was visiting the Volga area and witnessed the funeral of a chief of the Rus, a Swedish people, among whom heathenism remained long after their English kinsmen had become Christian. The ceremony he describes was gruesome and spectacular:

> I had always been told that when a chieftain of theirs died many things took place, of which burning was the least; I was very interested to get information about this. One day I heard that one of their leading men had died. They laid him in a grave and closed it over him for ten days, till they had finished cutting and sewing clothes for him. This is how things are done: for one of the poorer men among them they take a small boat and lay him in it and burn him, but when it is a question of a rich man, they gather his wealth and divide it in three parts—one third for his family, one third for making clothes for him, and one third to make the liquor they drink on the day his slave-girl is killed and burnt

98

with her master. They are indeed much addicted to liquor, for they drink day and night; often one has died with a beaker in his hand.

When a chieftain dies, his family say to his slave-girls and menservants: 'Which of you will die with him?' Then one of them says: 'I will.' When he has said this, he is forced to do it, and is not free to retract; even if he wanted to, it would not be allowed. It is mostly the slave-girls who do this. So when the man I am speaking of died, they said to his slave-girls: 'Which of you will die with him?', and one of them said: 'I will.' Two slave-girls were given the task of waiting on her and staying with her wherever she went, and often they would even wash her feet and hands. Then they began seeing to the man's things, cutting out his clothes and preparing everything that ought to be there, while the slave-girl drank and sang joyfully every day, and seemed to be looking forward to a coming happiness.

When the day came when he and his slave-girl were to be burnt, I went to the river where his ship lay. It had been dragged ashore, four props of birchwood and other wood had been set ready for it, and also something that looked like a great stack of wood had been laid all around. The ship was then dragged up on to this, and set in place on this woodpile. The men began walking to and fro, talking together in a language I could not understand; meanwhile, the dead man still lay in his grave, for they had not taken him out. Then they brought a bench, set it in the ship, and covered it with rugs and cushions of Byzantine silk; then an old woman whom they called the 'Angel of Death' came and spread these rugs out over the bench. She was in charge of sewing the clothes and arranging the corpse, and it is also she who kills the girl; I saw that she was an old, hag-like woman, thick-set and grim-looking.

When they came to his grave they cleared the earth off it, and also took the woodwork away. They stripped him of the clothes he had died in; I noticed that he had turned black, because of the cold in that land. They had laid liquor, fruit and a lute in the grave with him, and all these they now took out. Oddly enough, the corpse did not stink, and nothing about it had changed except the colour of the flesh. Then they dressed him in under-breeches, breeches, boots, coat, and a caftan of silk brocade with gold buttons on it; they set on his head a silk brocade hood with sable fur, and carried him into the tent that stood on the ship, and laid him on the rugs, and propped him up with cushions.

Then they brought liquor, fruit and sweet-smelling plants and laid them by him; they also brought bread, meat and leeks and threw them in front of him. Then they brought a dog, cut it in two, and threw it into the ship. Next, they brought all his weapons and laid them beside him. Then they took two horses and made them gallop about till they sweated, whereupon they cut them to pieces with swords and threw their flesh into the ship. In the same way they brought two cows, and these too they cut to pieces and threw into the ship. Then they brought a cock and a hen, killed them, and threw them in. Meanwhile, the slave-girl who had chosen to be killed was walking to and fro; she would go inside one or other of their tents, and the owner of the tent would make love with her, saying: 'Tell your master I did this simply for love of him.'

When it came to the Friday afternoon, they took the slave-girl to a thing like a door-frame which they had made. She sat herself on the palms of the hands

99

of some men, and stretched up high enough to look over the door-frame, and said something in her own language; at this they set her down. Then they lifted her up again, and she did as she had done the first time. At this they set her down, and lifted her up for the third time, and she did as she had done the first two times. Then they handed her a hen, and she cut the head off and threw it; they took the hen and threw it into the ship. I then questioned the interpreter about what she had done. He replied: 'The first time they lifted her up, she said: "Look, I see my father and my mother!" The second time, she said: "Look, I see all my dead kinsmen sitting there!" The third time, she said: "Look, I see my master sitting in Paradise! Paradise is fair and green, and there are men and young lads with him. He is calling me, let me go to him!"'

Then they went off with her towards the ship. She took off two arm-rings she was wearing and gave them to the old woman called the Angel of Death, the one who was going to kill her; then she took off two ankle-rings she was wearing and gave them to two other women, daughters of the one known as the Angel of Death. Next, they led her up on board the ship, but did not let her go into the tent. Then came some men who had shields and sticks, and they handed her a beaker of liquor; she sang over it and drank it off. The interpreter told me: 'Now with this she is bidding farewell to all her friends.' Next, another beaker was handed to her; she took it, and made her singing long drawn out, but the old woman hurried her to make her drink it off and go into the tent where her master was. I was watching her, and she looked quite dazed; she tried to go into the tent, but stuck her head between it and the ship's side. Then the old woman took hold of her head, and managed to get it inside the tent, and the old woman herself went inside with her.

The men then began to beat their shields with sticks, so that no sound of her shrieking should be heard, for fear other girls should become frightened and not want to seek death with their masters. Then six men went into the tent, and they all made love with her. After this they laid her down beside her dead master; two held her legs and two her hands, and the woman called the Angel of Death wound a cord with knotted ends round her neck, passing the ends out on either side and handing them to two men to pull. Then she stepped forward with a broad-bladed dagger and began to drive it in and pluck it out again between the girl's ribs, while the two men throttled her with the cord, and so she died.

After this, whoever was the closest kinsman of the dead man came forward. He took a wooden stick and set light to it, and then he walked backwards, with his back to the ship and his face to the people, holding the stick in one hand and with the other hand laid on his backside; he was naked. In this fashion the wood they had put just under the ship was set on fire, immediately after they had laid the slave-girl they had killed beside her master. Then the people came forward with wood and timber; each brought a stick with its tip on fire and threw it on to the wood lying under the ship, so that flames took hold, first on the wood, and then on the ship, and then on the tent, and the man and the woman and everything inside the ship. Thereupon a strong fierce wind sprang up, so that the flames grew stronger, and the ship blazed up even more.

A man of the Rus was standing beside me, and I heard him talking to the

100

interpreter, who was near him. I asked the latter what the man had said to him, and he answered: 'He said: "You Arabs are stupid." I said: "Why so?" He answered: "Why, because you take the people you most love and honour and throw them into the ground, and the earth and creeping creatures and growing things destroy them. We, on the other hand, burn them up in an instant, so that they go to Paradise in that very hour." Then he gave a roar of laughter, and when I asked him about that, he replied: "For love of him, his Lord has sent this wind to carry him away at the right time!"' And in fact, no great time passed before the ship and the timber and the slave-girl and her master had all turned into ashes, and so into dust.

After this, on the spot where the ship had first stood when they dragged it up out of the river, they built something that looked like a round mound. In the middle of it they set up a big post of birch-wood, on which they wrote this man's name, and the name of the King of the Rus; then they went on their way.

(*Beowulf and its Analogues*, pp.341–5)

The Arab witness makes no mention of pagan gods, but we may note traces of the cult of Woden in the method of the slave-girl's murder—stabbing and strangulation—and the raising of a mound. We may detect the cult of Freyr in the use of a ship and in the fruits and plants laid with the corpse.

There were also traces of the fertility cult in the ninth-century Oseberg ship burial. A royal barge was buried under a mound with the bodies of two women at Oseberg in Norway. The burial had already been plundered of its treasures when modern archaeologists found it, but it still contained wooden objects, among them a carved wagon such as Freyr might have ridden in (plate 25). A wagon was also represented on the tapestry found in the burial. Surviving grave-goods included a bucket of apples, another possible indication of the fertility cult. Golden apples are associated with Freyr in one of Snorri's stories.

Three ship-burials have so far been found in England. They are among the earliest in north-west Europe, only the sites at Vendel and Valsgärde in Sweden offering any contemporary parallels. The discovery made in 1939 at Sutton Hoo produced what was then the most valuable archaeological find ever to have been made in Britain.

All three English ship-burials were in Suffolk, one at Snape, two at Sutton Hoo, only nine miles away. This area was in the Anglo-Saxon kingdom of East Anglia, which was ruled by the Wuffingas, who were probably a Swedish family, a branch of the Scylfings who are mentioned in *Beowulf*. There may have been a close connection between the poem and the kings of East Anglia. Wuffa, from whom the dynasty took their name, was the son of Wehha. This Wuffa may be identified with Wiglaf, son of Weohstan, the young kinsman of Beowulf who survives the (fictional) hero at the end of the poem. Although fighting on the side of Beowulf, who was of the Geatish

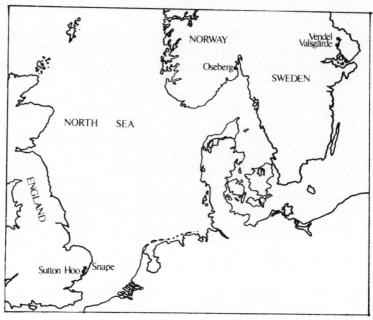

III   Sites of some major ship burials

race, Wiglaf was a Scylfing, a Swede. We understand from the poem that because of his father's past political involvement, Wiglaf is unlikely to find favour with the present king of Sweden once Beowulf, his powerful protector, is dead. The fall of the Geats to the Swedes and other enemies is predicted in the poem. This event may not have been poetic fiction, and if it really happened probably took place near the middle of the sixth century. The survivors may have founded a new dynasty in England. Certainly the Wuffing kings of East Anglia owned regalia which had been made in Sweden and it was from Sweden that they brought the ritual of the ship funeral.

The boat burials at Vendel and Valsgärde, Uppland, Sweden, which offer the closest parallels in date to the Suffolk examples, belong to persons of a lower social class than the English burials, which were all evidently rich, two of them royal. The first was found at Snape in 1862. The Snape boat grave had already been robbed when the nineteenth-century excavators found it, and their accounts of the discovery are sometimes conflicting. Nevertheless, from the few surviving grave-goods and the observations made by various witnesses to the excavation, it is possible to reconstruct a picture of the ship funeral as it took place at Snape.[1]

It was evidently the practice of the community at Snape to cremate their dead and place the ashes in urns, in a common burial ground. When a leader of the community died a more elaborate funeral was arranged, but his remains were laid to rest in the same cemetery as the ordinary people, and

---

1.   See R. Bruce-Mitford, *Aspects of Anglo-Saxon Archaeology*, pp. 114–40.

102

marked by a tumulus. There were between five and ten such tumuli on the site in the nineteenth century, varying in size from 6–7ft (1·8–2·1m) across, to the largest which was 85ft (25·9m) in diameter and 7–8ft (2·1–2·4m) high. Only one mound yielded a boat burial, but there may have been others on the site. Not all the barrows were excavated and most have now been destroyed by ploughing.

The boat which was used for the burial must have been brought along the River Alde to the nearest point to the cemetery of the Snape community. It would then be necessary to drag it, uphill, about half a mile to the trench which had been dug for it in the urn field. The boat was wooden, with iron rivets (which survived to be excavated). It was 50ft (15m) long and about 10ft (3m) wide at the widest point, so the manœuvring must have required considerable manpower and experience. The boat was lowered into its trench and the funeral deposit (grave-goods and, presumably, the body) was laid, unburnt, on the wooden floor of the vessel. The deposit was protected, either by planks or by a burial chamber as at Sutton Hoo (see p.111), and the rest of the boat was filled in with sand. A circle was marked out, 72ft (22m) in diameter, around the boat, and this area was built up into the funeral mound. As turf and soil were scraped from the surrounding ground to fill the tumulus area, earlier urn-burials were disturbed. These were laid in the barrow, which, at the time it was excavated, stood 4ft 6in (1·3m) high.

The grave-robbers had left only a few objects behind. These included two iron spearheads, one still attached to its wooden shaft. The other relics were luxury objects, giving some indication of the rank of the man buried there.

A well-worn ring, of a size suitable for a man's thumb or fore-finger, was found as the excavators were discarding sand from the boat area. The richest finger-ring yet found in an Anglo-Saxon context, it consists of an onyx intaglio of Roman workmanship in a setting made for it by Germanic craftsmen. The setting and the hoop of the ring are gold. It is possible that the ring was made on the continent, but Bruce-Mitford finds stylistic

Fig 18   Finger-ring from Snape, Suffolk

grounds for supposing it to be Anglo-Saxon: the S-shaped scrolls in the filigree are common in Anglo-Saxon work, as in Romano-British. The granulation in the filigree is found on the continent but was popular in Anglo-Saxon England from the seventh to the tenth centuries; in particular there are seventh-century parallels from Kent and from Sutton Hoo. The hook-and-eye shaped filigree is rare among Anglo-Saxon work, but finds its closest parallel on the sword clips from Sutton Hoo. Thus we see that the Snape ring, although unique, may fit into the artistic context of Sutton Hoo, our other ship burial site. Bruce-Mitford suggests that, if the ring is indeed English and not continental, it must have been made about AD 600, and, allowing for wear, buried in the Snape boat about AD 615.

Finger-rings have often been found in Scandinavian burials and they are not uncommon in Anglo-Saxon pagan graves (although more often associated with women than men); but they have not been found either at Sutton Hoo or in the near-contemporary boat graves in Sweden. Rings are frequently mentioned in Old English literature, where they are given by chiefs to loyal retainers. Indeed, some of the poetic epithets for a chief, such as *beaga brytta* (distributor of rings), directly refer to the lord's generosity in this respect. The man buried at Snape may have received this magnificent ring from his king as a sign of his rank and power.

Other luxury objects which evaded the grave-robbers were a fragmentary green glass beaker and a piece of blue glass from another vessel. The number of glass vessels to survive in Anglo-Saxon context is surprising in view of their fragility. They usually accompany burials of the richer sort. The Snape beaker is of the type known as a claw-beaker—blobs of glass, while still soft, were drawn down the vessel to form ornamental claws, which were then decorated with further trails of glass. The foot of the beaker was not found, but the vessel is of a well-known type and from other examples we can be sure that the foot would not be wide enough to support the vessel upright. It could only be laid down on its side or inverted (or, as displayed in museums, placed in a stand). The drinker, therefore, could not put it down until he had emptied it, a fact which coincides with the reputation for drunkenness enjoyed by the Germanic peoples (cf. *Germania*, 22). This vessel from Snape must have been about $7\frac{1}{4}$in (18cm) high, $3\frac{1}{2}$in (9cm) wide at the mouth, which means that full, it could have held about $\frac{2}{3}$ pint (380ml) of liquid. This type of drinking vessel is hard to date precisely, but the Snape example is probably late sixth century and was almost certainly imported from the continent. It may have been treasured for years before burial. The blue glass (now lost) probably derived from a squat jar, a type of vessel made in Kent in the seventh century.

The excavators at Snape found what they thought to be human hair of a 'dirty red' colour. This is now lost, but it seems probable that what they found was not part of the corpse but the remains of a fur cloak of a luxurious

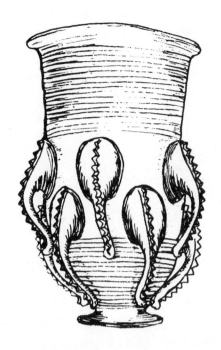

Fig 19   Glass beaker from Snape

kind. Shaggy woollen cloaks, made from tufts of fleece inserted into a cloth base, have been found at Sutton Hoo and at Broomfield (Essex), both seventh-century sites, the latter a grave of unusual and elaborate construction. Fur or hair remains have also been found at Taplow (Bucks.), Benty Grange (Derbys.) and Broome (Norfolk), all well-equipped, seventh-century, male burials (all, incidentally, lacking corpses—because the body was completely decayed or because it was never present). The burial of the fur cloak (possibly an import) may then have been a ritual which the Snape boat burial shared with other elaborate seventh-century funerals in various parts of England.

The cemetery at Sutton Hoo differs from that at Snape, in that it appears to have been, exclusively, a royal burial ground; specifically the cemetery of the Wuffingas, kings of East Anglia, whose royal dwelling was at Rendlesham, four miles north of the burial site in a direct line, four-and-a-half miles by river. Both Rendlesham and the burial site are on the east bank of the River Deben. The cemetery consisted of at least fifteen tumuli, possibly as many as seventeen, some of which are still visible. Some of them, probably the earliest, were arranged in a straight line, along the edge of an escarpment. Others, including the one containing the famous ship burial, were built on a spur of land where they could be seen from the river, which, in Anglo-Saxon times, was about 600 yards (550m) away. The mounds were flat-topped, and varied in size. The largest, which contained the rich ship burial, was originally a circular barrow about 100ft (30m) across, and 9ft (2·7m) high. The other ship burial, disturbed, was under a lower mound—7ft

(2·1m)—of similar width. The smallest identifiable barrow in the group is 50ft (15m) across, but less than 1ft (30cm) high.

The site had evidently been occupied in prehistoric times, but there is no sign of habitation by the Anglo-Saxons, who evidently cultivated cereals on at least part of the site, building the largest barrow directly on to ploughed soil, this being one of the last tumuli to be added to the cemetery. Three mounds were excavated in 1938, a fourth in 1939. The 1938 finds yielded two cremation graves and one robbed boat burial. The 1939 excavation revealed the rich ship burial. Other mounds, as yet unexcavated, may also contain ships.

The first boat found, in 1938, was under one of the mounds arranged in a line. The burial had been destroyed by grave-robbers, but a few iron rivets and the dark stain of the boat remained in the sandy soil. It was about 6ft (1·8m) wide at the widest point and about 3ft (91cm) deep. It was about 22ft 6in (6·9m) long, but while one end was pointed the other was blunt, apparently having been cut off short. The boat occupied a relatively small space under the large mound.

The fragments left by the grave-robbers indicate that the burial was rich and that of a man. Instead of the single knife which usually accompanied a corpse, there were three separate knives plus two more, placed in opposite directions in a double sheath of leather. There had been a sword, an object usually found only in richer burials. Only the tip remained, attached to its wooden scabbard, but this was sufficient to determine that the blade had been pattern-welded, as the best Anglo-Saxon swords were. Fragments from a shield suggest that it had been decorated like the shield found the following year in the rich ship burial. The remains consisted of a 2in (5cm) disc of gilded bronze decorated with zoomorphic ornament, and a strip ornamented with a dragon's head; teeth and an eye were visible. The dead man may have owned a battle harness, for there was a gilt-bronze stud which had probably come from a large buckle, as well as a smaller silver buckle and a bronze ring and tab which might have been stitched into leatherwork. Textile, traces of which were found on the sword-tip, was probably a diamond or chevron twill, a luxury fabric.

Probably there were arrangements for the dead man to eat and drink: wood and iron remains indicated that there had been an iron-bound wooden bucket, standing on three legs, which might have held food or liquor. There were also remains of a blue glass squat jar, similar to the blue glass from Snape. The vessel may have been of Kentish workmanship, dating from the late sixth or early seventh century. There were also fragments of silver-gilt foil, part of a triangular mount used to decorate the mouth of a drinking horn. The mount was stamped with the same zoomorphic pattern as that on the drinking horns found in the 1939 ship burial. All these horns derived from the aurochs, which in antiquity was a formidable beast of great size.

Julius Caesar, writing in the first century BC, records that among the Germanic people it was considered a feat of skill and courage to kill an aurochs, and that the horns of the dead animal were edged with silver and used as drinking vessels at splendid feasts. Even the smaller, degenerate specimens of aurochs were fearsome, and Bruce-Mitford suggests that the Sutton Hoo vessels made from their horns were symbolic of manly valour. The runic symbol ∩ (*ur*) is named from the aurochs, which suggests that the animal had symbolic, even superstitious, associations. In placing one of these drinking horns in a burial, then, the mourners were giving their dead king the most magnificent of drinking vessels and also a symbolic object (see *The Sutton Hoo Ship Burial. A Handbook*, pp.55–7).

The type and decoration of these few grave-goods are suggestive of a seventh-century date, and Bruce-Mitford suggests that the burial was made before about AD 620. (*The Sutton Hoo Ship Burial*, I, p.128.)

The mound which was excavated at Sutton Hoo in 1939 had been partially ploughed away and had been explored by treasure-seekers in Tudor times. Fortunately, neither plough nor robbers had touched the ship, and the excavators discovered the deposit intact. They were also able to establish the way in which the grave came to be constructed. The coins in the burial make it possible to date the deposit with more precision than is usual among archaeologists. This dating and the unique character and range of the grave-goods make it highly likely that the ship burial commemorates Rædwald, King of East Anglia, who died in 624 or 625.

Rædwald was the grandson of Wuffa and the most famous king of the Wuffing dynasty. According to Bede (*HE*, II, 5) and the *Anglo-Saxon Chronicle* (for 829) he was the fourth Anglo-Saxon king to hold the rank of Bretwalda, pre-eminence over other contemporary Anglo-Saxon kings, a position which, according to Bede, allowed him to 'hold sway over all the provinces south of the River Humber'. He succeeded King Æthelberht of Kent in the Bretwaldaship, and Bede, even while praising Æthelberht, admits that Rædwald 'won pre-eminence for his own people' even during the lifetime of that powerful king. Rædwald was converted to Christianity and baptized on a visit to Kent, but Bede tells us that on his return to East Anglia his wife and advisers persuaded him against deserting paganism.[2] Accordingly:

> ... he tried to serve both Christ and the ancient gods, and he had in the same temple an altar for the holy Sacrifice of Christ side by side with an altar on which victims were offered to devils.
>
> (*HE*, II, 15; p.128)

---

2. Possibly Rædwald's marriage would have been ruled incestuous by Christian standards. Certainly his wife had been married before, to someone in the royal family. See Bruce-Mitford, *The Sutton Hoo Ship Burial*, I, pp.700–1.

He evidently maintained this compromise for the rest of his life, and his son Eorpwald who succeeded him was a pagan until converted to Christianity in 627. Even then the East Anglian people must have remained heathen, for Eorpwald reigned only briefly. It was not until three years later, after the accession of his brother, or half-brother, Sigeberht, who had become a Christian and a scholar while in exile abroad, that East Anglia received its own bishop and paganism was finally abandoned (see p.143).

Rædwald provided a refuge for the Northumbrian Edwin during that king's years of exile. At one time tempted or intimidated into betraying his guest, Rædwald, according to Bede (*HE*, II, 12) was again dissuaded by his wife and proved a good friend to Edwin, killing his rival Æthelfrith and establishing Edwin on the throne of Northumbria in 616, losing his son, Rægenhere, in the same battle. Edwin succeeded Rædwald as Bretwalda as the Northumbrian kingdom became pre-eminent. East Anglia was never so powerful again. (It was to become dominated by Mercia and later settled by Vikings.)

Rædwald's funeral ceremony, with its ship, lavish provision of grave-goods and large tumulus, was obviously an elaborate tribute to a pagan king by his pagan subjects and successor. Its organization, like the other ship funerals here and at Snape, must have required a great deal of expertise and manpower, for this ship, the largest to have been found in such a burial, was dragged uphill from the River Deben for about $\frac{1}{3}$ mile (533m) before being lowered into the trench already dug for it in the sand near the other royal burials. The ship was probably moved on rollers and laid on rollers and cables over the trench. The rollers removed, it must have been lowered vertically into the trench, which it fitted closely.

The ship was 89ft (27·1m) long and 14ft (4·3m) across at the widest point, where it was 4ft 6in (1·3m) deep. It was an ocean-going rowing boat, probably a warship originally, propelled by twenty pairs of oars and steered by means of a tiller and steering oar in fixed position on the starboard side. It was open, without a deck, although it had a floor. It may have been adapted during its lifetime to carry sail, perhaps for use as a royal barge, since the tholes for oars were missing from the central area; but if there ever was a mast, that and other equipment connected with the sail had been removed to make way for the central burial chamber.

The ship was clinker-built, of overlapping oak planks secured by iron rivets and strengthened by internal ribs. It was probably caulked. The ship had no keel as such, merely a thick keel plank. Both ends of the ship were apparently similar in shape and dimensions. No stem- or stern-post survives, but there may have been a figure-head of carved wood, like the (slightly earlier) examples which have been recovered from the River Scheldt. The ship was not new; it had been repaired.

The burial chamber may have been constructed in advance, or at least

108

22 Cremation urn with 'wolf barking at ship' device from Caistor-by-Norwich, Norfolk (*Hallam Ashley, Norfolk Museum*)

23 Cremation urn with stamped swastikas and animals from Caistor-by-Norwich, Norfolk (*Hallam Ashley, Norfolk Museum*)

24 Two urns with runic or rune-like inscriptions from Loveden Hill, Lincolnshire and Lackford, Suffolk (*Trustees of the British Museum* and *The Faculty of Archaeology and Anthropology, Cambridge University*)

Fig 20 Ship's figure-head from the River Scheldt, near Appels, Belgium

made in parts ready to assemble, since there was no evidence that joinery work had taken place on the site. It took the form of a solid wooden chamber. Its steeply pitched roof, of double thickness, spanned the ship, and wooden walls enclosed the chamber. The chamber was about 18ft 3in (5·6m) long. It therefore occupied less than a quarter of the ship, which must have looked like the popular conception of Noah's Ark when the burial chamber was erected. The floor of the burial chamber was probably carpeted. Grave-goods were laid in the chamber and hung around the walls in a deliberate, H-shaped arrangement: in general the domestic items were found at the east end, the ceremonial items at the west, other objects occupying the space between.

The excavators in 1939 found no trace of a body, or of personal ornaments such as a finger-ring which would have been worn on the body, although the distribution of the grave-goods indicated an obvious place for a corpse, between the groups of objects at the east and west ends, among the jewellery, and with the sword at its right side. The positions of the belt fittings and shoulder-clasps, however, were not consistent with having been worn on the body, whether that body was lying on its back, sitting on a chair or propped on cushions. It was therefore suggested that the ship burial had never contained a body and was a cenotaph. The definitive publication of the ship burial (1975), however, cites scientific evidence that there was a major phosphate source in the body space. The most likely solution to this much-discussed question seems to be that there was a body present, but it was not wearing elaborate costume and personal jewellery.[3] Some of the jewellery found in the burial chamber was not worn; the harness with its jewelled fasteners was probably hung up and the shoulder-clasps were detached from the leather cuirass they were designed to fasten. A tapestry may have hung around the dead man; threads of it survived. But the combination of acid soil and water-logged conditions in the buried boat must have caused his body to disappear entirely.

Neither did the excavators find any traces of the animal sacrifices which feature in Ibn Fadlan's account of a ship funeral, although there was apparently room for other things in the burial chamber. A fossil which was once cremated bone was found on a silver dish, but its origin (human or animal) is unknown. It could have been a primary cremation or ritual sacrifice. It could equally derive from a piece of overcooked meat from the funeral feast or from the food provided for the dead man's journey.

Once the body was laid in the chamber, the grave-goods arranged and any other rituals completed, the chamber was strewn with bracken. Possibly all these arrangements were carried out ceremonially. Difficulty of access would prevent many people being closely involved, but probably the final rituals were carried out by the next of kin or someone appointed to stage-manage the occasion. (Cf. Ibn Fadlan's narrative.)

The rest of the ship, outside the burial chamber, and the surrounding trench, were then filled in with the sand that had been dug out of the trench. The roof of the chamber may have been covered with turf. A circular barrow was then built over and round the ship, the length of the ship's trench determining the diameter of the barrow. (The ship therefore occupied a proportionately larger space in its barrow than the 1938 ship did.) The barrow was made of turf and topsoil, carted to the site and tipped. It has been estimated that between 17,000 and 20,000 cubic feet of material was moved. (About 5ft (1·5m) above the deposit the excavators found a clay pan, not a man-made object, but suggestive of ritual libations. Such an object would be unique, however, and current opinion is that the clay feature is a natural formation caused by the collapse of the burial chamber and therefore having nothing to do with the ship funeral.) The surface of the barrow may have been turfed. Its top was fairly flat, the highest point not directly over the burial chamber but to the east of it, which misled the Tudor grave-robbers who explored it. The stem- and stern-posts and the top of the burial chamber were quite close to the surface of the barrow.

The chamber must have stood for a considerable time, perhaps half a century, allowing the metal objects to rust. When it collapsed it fell violently,

---

3. Professor Evison has recently stated her conviction that there *was* a body, possibly resting on its right side, in a rectangular coffin which is evidenced by iron clamps. She finds the positions of grave-goods consistent with this interpretation, given some activity by rabbits in the soil. See 'The body in the ship at Sutton Hoo'.

smashing the oxidized lumps of metal and bending other metalwork. Upright objects were toppled and articles hanging on the walls fell to the floor. The reconstruction of the grave-goods has therefore been like the assembly of numerous delicate jigsaw puzzles.

Many of the grave-goods reflected their owner's role as king and Bret-walda, descendant of a race of heathen Scandinavians. The Bretwalda's sceptre consisted of an enormous four-sided stone bar (see plate 6 and fig. 7). It is $32\frac{1}{4}$in (82cm) long and weights 6lb $4\frac{1}{2}$oz (2·8kg). The stone is that type commonly used for whetstones, but this object has never been used to sharpen anything. At each end are carved four human faces. Four of the eight faces are bearded, so certainly represent men; the other four are probably intended to be feminine. At each end the stone bar is shaped into a knob, which is painted red and surrounded by a bronze cage. At the bottom end this cage is joined to a saucer, which could have rested on the king's knee to support the heavy object during ceremonies. At the top an iron ring was surmounted by a free-standing, bronze stag.

Functional whetstones have been found in Scandinavian burials of the Vendel period, and whetstones with carved heads have been found in England in Anglo-Saxon and Celtic contexts, but none is so elaborately or skil-fully decorated as this. In the nineteenth century a massive but undecorated whetstone, unused, was found set upright in the ground near a group of Anglo-Saxon barrows. Clearly this fine-grained stone was of ritual significance.

The Sutton Hoo sceptre is an awesome object, and has caused the most careful of scholars instinctively to think of paganism. Bruce-Mitford, noting that the knobs are painted the colour of blood, writes:

> ... there can be little doubt that this great ceremonial stone is an object of magic and potency, whether in enlisting the aid of ancestors or warding off evil. With no redeeming sign of Christianity added to it, it seems to reflect essentially a pagan outlook.
>
> (*Handbook*, p.31)

Soon after its excavation Kendrick recognized the object as:

> a unique savage thing; and inexplicable, except perhaps as a symbol, proper to the King himself, of the divinity and mystery which surrounded the smith and his tools in the northern world.
>
> (*British Museum Quarterly*, XIII, 1939, p.128)

We may remember the fame of the mythical smith Welund and the savage revenge he took on his enemy (see p.38). Others have been reminded of Woden/Odin by the sceptre:

Our view is that those especial powers and influences that established the fortunes of the Sutton Hoo royal house were incapsulated in this staff, as Odin's divine strength was in his spear.

(Quoted in Bruce-Mitford, *Handbook*, p.31)

Let us recall, too, the association of whetstone with the god Thunor, or Thor, god of thunder (see p.25).

The stag, an example of which stands on top of the sceptre, seems to have been a symbol of royalty in the northern world. In *Beowulf* the King of Denmark builds the most magnificent hall that has ever been seen and calls it *Heorot*—'hart' or 'stag'.

Another symbol of this East Anglian king's power and position was the iron standard found close to the sceptre at the west end of the burial deposit. The standard consists of an iron shaft 5ft 7in (1·7m) long, with a spike at the bottom to enable it to stand in the ground, or to be carried in a holster. At its upper end is a plate with four projecting arms terminating in stylized ox-heads. An iron grill, 9in (23cm) lower, is also ornamented with ox-heads. The grill would probably be filled with feathers, perhaps colourful ones such as peacock feathers. Bede tells us that King Edwin of Northumbria was habitually preceded by his standard:

The king's dignity was highly respected throughout his realm, and whether in battle or on a peaceful progress through city, town, and countryside in the company of his thanes, the royal standard was always borne before him. And whenever he passed through the streets on foot, the standard known to the Romans as *Tufa*, and to the English as a *Tuf*,[4] was also carried in front of him.

(*HE*, II, 16; p.130)

The Sutton Hoo standard may well have been a *Tufa*. Edwin may have copied the use of standards from Rædwald, his predecessor as Bretwalda, during his stay in East Anglia.

The bearing of the standard before a great man was, like the carrying of a sceptre, a custom borrowed from the Roman Empire. Standards of a different kind, however, were traditionally associated with royalty and with deposits of treasure in Germanic literature. A gold standard (*segen gelden*) was raised over Scyld Scefing when his treasure ship was sent out to sea (*Beowulf*, line 47, *ASPR*, IV, p.4), and a standard, woven in gold (*segn eallgylden*), hung over the dragon's hoard of treasure (line 2767, p.85). The Sutton Hoo standard never carried a banner of textile, and certainly not cloth of gold (this would have survived); but it is possible that the Anglo-Saxon Bretwaldas were conflating Germanic tradition with Roman when they adopted Roman-type standards, and when Rædwald's standard was laid in his ship burial.

---

4. OE *þuf* (*thuf*) means a tutt of leaves or feathers.

 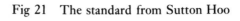
Fig 21   The standard from Sutton Hoo

The shattered remains of the king's helmet (plate 1) lay a few feet away from the standard and sceptre. It had consisted of an iron cap, neckguard, face-mask and cheek-pieces which would have been tied down with tape. It had been padded, probably with leather. As restored, it stands $12\frac{2}{5}$ in (32cm) high and its circumference at the widest part is $29\frac{2}{5}$ in (75cm). A protective crest runs from front to back (the *wala* mentioned in *Beowulf*, line 1031, *ASPR*, IV, p.33); it is inlaid with silver wire and terminates in dragons' heads, with garnet eyes. A stylized face is depicted on the mask with eyebrows, nose and moustache of gilt-bronze. Square garnets decorate the eyebrows, which terminate in boars' heads. The eyebrows also form the wings of a flying creature, apparently a dragon, not a bird, since the head bears the same savage teeth as the heads on the crest.

The helmet was originally covered with stamped plaques of tinned bronze. Three different designs have been reconstructed, and there is evidence for a fourth. The figures of twin warriors performing some ritual appear on

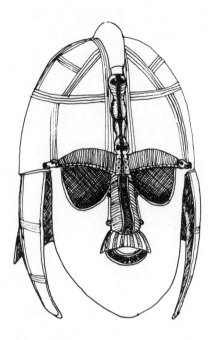

Fig 22 The face-mask of the helmet from Sutton Hoo

the cheek-pieces and forehead, and the mounted warrior appears on plaques running round the helmet and up the sides of the cap (see figs. 1 and 2). Other panels were decorated with interlacing animal ornament of the type known as Salin Style II.

It has already been suggested (see pp.13–14) that the figural scenes are related to the cult of Woden, showing some ritual of weapons associated with the god and a warrior helped by Woden's agent. We may recall that the nickname of Woden/Odin was *Grim* and that this derived from his custom of wearing a mask. This helmet includes a mask.

The boars on the cheek-pieces reflect a Germanic tradition as found on the (very dissimilar) helmet from Benty Grange and in the poem *Beowulf* (see p.31). They also recall the cult of Freyr. We see that the full boar figure was not necessary, and that the boars' heads alone were considered sufficiently symbolic, perhaps, like the ox-heads on the standard, a reflection of the belief in animal head magic already discussed (see pp.46–8).

The helmet also bears the dragon, the terrifying *wyrm* or *draca*, which features in Old English literature and popular belief (see pp.65–6, 90). The dragon appears in its flying form on the face-mask, and in serpentine form on the crest and the zoomorphic interlace.

Thus the helmet bears a variety of symbols conveying pagan beliefs. In type it resembles helmets found in near-contemporary graves in Sweden, and like them owes its basic design to late Roman influence. It was probably an import, an heirloom of the Wuffing kings, part of their Scandinavian, heathen heritage.

116

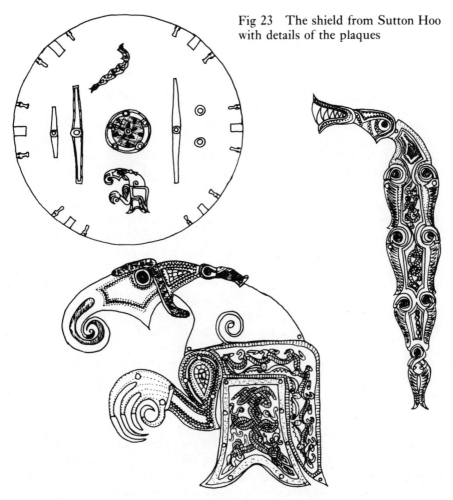

Fig 23   The shield from Sutton Hoo
with details of the plaques

The shield, like the helmet, must have terrorized any enemy coming face
to face with it. It consisted of a concave circle of leather-covered wood 3ft
(90cm) in diameter, with a central boss of iron and a metal rim. The boss
was functional—it protected the hand—but it was elaborately decorated:
with a central stud embellished with garnet and a circle of interlacing beasts;
with animal heads on the curved surface; and with a rim in which pairs
of horses in gilt-bronze reared up between gilt-bronze domes. Twelve
dragon heads decorated the rim of the shield board. The front of the shield
was decorated with metal devices including a flying dragon with three pairs
of folded wings and a fierce bird of prey. A dragon's head is incorporated
into the crest of the bird of prey, and a human face, pear-shaped like those
on the sceptre, in the leg. A gilt-bronze mount, like a ring, was attached
to the shield, symbolic of the owner's rank. At the back of the shield, the
hand-grip passed across the hollow boss, terminating in dragons' heads and

117

the heads of birds of prey. The shield could be suspended by means of a leather strap. It is a type known in East Scandinavia, and may be another heirloom of the Wuffing dynasty, imported from Scandinavia, or it may have been made in East Anglia by an immigrant who had brought his tools with him.

Many weapons were provided for this king, like the legendary Scyld Scefing, but unlike the ordinary Anglo-Saxon man, who was equipped for the grave with only one spear. Three throwing-spears (angons) had been thrust through the handle of a bronze bowl at the west end of the burial chamber. At least one was tipped with an iron ferrule. The angons were about 7ft (2·1m) long. Five other spears were found with them. Further east there was a scramasax—a sword-like weapon with one cutting edge, typical of the seventh century. The blade was 16½in (42cm) long and had been contained in a leather sheath. Parallel to it, northward, in the space where the body might have been, lay the sword.

The sword was quite short, 33in (84cm) long. The blade was pattern-welded: that is, it was not hammered out of a single piece of metal, but from metal rods, twisted and beaten to form a strong, ornamented blade. It had been contained in a wooden scabbard, lined with fur. The sword pommel was made of gold and garnet, as were two bosses which decorated the scabbard and two pyramidal studs of outstanding workmanship which were probably attached to the suspension-strap of the sword. Millefiori glasswork was used in the tops of these studs. There were also two clips decorated with filigree. The sword and its pommel were probably of Swedish workmanship, although the accompanying jewellery was probably English.

An iron-shafted axe-hammer may also have been a weapon; alternatively, it might have been a tool. It was found, about the middle of the burial deposit, under the rusted remains of a coat of mail. The mail-coat is an object unique in Anglo-Saxon archaeology. The chain-mail corselet (*byrne*) is frequently mentioned in Old English poetry, but in the heroic context of aristocratic society. Ordinary Anglo-Saxon men were not buried with such objects. Possibly they were comparatively rare in the Dark Ages although they are regularly depicted on Anglo-Saxons and Normans in the eleventh-century Bayeux Tapestry. The Sutton Hoo mail-coat was apparently knee-length. The rows of chain-mail were alternately riveted and welded.

A leather harness, secured by elaborate jewellery, had apparently been hung up in the burial chamber, to fall, when the chamber collapsed, into the space where the king's body may have been. The associated jewellery was gold, set with garnets in intricately shaped cloisons. We may note the mushroom-shaped cell characteristic of the Sutton Hoo jeweller, on five of these pieces, and the cable-twist effect on the others. The jewellery associated with the (presumed) harness includes two pairs of strap mounts, each 2in (5cm) long, a rectangular buckle 3in (8cm) long, a T-shaped strap distri-

118

butor $2\frac{2}{5}$in (6cm) and a clasp, curved and designed to look like a buckle $2\frac{9}{10}$in (7cm) long.

There was another set of gold and garnet belt equipment, comprising a buckle and two strap-ends, all with rounded ends, the buckle $1\frac{4}{5}$in (5cm) long and the strap-ends $1\frac{1}{5}$in (3cm) long. A triangular strap-mount $1\frac{1}{5}$in (3cm) long was suggestive of an animal's head, with circular garnets representing eyes and nose (plate 26).

Also in the body-space there was a pair of jewelled clasps (see plate 8), curved to fit the shoulders. Each clasp was in two parts which could be linked together by means of a gold pin, forming a unit about 5in (13cm) long. They had probably fastened together the front and back of a leather cuirass, but although there are loops on the backs of the clasps, for attachment to the garment as mentioned above (p.112), the positions of the clasps in the burial deposit suggested that they had been detached from the garment before burial. The main body of each clasp is composed of a neat chequer-board of cloisonné. Garnet and millefiori glass are set into the cells. As a border, interlacing animals in Salin Style II bite upon their own bodies. They too are executed in cloisonné, the jeweller having provided gold lids for some of the cells, to give the effect of red serpents against a gold background. At the D-shaped ends of the clasps full-length boars, executed in garnet and millefiori glass, intertwine against a filigree background (fig. 10). Thus the symbol of Freyr, a god particularly associated with the ship and ship funeral, appears on these English-made clasps as well as on the Swedish-made helmet.

The garnet is a brittle stone and the intricacy of the shapes cut by the Anglo-Saxon craftsmen who made all this garnet jewellery is remarkable. Before the discovery of the Sutton Hoo treasure Kent was the source of our best cloisonné jewellery, but the Sutton Hoo jewellery, with over four thousand individual garnets, equals the Kentish work in its skill and shows more versatility.

The single most valuable piece of jewellery in the ship was not, however, cloisonné. It was a gold buckle $5\frac{1}{5}$in (13cm) long, $2\frac{1}{5}$in (6cm) wide and weighing $15\frac{5}{8}$oz (443g). The buckle is triangular, with three bosses and a disc. It is decorated with interlacing serpentine animals, which, on the disc and buckle-plate, are elaborated with black niello. Here are the *wyrmas* (snakes or dragons) of Old English literature. The head of the bird of prey appears on the buckle also, and there is a small beast crouching at the narrow end. The buckle is hollow, and, considering its magnificence, seems to have fastened a surprisingly thin strap, not a heavy battle harness. Bruce-Mitford has suggested (in a lecture to the Manchester Medieval Society, 1978) that the buckle fastened the strap which suspended the purse.

The purse itself is of particular interest, not only because it is a unique object particularly evocative of northern paganism, but because it contained

Fig 24 The gold buckle from
Sutton Hoo

the coins that enable the ship burial to be dated. The purse consisted of
a perishable container and a lid, which had a gold frame and was decorated
with raised plaques of gold and garnet cloisonné. The lid, the only part to
survive, was $7\frac{1}{2}$in (19cm) long and $3\frac{1}{4}$in (8cm) wide. The gold and jewelled
parts of the lid were found face down in the earth, the coins scattered upon
the remains of the purse lid.

The outermost plaques in the upper row are geometric. The innermost
represent in garnet the same interlacing and confronting horses as appear
on the shield-boss (see fig. 8). The outermost plaques of the bottom row
apparently represent a scene from northern mythology, since the moust-
ached man, flanked by biting beasts with collars, is paralleled in Swedish
art. In the centre, the now familiar bird of prey claws an innocent-looking
bird, the jeweller achieving a realistic effect in cloisonné (see fig. 5).

The purse had contained thirty-seven coins, three pieces of gold the same
size as the coins but blank, and two small ingots. The coins were continental,
from the Merovingian Empire. As they are all from different mints
covering a wide area, they are clearly not the casual accumulation a traveller
might acquire in his purse, but a deliberately selected collection. It is unlikely that coins were minted or in general circulation in East Anglia at this

time. It seems, therefore, that the coins were not placed in the ship for their monetary value (which, for a royal occasion, would have been relatively little) but for a symbolic purpose. The coins were probably a symbolic payment for the forty oarsmen needed to row the ship (the three blanks making up the required number with the thirty-seven genuine coins); the ingots paid the steersman who would guide the king in his ship on the journey into another life.

To 'pay the ferryman' is a pagan practice, but one not otherwise associated with the Anglo-Saxons. It normally belongs with Greek and Roman paganism, where the common practice was to place a coin in the corpse's mouth. The custom had percolated into the Germanic world, apparently, since similar 'payments' occur in a small number of rich Frankish graves; but the deposition of such a payment in a ship burial is, so far, unparalleled. To associate the classical ferryman Charon, who conveyed the dead over the River Styx, with the Germanic funeral ship was a brilliant sleight of hand comparable with the later absorption of the Germanic Sceaf into biblical tradition as son of Noah (see p.33). It is consistent with what we know already of Rædwald, who was able to absorb something of Christianity without abandoning the ancient gods.

Feasting played an important part in Germanic life, as we know from Tacitus. Old English poetry, especially *Beowulf*, provides us with details of the banquets, when tapestries hung around the walls of the great hall, and the queen ceremonially carried the drinking vessel to her husband, at the high table, and to honoured guests. The minstrel sang legends of heroic deeds, accompanying himself on a stringed instrument; young men pledged their allegiance and boasted of the brave deeds that they would perform; heroes were rewarded with splendid gifts.

Many of the Sutton Hoo grave-goods confirm this splendid way of life at the royal court. A set of drinking vessels, comprising a pair of aurochs horns and six maple-wood bottles, are decorated with silver-gilt mounts. The mounts circle the rims and spread out in triangular panels. They are covered with zoomorphic interlace. The horns were originally about 24in (61cm) long and the bottles about $5\frac{7}{8}$in (15cm) high. There are seven small cups of walnut burr-wood, also with silver or silver-gilt rims, two decorated with matching animal ornament. A horn cup, a wooden bowl and a pottery bottle would also have held liquid. The burial chamber also contained vessels of silver: a small cup, 3in (8cm) in diameter, $1\frac{1}{2}$in (4cm) high, a ladle and two larger vessels, remarkable because they were clearly imports from the Roman world. One, a fluted bowl with two handles, is decorated with a classical head. It measures 16in (41cm) across. The other is a large salver $28\frac{1}{4}$in (72cm) across. It is known as the Anastasius Dish since it bears, on its base, control stamps showing that it was made in the Byzantine Empire and probably assayed in Constantinople, during the reign of Anastasius I

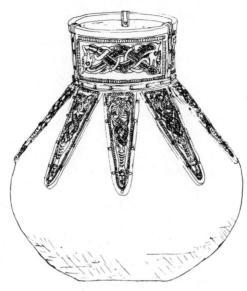

Fig 25   Drinking vessel with zoomorphic mounts from Sutton Hoo

(491–518). Burnt bone was found on the dish, probably from a cremation, but possibly from a funeral feast. Bede tells us that at the court of the Northumbrian King Oswald, who succeeded Edwin as Bretwalda, the food for the Easter feast was served on a silver platter (*HE*, III, 6). Probably Rædwald dined in similar splendour off an imported dish made of silver.

There was also a bronze bowl of Coptic type, $15\frac{1}{8}$in (39cm) across, decorated inside with naturalistic animals. A wooden tub, $20\frac{1}{2}$in (52cm) high and 20in (51cm) across at the top, and three smaller buckets may have held food and drink. The wood, where it could be analysed, was found to be yew. The vessels were all bound with iron and had decorated handles. Birds' heads appeared on two of them. There were also three bronze cauldrons. The largest of them was 17in (43cm) deep and 27in (69cm) across, large enough, as Bruce-Mitford points out, to hold a sheep (*Reflections*, p.26). A length of elaborate chainwork had suspended this cauldron. The chain was 11ft 4in (3·5m) long. An iron lamp consisting of a bowl containing beeswax, mounted on three legs, gives us some idea of how the great hall was illuminated. It was $7\frac{1}{2}$in (19cm) high, the bowl 6in (15cm) across.

A musical instrument (fig. 4) had been placed in a beaver-skin bag. It may have been the king's personal instrument, since Bede leads us to believe that a competent performance was expected of every man (*HE*, IV, 24). The instrument was a lyre. The frame was maple-wood, decorated and secured by two gilt-bronze plaques, each consisting of a circle of zoomorphic interlace and the head of a bird of prey. There had been six strings, presumably of gut, secured by pegs of poplar or willow-wood. The lyre was 29in (74cm) long, $8\frac{1}{6}$in (21cm) wide. Lyres have been found in graves in Germanic areas

122

of the continent, but they are rare. This find is interesting in confirming the impression we get from literature of the importance of the stringed instrument in Anglo-Saxon life.

Rædwald's survivors provided further for their dead lord's recreation in his future existence by including a set of gaming pieces among his grave-goods. Only a few fragments survive from what may have been a set of twenty-four or more ivory pieces, each about $1\frac{4}{5}$in (5cm) high, $1\frac{1}{10}$in (3cm) across.

Apart from the textiles which covered the floor of the burial chamber and which were possibly hung around the body area, archaeologists found remains of fabrics which may derive from bedding and clothes. There had been a pillow filled with down, covered perhaps by two textiles—a plain linen and a more luxurious twill-woven linen. Woollen fabrics in uncommon and luxurious twill weaves probably derive from blankets and a cushion cover. There were the remains of a pile-woven cloak, and possibly a pile-woven cap, and evidence to suggest an otter-skin cap, lined with woollen fabric. Fine, luxurious cloth, in broken diamond twill weave, probably derived from a tunic. There were four leather shoes, which had been fastened by laces and woven tape. Small silver buckles and strap ends were associated

Fig 26   Wooden tub from Sutton Hoo

with the shoes. Other personal possessions placed in the vessel include two pairs of knives with horn handles, in leather sheaths, and three combs, one double-sided, the others single.

Thus we see that the king buried in this ship was laid to rest in a truly pagan manner, with personal possessions befitting his noble status and with objects symbolic of his power, his military might and his Swedish heritage. Yet there was evidence that this king had experienced rituals other than the pagan and heroic. He had come into contact with the Christian Church, an institution which would have strongly disapproved of ship burial, the provision of grave-goods and the heathen rites involved in such a funeral.

Rædwald, we know, had been converted to Christianity on a visit to Kent. Adult baptism, in the early days of English Christianity, was an elaborate ritual spread over twenty-eight days. When a royal convert was sponsored by a royal godfather elaborate baptismal gifts were made. Rædwald, paradoxically, took his Christian possessions to his pagan grave. A pair of silver spoons, of Roman not Anglo-Saxon type, each 10in (25cm) long, may have been a christening gift to Rædwald, for their handles are inscribed in Greek letters 'Saulos' and 'Paulos'. (St Paul, previously called Saul and a persecutor of the disciples, was converted to Christianity as an adult by a mystical experience while travelling to Damascus.) Even if, as has been suggested, the 'Saulos' spoon was a barbaric craftsman's attempt to copy 'Paulos', the reference to Paul alone is enough to signify adult baptism. Ten silver bowls (five pairs) decorated with cruciform motifs may also have been baptismal gifts. They were about 9in (23cm) in diameter.

Among the grave-goods were three bronze hanging bowls. Bowls of this type are of Celtic origin, made either in Ireland, or in Celtic establishments in England. They obviously appealed to the Anglo-Saxons, since similar vessels, or sometimes just the escutcheons from such bowls, have been found in several Anglo-Saxon graves. The smaller Sutton Hoo bowls are decorated with enamelled escutcheons. The largest bowl, which measures $12\frac{1}{4}$in (31cm) across and is $5\frac{1}{2}$in (14cm) deep, has six external escutcheons, decorated with enamel and millefiori glass, three square and three circular (plate 27). Beneath the latter are bronze boars' heads. (The boar was a popular Celtic motif as well as a Germanic one.) Inside the bowl, and rising from a pedestal attached to the base escutcheon, is a naturalistic fish. This can be rotated by the finger. The fish, an early Christian symbol, marks out the bowl as a Christian object. The bowl was probably designed to be filled with water since then the fish would be in its natural element. The bowls would be hung by their three suspension rings by means of leather straps. (The remains of one strap was attached to one of the smaller bowls.) They must have played some part in Christian ceremonies. Perhaps they contained holy water, or were used for ritual hand-washing.

We do not know whether their Anglo-Saxon owners' appreciation of the

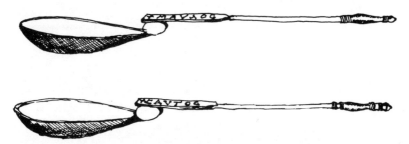

Fig 27   Christening spoons from Sutton Hoo

hanging bowls was divorced from their original Christian function, or if the bowls played some part in the strange compromise worship which Rædwald practised. One point is clear—the bowls were cherished by the Anglo-Saxons. The largest bowl was patched with a piece of silver from the Sutton Hoo workshops: it is stamped with the fierce bird-heads which occur so often in the jewellery. Furthermore, the Anglo-Saxon jeweller had placed gold foil and garnets in the eyes of the boars, using his habitual cloisonné technique, to replace the original eyes, which were probably of enamel.

We find then, that Rædwald's grave-goods exhibit exactly the kind of compromise he himself achieved in his religion. Possibly the absence of sacrifice is also a concession to Christianity, a concession also found in the poetic description of a ship funeral in *Beowulf*; but perhaps sacrifice was never a part of ship funerals in England. The ship burial found in 1939 at Sutton Hoo must have been the last, or one of the last, royal East Anglian burials to be predominantly pagan, for although King Ecgric (killed *c*.635) may have been a pagan, Christianity influenced all Rædwald's other successors and was soon firmly established in the kingdom. If there are earlier ship burials on the site—and the presence of other mounds and the expertise with which our two ships were buried suggest there may be—then these, when excavated, may provide us with pagan funerals undiluted by Christianity, and could answer the question about sacrifices.

It seems that the symbolism of the boat taking the dead on a journey persisted in East Anglia even into Christian times, for at Caistor-by-Norwich (Norfolk) pieces of boats were used as cradles or lids for burials in graves as late as the seventh or eighth century. This token acknowledgement of the old custom is comparable with a practice observed in Scandinavia: stones were laid out in the shape of a boat surrounding the remains of the dead. In these cases the belief in the funeral ship has been reduced to a symbolic gesture. It is at the opposite pole to the conception of the poet who described the dead hero Scyld Scefing as literally drifting across the ocean with a ship-load of treasure.

5

The Arrival of Christianity

The author of the English conversion was a Roman named Gregory. An able man, who had risen in the Roman civil service before deciding to devote himself to Christianity, Gregory encountered pagan Anglo-Saxons being sold as slaves in Rome in about 585. Bede's account of this meeting has become famous:

> We are told that one day some merchants who had recently arrived in Rome displayed their many wares in the crowded market-place. Among other merchandise Gregory saw some boys exposed for sale. These had fair complexions, fine-cut features, and fair hair. Looking at them with interest, he enquired what country and race they came from. 'They come from Britain,' he was told, 'where all the people have this appearance.' He then asked whether the people were Christians, or whether they were still ignorant heathens. 'They are pagans,' he was informed. 'Alas!' said Gregory with a heart-felt sigh: 'how sad that such handsome folk are still in the grasp of the Author of darkness, and that faces of such beauty conceal minds ignorant of God's grace! What is the name of this race?' 'They are called Angles,' he was told. 'That is appropriate,' he said, 'for they have angelic faces, and it is right that they should become fellow-heirs with the angels in heaven. And what is the name of their Province?' 'Deira,' was the answer. 'Good. They shall indeed be *de ira*—saved from wrath—and called to the mercy of Christ. And what is the name of their king?' he asked. 'Aella,' he was told. 'Then must *Alleluia* be sung to the praise of God our Creator in their land,' said Gregory, making play on the name.
>
> (*HE*, II, 1; pp.98–9)

Gregory did more than make puns; he immediately conceived the idea of a mission to England and received the approval of the then Pope, Pelagius II. Gregory wished to undertake the journey himself but was prevented by the citizens of Rome, and the scheme was not put into operation until Gregory was himself elected Pope in 590. Unable now to carry out the mission personally, Gregory selected as leader of the expedition the monk Augustine, who was his friend and also prior of the monastery that Gregory had founded on his own family estate.

The missionaries set out for Britain and travelled as far as Provence, where Augustine's companions became afraid of the dangers they were to face and sent him back to Rome with the request that they be recalled. Gregory's

126

25 Wooden wagon from Oseberg, Norway. This elaborately carved cart was found in a ninth-century ship burial (*University Museum of National Antiquities, Oslo, Norway*)

(*left*) 26 Strap mount from Sutton Hoo, Suffolk. A stylized animal's head is represented in this gold and garnet cloisonné piece (*Trustees of the British Museum*). (*right*) 27 Bronze hanging bowl from Sutton Hoo, Suffolk. A Celtic object, the bowl had been repaired by an Anglo-Saxon using a piece of metal stamped with birds' heads. Six enamelled escutcheons decorate the outside. Inside swims a fish, symbol of Christianity (*Trustees of the British Museum*)

28 Scenes from the life of Christ, in CCCC MS 286, fol. 125. The book is known as 'The Augustine Gospels' and was probably brought from Italy by or for Augustine to help in his mission to the Anglo-Saxons (*The Master and Fellows of Corpus Christi College, Cambridge*)

response was not defeatist but encouraging; he appointed Augustine abbot, perhaps to give him more authority over the reluctant missionaries (*HE*, I, 22), and also wrote to leading ecclesiastical and secular figures in Gaul ensuring their co-operation. The missionaries made the hazardous journey across Gaul without mishap and landed on the island of Thanet, in the Anglo-Saxon kingdom of Kent, early in the year 597.

Kent had no doubt been carefully chosen. It was a wealthy kingdom, and its ruler at that time, Æthelberht, was Bretwalda and so had influence over other kingdoms. Being the closest of the Anglo-Saxon kingdoms to the continent, Kent had strong ties of culture and kinship with her Frankish neighbours. Æthelberht himself was married to a Frankish woman, Bertha, daughter of Charibert, King of Paris. She was a Christian and the continued observance of her faith had been a condition of her marriage. The Frankish bishop Liudhard had come to Kent as her chaplain, and she worshipped in the old church of St Martin which had been built near Canterbury in Roman times.

Æthelberht at first kept the visitors confined to Thanet and superstitiously insisted that his first meeting with them be in the open air, for he apparently believed that if the newcomers were magicians they could do him harm in a house (*HE*, I, 24); but he treated them courteously, providing for them and coming to Thanet to meet them. The first meeting must have been carefully stage-managed and dramatic:

> ... the monks ... approached the king carrying a silver cross as their standard, and the likeness of our Lord and Saviour painted on a board. First of all they offered prayer to God, singing a litany for the eternal salvation both of themselves and of those for whose sake they had come.
>
> (*HE*, I, 25; p.69)

Their appearance, tonsured and in unfamiliar costume, their chant, and the cross and icon they carried must have seemed exotic to the barbarian people accustomed to Germanic culture, the music of the lyre and geometric art.

After hearing Augustine preach, Æthelberht refused to abandon immediately his traditional beliefs in favour of something new, but he permitted the missionaries to enter the mainland of Kent and gave them a dwelling in Canterbury. Despite his reticence it seems that the king was not reluctant to hear the Christian message. Pope Gregory's letters to Frankish rulers state that the English wished to become Christians, so it is possible that Æthelberht had already put out feelers and was not unwilling to embrace the religion of his powerful neighbours. The arrival of the missionaries, then, may have been expected (see J. Godfrey, *The Church in Anglo-Saxon England*, pp.73–5).

The missionaries utilized St Martin's church, which Queen Bertha and Bishop Liudhard had been using. The Roman monks soon made converts.

King Æthelberht's baptism must have taken place quite soon since he early endowed the mission with property in Canterbury and other possessions. On the Christmas Day after his arrival in Kent, Augustine was able to baptize more than ten thousand converts. Bede tells us (*HE*, I, 26) that at first the missionaries baptized in St Martin's church, but these large-scale ceremonies, now and later, probably took place in the open air in rivers or streams, for the tiny missionary churches the Roman monks built could not accommodate large congregations. No archaeological evidence found so far suggests that baptisteries were built at this time either within the churches or independently, or that the churches contained fonts.

By the autumn of 597 it had become opportune that Augustine be consecrated bishop. He accordingly travelled to Arles in Gaul for the ceremony (which had to be performed by a bishop, normally in the presence of at least two others). He made his episcopal seat at Canterbury, rebuilding a Romano-British church and consecrating it in the name of Jesus Christ. (Its design is not known, since subsequent building has obliterated the Anglo-Saxon architecture.) At Christ Church Augustine established his household, or *familia*, of men committed to the Church but not to monasticism. If the Church were to survive and expand it was necessary to train native clergy, an education which largely depended on the bishop. Only a minority of clerics rose to the rank of presbyter (or priest) and then only at maturity. (Bede tells us, *HE*, V, 24, that he was ordained priest at the age of thirty.) The minor clergy (lectors, acolytes, subdeacons and deacons) consisted of boys from the age of seven and young men moving up the hierarchy, as well as older men who were not sufficiently learned for promotion. All wore the tonsure in which, in the Roman fashion, the hair was shorn at the nape of the neck and at the top of the head, leaving a circular fringe of hair in imitation of the crown of thorns (see plate 35). The minor clergy provided the domestic labour necessary for the maintenance of the household and church but their more important duty was to take part in the rituals of the Christian religion.

While some, no doubt, learned Latin prayers and psalms parrot-fashion, the art of reading was now taught to the Anglo-Saxons for the first time and their own language was set down in the Roman alphabet. It was important, however, that the pupils learned to read Latin so that they could read or chant in church and eventually perform ceremonies such as exorcism, baptism and burial.

For those of Augustine's party who remained in the confines of monastic life, the monastery of St Peter was built to the east of Canterbury. Its original dedication to Peter (it was later to be known as St Augustine's) was a constant reminder of the Church of Rome. Within the monastery King Æthelberht founded a church dedicated to SS Peter and Paul. It was a building of modest proportions (the nave 39ft (11·9m) long, 27ft (8·2m) broad), but in its materials and design must have seemed as alien to the less sophisticated of the Anglo-Saxons as the missionaries who occupied it. The walls were of Roman brick and the floor of *opus signinum* (mortar and pounded brick). The design was not Roman, since there was little church-building going on in Rome at that time; instead the architecture of this and other early missionary churches was derived from the Adriatic and North Africa, ultimately Syria. Archaeologists have found similar features in the plans of several early churches: St Mary's at Canterbury, built *c.*620 by Æthelberht's son Eadbald on the same axis as SS Peter and Paul, and joined to it by an octagonal rotunda in the eleventh century; and, also at Canterbury, in line with the other two, the church of St Pancras, probably part of the same monastery, although (according to a late medieval scholar) King Æthelberht had had a pagan temple on this spot before Augustine rededicated it. On a similar pattern was built St Andrew's church at Rochester, where Justus, who arrived from Rome in 601, was the first bishop; and St Mary's at Lyminge, built in 633 for Æthelburg, daughter of King Æthelberht and widow of King Edwin of Northumbria. Of the same type are the later churches at Reculver (built in 669 on land given by King Egbert, Æthelberht's great-

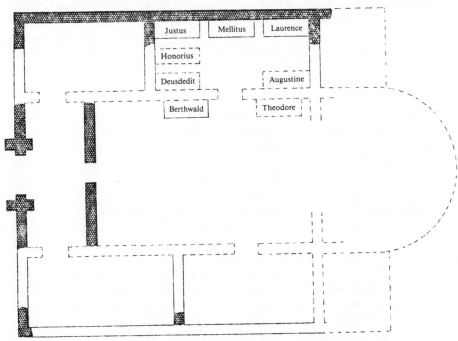

Fig 28   Plan of the church of SS Peter and Paul, Canterbury. Produced from H. McC. and J. Taylor, *Anglo-Saxon Architecture*, Fig 62 (*by permission of Cambridge University Press*)

grandson), and the only one outside Kent, Bradwell-on-Sea, Essex (built for Bishop Cedd in 653).

In these early churches a wide *narthex* or porch led to a rectangular nave and, at the east end, a chancel, which took the form of a semicircular (stilted) apse. A stone bench lined the apse at Reculver, suggesting that the clergy sat round this curve. In at least some of these churches the apse, which contained the altar, was separated from the nave by a triple arcade. At Lyminge the central archway was 6ft (1·8m), the flanking ones only 2ft (61cm) wide. From Reculver there survive the tapering cylindrical columns with ornamented bases and capitals which had supported the arcade.

Archaeological evidence, confirming in some cases what we know from literary sources, indicates that all these churches except St Mary's, Canterbury, were provided with additional chambers. These were not part of the nave separated from the body of the church by screens or arches, but independent rooms built to the north or south and entered by doorways within the church. These chambers, or *porticus*, derived from the church architecture of Syria where they had ritual significance: the northern chamber, the *diaconicon*, functioned as a sacristy; vestments and vessels were kept there and the clergy robed themselves there; in the southern chamber, the *prothesis*, offerings were prepared.

It is clear, however, that at least the earliest *porticus* in the missionary churches were designed as mausoleums. Roman civil law, at the time of the mission, forbade burial in church except in the cases of infants; so the chambers attached to the church were used as a suitably honourable resting-place for the highest-ranking clergy and for the Kentish royalty most intimately associated with the church. In the *porticus* dedicated to St Gregory, on the north wall of the Church of SS Peter and Paul, were buried Augustine and five successive archbishops of Canterbury. (Augustine died before the completion of the church but his body was translated to the *porticus* when it was built.) In a slightly smaller *porticus* dedicated to St Martin, on the south wall, lay King Æthelberht, Queen Bertha and Bishop Liudhard. Similarly Queen Æthelburg, according to the post-Conquest writer Goscelin, was buried in a *porticus* on the north side of the church she had founded at Lyminge, and Bishop Tobias of Rochester was buried in a similar structure at St Andrew's church (*HE*, V, 23).

Other flanking chambers may have had ceremonial use: an additional pair of chambers at SS Peter and Paul, to the west of the burial chambers, opened on to the *narthex*. Not more than a century after it was built the Reculver church was surrounded by flanking chambers. At Reculver two chambers, one on each side, opened on to the outside of the building as well as on to the chancel; while at Bradwell a pair of chambers overlapped the nave and chancel, the northern one opening on to the chancel, the southern on to the nave, in a close copy of the Syrian arrangement. It would have been possible for the clergy to process from one to the other in the manner of the eastern Church, but we have no evidence that the English clergy did so, or that the chambers were any more than a vestigial feature of eastern architecture.

In the churches, more than anywhere, the people of Kent would witness the rituals of the new religion which was among them. Mass was celebrated on Sundays and many other occasions. Meanwhile the monastic churches were in daily use for the singing of the canonical hours. The trappings of Christianity were simpler and the practice less uniform than they became in later medieval times. Augustine, although a bishop, would not have worn a mitre or episcopal gloves, but he may have had a ring and staff as insignia of his position. He lived monastically, and so, no doubt, dressed simply on most occasions, but for celebrating mass he would wear a chasuble (a cloak put on over the head) over a white linen alb and the narrow strip of cloth known as a stole. The flowing white alb was worn by all the lesser clergy; those of the rank of deacon and above also wore the stole; priests wore the chasuble. The maniple (originally a handkerchief held in the hand for wiping vessels or the face but which evolved into a symbolic strip of cloth) may have been carried over the left wrist, and sandals were probably worn on the feet. Anglo-Saxon men normally wore short tunics of wool; linen was a luxury. This full-length Italianate costume of the processing clergy must have looked very different from what the layfolk were used to.

The celebrant and other ministers would process to the altar singing a psalm in Latin, bearing candles and incense.[1] The altar, which would be covered by a cloth, held the chalice or cup for the eucharistic wine and the paten or dish for the bread. A cross may have stood on the altar and the gospel book may have been laid on it. There is a gospel book in Cambridge (Corpus Christi College MS 286) which is believed to have belonged to Augustine, either brought to England by him or sent as a subsequent gift by Pope Gregory. It was illustrated with scenes from the life of Christ and with 'portraits' of the evangelists who wrote the gospels (plate 28). It must have provided a model for later Anglo-Saxon illuminators at Canterbury.

At the altar Latin prayers and readings took place. A litany—a series of petitions by the clergy answered by formulaic responses—may have been recited before the collect, a prayer preceding the epistle. The epistle and gospel may have been introduced by a procession from the altar to a pulpit in the nave, to the accompaniment of a chanted psalm. The offerings of the congregation were used for the eucharist, the celebrant washing his hands and giving a prayer of thanksgiving and consecration. All could communicate except penitents, and the eucharist, with its reverence and mystery, must have been the climax of the converts' Christian experience.

---

1. This description is largely derived from M. Deanesly, *The Pre-Conquest Church in England*, 2nd ed., pp.146 ff.

There was as yet no single book of prayers for the whole Christian Church. Different sects used different sacramentaries but did not necessarily confine themselves to any one book. Augustine himself seems to have been disturbed by this variation. He must have come across different services in his journey across Gaul; while in Kent itself, Bishop Liudhard, who was a Frank, almost certainly used the Gallican liturgy and so differed from the Roman missionaries in his prayers and practices.

Augustine seems to have used the Gelasian sacramentary. This book contained masses for use on the major feast days and Sundays of the Church year (Christmas, Easter, Pentecost and so on) and for other specified Sundays, for Saints' Days, and for use on other (unspecified) Sundays. It also contained prayers and blessings for occasions we are still familiar with, such as marriage and burial, and for circumstances less common now, for example, blessing of trees and prayers against enemies. Augustine must have used the sacramentary in praying for catechumens and baptizing them, and in ordaining the priests and other clergy for the Church in England.[2] Augustine may have also owned a copy of the newer 'Gregorian' sacramentary in which the Sundays and feasts were catalogued according to the Julian calendar, which began on 1 January (rather than in relation to the ecclesiastical year which categorized Sundays in relation to the major feasts and began with Christmas). Augustine's other 'text books' must have consisted of a book of chants,[3] a psalter and the gospels.

Those members of Augustine's mission who did not receive ordination or join the episcopal *familia* lived a life of strict routine within the confines of the monastery. St Benedict (who died *c*.547) had already formulated for the monks at his Italian monastery of Monte Cassino the 'Rule', which later became widely accepted as the basis of monastic life in the west, but at the time of the Anglo-Saxon mission standardization had not been imposed and each monastery was guided by its own abbot. Augustine's monks probably knew the Benedictine Rule, but their lives may not have conformed to it exactly.

It was the daily duty of the monks to recite the canonical hours. The full timetable could consist of Vigils, Lauds, Prime, Terce, Sext, None, Vespers, Collation and Compline, although St Benedict lists only eight hours, omitting Collation. These services were performed simply, chanted rather than spoken for the sake of clarity, but probably without the elaborate variation of tone and rhythm learned by later generations of Anglo-Saxons. The hours consisted mostly of psalmody—psalms and canticles (songs selected from the Old and New Testaments, such as the Song of the Three Children)— and prayer, for instance the Lord's Prayer and collects, and readings from

---

2. See H. A. Wilson, *The Gelasian Sacramentary*.
3. See W. Apel, *Gregorian Chant*, p.48.

scripture. The hours could be performed without the presence of a priest (indeed a monastery did not always contain a priest). Between their duties in church, the monks' time would be filled with study and manual work; meals would be frugal and sleep short. Clothing was provided at the discretion of the abbot who could vary the allowance according to season and climate. The monks may not have worn a uniform habit but all would be simply dressed. They would wear a cowl and carry the minimum of personal belongings. Augustine's monks, being Italians, would have worn long habits, but Anglo-Saxon monks may have dressed in the shorter garments of Germanic culture, and were not compelled to wear long habits until 873.[4]

Augustine's monks may not have embraced the extreme asceticism of their Celtic brethren (see p.139) but their simple piety impressed the people of Kent:

> As soon as they had occupied the house given to them they began to emulate the life of the apostles and the primitive Church. They were constantly at prayer; they fasted and kept vigils; they preached the word of life to whomsoever they could. They regarded worldly things as of little importance, and accepted only necessary food from those they taught. They practised what they preached, and were willing to endure any hardship, and even to die for the Faith which they proclaimed.
>
> (*HE*, I, 26; p.70)

The year after his arrival in Kent, Augustine sent two of his party, Laurentius a priest and Peter a monk, back to Rome to report progress and to ask for reinforcements. They carried with them a letter from Augustine asking Gregory's advice on various matters. It seems from his questions that he was anxious about his own authority as bishop. It must have been difficult for one who arrived as a monk among monks to reconcile that role with the episcopal one in which he maintained his own household and received the offerings of the faithful. He sought Gregory's authority to consecrate new bishops without the presence of other bishops since all his peers were so far away, and he asked for clarification of his position in relation to the bishops of Gaul and Britain. He expressed his surprise that Church ritual in Gaul differed from that of Rome. He was probably unaware, as yet, of the even greater differences between the Roman Church and the Celtic. Gregory advised flexibility:

> ... if you have found customs, whether in the Roman, Gallican, or any other Churches that may be more acceptable to God, I wish you to make a careful selection of them, and teach the Church of the English, which is still young in the Faith, whatever you can profitably learn from the various Churches.
>
> (*HE*, I, 27; p.73)

---

4. E. Caspar (ed.), '*Fragmenta registri Iohannes VIII, papæ*', *MGH, Epistolæ*, 1, VII, Berlin, pp.293–4.

The Pope showed similar tolerance in permitting marriage among the lower clergy, and in dealing with those who had contracted, before their conversion, marriages that the Church considered unlawful. These people were to be warned that they were committing an offence and that they should not continue with it, but they were not to be denied Holy Communion since they had sinned in ignorance:

> For in these days the Church has to correct some things strictly, and allow others already established by custom; others have to be tolerated for a while, in the hope that forbearance may sometimes eradicate an evil of which she disapproves.
>
> (*HE*, I, 27; p.74)

The sin of incest proved tenacious. When Æthelberht died, his pagan son Eadbald married his stepmother (not Bertha, but Æthelberht's second wife). Augustine had evidently come across this specific problem, for he questioned Gregory about marriage between kin, especially the stepmother and sister-in-law relationships.

The new bishop, shocked by the Anglo-Saxon lack of refinement, sought the Pope's advice on matters of childbirth and marital relations:

> May an expectant mother be baptized? How soon after childbirth may she enter church? And how soon after birth may a child be baptized if in danger of death? How soon after childbirth may a husband have relations with his wife? And may a woman properly enter church at certain periods? And may she receive Communion at these times? And may a man enter church after relations with his wife before he has washed? Or receive the sacred mystery of Communion? These uncouth English people require guidance on all these matters.
>
> (*HE*, I, 27; p.76)

Again Gregory's attitude was flexible. He was obviously reluctant to deny anyone baptism or Communion at any time, but seemed to hope that peoples' own sense of reverence would develop sufficiently for them to refrain from religious activities when their bodies were unclean.

In 601 Laurentius and Peter returned to Kent with Gregory's answers and with reinforcements. This second party of missionaries included such important men as Mellitus and Justus, who, like Laurentius, were future archbishops of Canterbury. The Pope sent to Augustine with this mission the pallium (or pall), which was the insignia of an archbishop. The pallium was a narrow strip of material (not unlike the stole) which was woven for the Pope from the wool of specially reared white lambs. It was sent by the Pope only to archbishops (and a very few, special bishops) and each pallium was personal to its owner—it could not be lent.[5] Archbishops were permitted

---

5. R. A. S. Macalister, *Ecclesiastical Vestments*, pp.96–102.

Fig 29   Early form of the pallium, from a mosaic at Ravenna, Italy

to wear the pallium only at mass. Augustine probably wore his pallium wound loosely round his neck so that one end hung down at the front and the other at the back (in the manner of a college scarf) as we see it worn on mosaics at Ravenna. The Y-shaped pallium (see plate 34) had not yet become fashionable.

The Pope ordered Augustine to consecrate twelve bishops, and to send to York a bishop who was in turn to consecrate twelve further bishops. Gregory's intention was that the English Church should be administered as *Britannia* had been governed when it was a Roman province, that is, from London and York; but London was in the East Saxon kingdom and in the years immediately following the mission the Church's hold on Essex was never strong enough for Augustine to move his headquarters to London; so Canterbury, although it was threatened in the eighth century (see p.152), remained, and remains to this day, the see of England's senior archbishop. York did eventually receive its archbishop but not as quickly as planned. The missionary Paulinus was consecrated bishop when he accompanied Æthelberht's daughter Æthelburg to Northumbria on her marriage to the heathen King Edwin in 625. When Edwin was converted, Paulinus duly received York as his see; his archiepiscopal pallium was sent by Pope Honorius in 634, but before it arrived from Rome Edwin was dead and Northumbria had lapsed into paganism.

Undoubtedly the patronage of King Æthelberht of Kent was an important factor in the conversion. Bede tells us (*HE*, I, 26) that the king showed favour to converts and it was through this powerful king's connections that the missionaries sought to bring Christianity to the other Anglo-Saxon kingdoms. It was at Æthelberht's court that King Rædwald of East Anglia received baptism. Æthelberht's nephew, Saberht, king of the East Saxons, received Mellitus into Essex as Bishop of London in 604; and it was through the marriage of Æthelberht's daughter (after his death) that Christianity

137

was introduced into the powerful kingdom of Northumbria. Possibly the Northumbrian people recalled traditions of Christianity from Romano-British days and King Edwin may have come into contact with it while in exile at the court of Rædwald of East Anglia (*HE*, II, 12). He was still heathen at the time of his marriage to Æthelburg, but he promised tolerance of his Kentish bride's religion. It was not Edwin himself but his infant daughter who became Northumbria's first Christian: at Easter 626, an attempt was made on Edwin's life but the assassin was foiled, and in gratitude the king permitted the baptism of the newly born Eanflæd. He promised that his own conversion would follow if he was successful in a punitive expedition against the king of Wessex, who had planned the murder. He eventually accepted Christianity after instruction from Paulinus. The councillors of Northumbria debated and formally rejected paganism, the high priest desecrating the heathen temple (see pp.50–1). Edwin was baptized on Easter Day 627, at York, in a wooden oratory built during his period of instruction. Baptismal ceremonies took a week, during which the convert appeared in church each day robed in white. During this time the chrism or consecrated oil was bound to the head by a baptismal fillet which was ceremonially removed.

Around Edwin's small wooden church a more splendid stone church was begun. Members of the royal family, following Edwin's lead, were baptized, including his kinswoman Hild, then aged thirteen, his sons by an earlier wife and his subsequent children by Æthelburg. Two of these, a son and a daughter, died in infancy and were buried in the York church, presumably still in their white robes of baptism, as was customary. For six years the missionary Paulinus preached zealously. He spent thirty-six days at Yeavering, and it was no doubt at this time that the pagan temple there was rededicated as a church. Paulinus did not, however, use it for baptism, preferring the river. He also, Bede tells us, baptized in the River Swale near Catterick since there was no church or baptistery in the area (*HE*, II, 14). In these prosperous times Paulinus also preached in Lindsey, and Eorpwald of East Anglia, son of the lapsed Rædwald, was converted. In 632, however, Edwin was killed by King Cadwallon of Gwynedd, in alliance with the pagan King Penda of Mercia. Paulinus escorted the widowed queen and the royal children back to her brother's kingdom of Kent, where she founded England's first convent at Lyminge and Paulinus himself became Bishop of Rochester. Northumbria temporarily reverted to heathenism. Only the deacon James, remaining near Catterick, continued the Roman mission to Northumbria. He was very knowledgeable about Church music, and in more peaceful times, when Christianity was re-established, he taught people to sing in the Roman manner (*HE*, II, 20).

The restoration of Christianity in Northumbria owed its inspiration to Edwin's nephew Oswald. He succeeded to the throne in 633 after a period of anarchy and the deaths of two other Northumbrian kings. During Edwin's reign Oswald had been exiled in Scotland, almost certainly on the island of Iona, and had been converted to Christianity by Celtic clergy. Once he had established himself as king he sent for a missionary from Iona. He received the monk Aidan and founded a monastery for him on Lindisfarne, an island off the coast of Northumbria connected at low tide to the mainland near Bamburgh, a royal residence. The king himself acted as interpreter for the Celtic missionary, who impressed all by his unworldliness. He fasted until None (3 p.m.) on Wednesdays and Fridays, and travelled widely preaching and teaching, by preference walking rather than riding (*HE*, III, 3, 5).

Aidan's home monastery of Iona was a famous centre of learning and missionary work. It had been founded by St Columba in 563 and was an Irish establishment. The Irish Church had originally been episcopal, as the Roman Church was, but in the sixth century (while England was inhabited by pagan Anglo-Saxons) the increasing importance of monasticism had changed its character. There were fewer bishops and many priests, all of whom lived under the rule of an abbot in the monastery. Their monasticism was extremely ascetic, and, although the monks lived in closed communities, there was an emphasis on individualism which was later to produce hermits and anchorites. Many Irish monks, of whom St Brendan is the most famous, traditionally travelled great distances in boats with little provision for their own safety. This eagerness to journey and the lack of care for personal comfort made the Irish enthusiastic missionaries and was to influence English Christians. The Old English poem *The Seafarer*, which may express the thoughts of a *peregrinus* or pilgrim, captures the typically Celtic embracing of physical discomfort for the love of God:

> '... ic geswincdagum
> earfoðhwile   oft þrowade,
> bitre breostceare   gebiden hæbbe,
> gecunnad in ceole   cearselda fela,
> atol yþa gewealc,   þær mec oft bigeat
> nearo nihtwaco   æt nacan stefnan,
> þonne he be clifum cnossað.   Calde geþrungen
> wæron mine fet,   forste gebunden,
> caldum clommum,   þær þa ceare seofedun
> hat ymb heortan;   hungor innan slat
> merewerges mod.'

(ASPR, III, p.143, lines 2–12)

'... I often suffered in days of toil, a time of hardship, I have endured bitter heart-care, experienced many places of sorrow in a boat, the bitter tossing of waves, where anxious night-watch often kept me at the prow of the ship when it tosses by the cliffs. My feet were pinched with cold, bound with frost, there cares surged hot about my heart; within, hunger rent the spirit of the one weary of the sea.'

Irish monks looked different from Roman monks since they wore a distinctive tonsure. The hair was cut from ear to ear, apparently from the forehead to the crown, the back hair being worn longer. Possibly we have a picture of this tonsure in the depiction of a man (symbolic of St Matthew) in a seventh-century Anglo-Irish gospel book, the Book of Durrow (plate 29).

Celtic clergy used the Gallican sacramentary rather than the Gelasian, and although the two had certain similarities there were significant differences: baptism took a different form; there were individual prayers, such as thanksgiving after Communion; there was a blessing for the Pascal candle; and the hands of priests were anointed at ordination.[6] Celtic psalters (books of psalms) seem to have omitted canticles.[7]

The most significant difference between Celtic and Roman Christianity, as far as the Anglo-Saxons were concerned, was in their method of calculating Easter, a mathematical as well as a theological conundrum. Easter is a movable feast, the date of which is calculated, as an inheritance from the Jewish Passover, according to the first full moon after the spring equinox. The Celts, calculating according to an eighty-four-year cycle, celebrated Easter between the fourteenth and twentieth days of the month, sometimes, therefore, beginning on the evening of the thirteenth day. The Romans, working to a more recently established nineteen-year cycle, calculated that Easter fell between the fifteenth and the twenty-first days of the month.

Augustine had attempted to discuss the discrepancy over Easter, among other things, at a meeting with Celtic clergy (probably Welsh) held in the west of the Anglo-Saxon territory in 603; but the British bishops were antagonized by Augustine's attitude, which they interpreted as discourtesy, and they refused to co-operate with him. Augustine had then, in a rather unchristian way, prophesied their destruction, and indeed many Celtic monks were later killed in a battle (*HE*, II, 2). Now, by means of an independent mission, Celtic monks were at last working among the Anglo-Saxons.

When Roman Christianity returned to Northumbria after Paulinus's setback, the discrepancy between Celtic practices and those of Canterbury was naturally found to be awkward, but there was tolerance in Aidan's lifetime because the man was so respected. Matters came to a head, however, in 664. King Oswiu, who was then on the throne of Northumbria, was Oswald's brother and, like him, had been converted to the Celtic brand of Christianity during his exile; but he had married Eanflæd, that daughter of King Edwin

6. See M. Deanesly, *The Pre-Conquest Church in England*, p.188.
7. J. Mearns, *The Canticles of the Christian Church, Eastern and Western, in Early and Medieval Times*, p.68.

who had been baptized as an infant by Paulinus and who had probably been brought up in Kent. Bede vividly depicts the theological complications of the marriage:

> It is said that the confusion in those days was such that Easter was kept twice in one year, so that when the King had ended Lent and was keeping Easter, the Queen and her attendants were still fasting and keeping Palm Sunday.
>
> (*HE*, III, 25; p.182)

(In 664 Easter for the Celts fell on 14 April, for the Romans on 21 April, a date outside the Celtic calculation.)

Bede tells us that Aidan's successor Finan was 'hot-tempered' and 'obstinate'. A Mediterranean-trained cleric, Ronan, opposed him on the question of Easter, so did James, formerly Paulinus's deacon. Most important, Oswiu's son Alhfrith had been convinced of the rightness of the Roman cause by Wilfrid, the strong-minded churchman whose later career was to range between high position and exile.

A synod was held in 663 or 664[8] at Whitby, where Oswiu's kinswoman Hild was abbess. The Celtic viewpoint was argued by Colman, Finan's successor as Bishop of Lindisfarne. The Romans were represented by Agilbert, Bishop of the West Saxons, but since his command of English was poor, Wilfrid spoke for him. He was persuasive, and Oswiu decreed that all should adhere to the Roman customs. Colman and those monks who could not bring themselves to comply withdrew to Iona. Others, choosing to stay, changed their tonsure and their computation of Easter; but the Celtic mission had left a stamp on the Christianity of Northumbria which could not disappear overnight.

The asceticism of the Celts is demonstrated most profoundly by the life of St Cuthbert. The man was a Northumbrian by birth and accepted the decision of the Whitby synod; but he had been raised in a Celtic monastery at Melrose, and the craving for a life of simple spirituality persisted even after he had been raised to the rank of Bishop of Lindisfarne. We are told that when his skin boots had been removed on Maundy Thursday for the annual foot-washing ritual, thick callouses were found on his legs, the result of the friction caused by constant genuflexions (B. Colgrave (ed. and trans.), *Two Lives of St Cuthbert*, p.218). He built a hermitage on remote Farne Island and died there, sustained in his final hours with only raw onions for nourishment (Colgrave, p.276). In complete contrast is Wilfrid, who was ordained with lavish ceremony in Gaul and was openly contemptuous of Celtic customs. He built elaborate churches and was ambitious for his epi-

---

8. The date is disputed, and depends on Bede's calculation of the year. Bede gives 664, but by modern reckoning 663 may be the more accurate date.

141

scopal see. On his death-bed, he ordered his treasure to be brought to him and he divided it among the religious houses he had founded, rejoicing in the material wealth he had brought to his Church.

Another enthusiast for the ways of Rome was Wilfrid's friend Benedict Biscop. Like Wilfrid, he travelled and studied on the continent and when, in 674 and 681, he founded the twin monasteries of Wearmouth and Jarrow (home of Bede), he brought books and pictures to enrich them, introducing an art that was wholly Mediterranean and quite unlike the complex patterns beloved by the Celts. His religious houses had *opus signinum* floors and painted, plastered walls. Glaziers were brought from Gaul to make glass for the windows. Benedict Biscop's monks could write in uncial, a continental hand unlike the Irish scripts produced at nearby Lindisfarne. They may have been taught the uncial hand by John, the arch-cantor from St Peter's in Rome, who was brought over to teach the monks in Benedict Biscop's establishments to chant in the Roman manner. It was not customary, in those days, to write down musical notes, so John's pupils had to learn their work by heart. He remained at Wearmouth for a year, and monks from other Northumbrian monasteries visited him and learned Gregorian chant. The presence of a resident teacher from Rome must have strongly influenced Benedict Biscop's community, and its visitors, to follow Roman ways rather than Celtic. John the cantor was an expert in liturgy, and it is known that he wrote down for his Northumbrian pupils all the Christian festivals as celebrated in Rome.

The Northumbrians were exposed to two extremes of Christianity: Celtic asceticism as well as the most lavish enrichment that well-travelled Englishmen could contrive with help of imported craftsmen and treasures. The people might worship in small village churches like the one which still stands at Escomb (Co. Durham), or in the elaborate basilicas erected by Wilfrid. The Escomb church has high walls, a rectangular nave and a chancel only 10ft (3m) square, joined to the nave by a narrow archway. It may, of

Fig 30 Plan of the church at Escomb, Co. Durham. Reproduced from H. McC. and J. Taylor, *Anglo-Saxon Architecture*, Fig 105 (*by permission of Cambridge University Press*)

course, have been decorated with pictures and hangings, but its architecture gives an impression of simple austerity. In contrast, we might compare the description given by Eddius Stephanus, Wilfrid's biographer, of the church of St Andrew at Hexham:

> My feeble tongue will not permit me to enlarge here upon the depth of the foundations in the earth, and its crypts of wonderfully dressed stone, and the manifold building above ground, supported by various columns and many side aisles, and adorned with walls of notable length and height, surrounded by various winding passages with spiral stairs leading up and down; for our holy bishop, being taught by the Spirit of God, thought out how to construct these buildings; nor have we heard of any other house on this side of the Alps built on such a scale. Further, Bishop Acca of blessed memory, who by the grace of God is still alive, provided for this manifold building splendid ornaments of gold, silver and precious stones; but of these and of the way he decorated the altars with purple and silk, who is sufficient to tell?
>
> (*Vita Wilfridi*, XXII; Colgrave (ed. and trans.), p.47)

Wilfrid's crypt, which still exists beneath Hexham Abbey, bears witness to the splendour of the seventh-century building.

The Celtic and the Roman elements were not always at variance in Northumbria. The clerics certainly met and exchanged ideas, and the resulting cross-fertilization produced great masterpieces of art such as the Lindisfarne Gospels, the Ruthwell Cross and the Franks Casket. The seventh and eighth centuries have often been labelled the Golden Age of Northumbria.

Meanwhile, the other Anglo-Saxon kingdoms had gradually been won over to Christianity. Two East Anglian kings, Rædwald and Eorpwald, had been baptized at the persuasion of royal friends, but their kingdom lapsed into heathenism until the 630s. Sigeberht, Eorpwald's half-brother, was then on the throne. He himself had been converted during exile in Gaul, and at his own request received in East Anglia the missionary Felix, sent by Honorius, the fifth archbishop of Canterbury. Felix made his episcopal see at Dunwich, where King Sigeberht founded a school for boys which Felix provided with teachers from the school already established in Canterbury. Felix was a Burgundian and no doubt the practices introduced by him and supported by Sigeberht were much influenced by Gaul; but East Anglia also experienced Celtic Christianity through the Irish monk, Fursey, who made many converts in the kingdom. On land given by the king, he established a monastery which continued to enjoy royal patronage. Fursey's life exemplified Irish traditions of asceticism and scholarship. Bede tells us (*HE*, III, 19) that during an illness Fursey fell into trances, in one of which he experienced the fires of purgatory and was left with a burn which permanently scarred his shoulder and jaw. He later lived the austere life of a hermit for a year and ended his days in Gaul where, twenty-seven years

143

after his death, his body was found to be incorrupt. (We find that similar miracles are associated with several pious characters in early Anglo-Saxon history, see p.153.)

The pious King Sigeberht of East Anglia retired to a monastery, leaving the kingdom to his kinsman Ecgric; but in 635 East Anglia was attacked by Penda of Mercia. Sigeberht was dragged from the monastery by his people, in an attempt to boost morale, but, adhering to his monastic vows, the former king would not arm himself except with a stick. Inevitably he was killed, as was Ecgric. The conversion seems to have been unaffected, however, since East Anglia was committed to Christianity during the reign of their successor Anna. A pious man himself, he fathered four future nuns, two of whom became famous as saints. Like his predecessors, Anna was killed by the pagan Penda of Mercia, in 654.

Wessex, which was eventually to emerge as the most important Anglo-Saxon kingdom, was not converted as a direct result of the Augustinian mission, but by an independent venture. The missionary Birinus, who had been consecrated in Genoa, was sent to England by Pope Honorius I. He baptized King Cynegils of Wessex in 635, and King Oswald of Northumbria, who was in Wessex at the time to marry Cynegils's daughter, stood as godfather to the West Saxon king. Birinus was made Bishop of Dorchester-on-Thames, but although Bede tells us he made many converts (*HE*, III, 7), his see does not seem to have been influential and the conversion was not consolidated. Cynegils's successor, Cenwalh, at first refused to accept Christianity, but was converted during three years of exile at the court of Anna of East Anglia. The Frankish cleric Agilbert then served him as bishop, but it was some time before the Church in Wessex settled down. That lack of competence in the English language which handicapped Agilbert at the Synod of Whitby (see p.141) finally so annoyed King Cenwalh that he divided the see, creating the additional bishopric of Winchester. He appointed to it an English cleric, named Wine, who had been consecrated in Gaul. Agilbert, offended, returned to Gaul, where he became Bishop of Paris. In time, Wine also displeased the king and was dismissed. Cenwalh asked Agilbert to return. Commitments in Paris prevented him, but he sent instead his nephew Leuthere, who became Bishop of Winchester. It is clear that the influence of the continent, especially Gaul, was very strong in the early Wessex Church, and doubtless the prayers and ceremonies differed accordingly from the Roman-based practices of Kent, and the Celtic-influenced customs of Northumbria.

That notorious pagan, King Penda of Mercia, enemy of so many devout Christian kings, died without retracting his heathenism; but Christianity had already infiltrated his domain. His son, Peada, King of the Middle Angles, was baptized when he married the daughter of King Oswiu of Northumbria. The baptism took place in Northumbria and four priests were

29 Symbol of St Matthew from The Book of Durrow, *Codex Durmachensis*, fol. 21v, a gospel book illuminated in Hiberno-Saxon style. A ribbon-like frame surrounds the stylized figure. His garment resembles millefiori glass work (*The Green Studio Ltd, The Board of Trinity College, Dublin*)

30 St Etheldreda ('Æþeldrype' in the picture) from The Benedictional of St
Æthelwold, BL MS Additional 49598, fol. 90v. The long hands, fluttering gar-
ments and heavy frame of acanthus leaves on a trellis are typical of the Winchester
Style (*British Museum, British Library*)

taken back to Peada's kingdom. Three were English, one of them at least (a man named Cedd) a Lindisfarne monk. The fourth, Diuma, was Irish. There was therefore a strongly Celtic flavour to the early Christianity of this region. In 654 Diuma was consecrated bishop. He does not seem to have had any one city as his see, but his sphere of influence encompassed Middle Anglia and Mercia proper, as well as Lindsey, the province that had been converted by Paulinus back in 628.

Heathenism seems to have been persistent in Essex. The East Saxons had tasted Christianity soon after Augustine's mission, but lapsed into paganism soon after the death of King Saberht, driving out the first bishop, Mellitus, in 616. It was another king, Sigeberht, who brought the kingdom back to Christianity. He was converted in 653 on a visit to his friend Oswiu of Northumbria, when, according to Bede, Oswiu himself argued persuasively. The speech Bede paraphrases interestingly implies that the pagan Angles had been accustomed to make idols of wood, stone and even of metal:

> Oswiu used to reason with him how gods made by men could not be gods, and how a god could not be made from a log or block of stone, the rest of which might be burned, or made into articles of everyday use, or possibly thrown away as rubbish to be trampled underfoot and reduced to dust. He showed him how God is of boundless majesty, invisible to human eyes, almighty, Creator of heaven and earth and of the human race. He told him that he rules and will judge the world in justice, abiding in eternity, not in base and perishable metal ...
>
> (*HE*, III, 22; p.174)

Oswiu arranged for the East Saxon king to receive Cedd, who was then working in Middle Anglia. Cedd seems to have retained the typically Celtic urge to travel: we find him baptizing Sigeberht's successor Suidhelm at Rendlesham in East Anglia (*HE*, III, 22), and he is known to have made journeys back to his native Northumbria. On one of these visits Bishop Finan consecrated him Bishop of the East Saxons, and in 663 or 664 he attended the Synod of Whitby. Another time he received a gift of land at Lastingham, in Northumbria, to build a monastery. His behaviour on this occasion demonstrates the asceticism of the Celtic monks and gives us a unique insight into the customs associated with the dedication of early monasteries:

> The man of God wished first of all to purify the site of the monastery from the taint of earlier crimes by prayer and fasting, and make it acceptable to God before laying the foundations. He therefore asked the king's permission to remain there throughout the approaching season of Lent, and during this time he fasted until evening every day except Sunday according to custom. Even then, he took no food but a morsel of bread, an egg, and a little watered milk. He explained that it was the custom of those who had trained him in the rule

147

of regular discipline to dedicate the site of any monastery to God with prayer and fasting.

(*HE*, III, 23; p.177)

Cedd died of the plague at Lastingham in 664, but before then he had enjoyed success in Essex, building churches, ordaining clergy and baptizing, particularly, Bede tells us, at Tilbury. Nevertheless, some of the East Saxons briefly apostasized in 665 when their kingdom was afflicted by plague. There were at that time two kings ruling Essex: Sebbi remained firm in his Christianity (he later became a monk); Sighere and his followers relapsed into heathenism, rebuilding ruined temples. Bishop Jaruman was sent from Mercia, however, and soon restored the faith. London was re-established as the episcopal see of Essex, but was doomed to further indignity: Wine, first Bishop of Winchester, after his disagreement with the King of Wessex, purchased the see of London from King Wulfhere of Mercia and occupied it for the rest of his life (*HE*, III, 7).

By the middle of the seventh century, Christianity was well established in England, despite these occasional backslidings. All the kingdoms had been converted except Sussex and the Isle of Wight (which were rather off the beaten tracks from Rome and Ireland), and in 654 Deusdedit, a man born in Wessex, became the sixth archbishop of Canterbury. The missionaries had fulfilled their obligation and a native Anglo-Saxon had risen to the highest rank in the hierarchy.

This was not, as it happened, the beginning of self-government by English clerics. Deusdedit's elected successor, Wighard, died in Rome, whither he had gone for consecration. Pope Vitalian proposed replacing him with Hadrian, the learned abbot of a monastery near Naples, a man of African birth. Hadrian modestly suggested the monk Andrew instead, but Andrew's ill-health prevented him from taking on the office and so Hadrian proposed the scholar Theodore, a bold choice which was to prove highly successful. Theodore had been born in Tarsus and trained in the Christianity of the east. The Churches of the east and the west had disagreed bitterly over theological doctrine; eastern monks, like Celtic monks, wore a distinctive tonsure unlike that of their Roman brethren. (When Theodore was appointed Archbishop of Canterbury he waited four months in Italy for his hair to grow, then he took the Roman tonsure.) The Pope must have feared that Theodore would take controversial theology with him, so he arranged that Hadrian should go with him to England. The Englishman Benedict Biscop accompanied the foreign scholars from Rome, instructing them in the English language. They arrived in 669. Theodore appointed Benedict Biscop as abbot of the monastery of SS Peter and Paul in Canterbury. (He was later to found the Northumbrian monasteries of Monkwearmouth and Jarrow.) Hadrian succeeded him as abbot in Canterbury in 671. Under great men such as these, foreign and English scholars steeped in continental tradition, the young English Church was to be firmly organized, and learning and the arts were to flourish. Bede writes enthusiastically about Theodore's rule:

> Soon after his arrival, he visited every part of the island occupied by the English peoples, and received a ready welcome and hearing everywhere. He was accompanied and assisted throughout his journey by Hadrian, and he taught the Christian way of life and the canonical method of keeping Easter. Theodore was the first archbishop whom the entire English Church obeyed, and, as I have observed, since both he and Hadrian were men of learning both in sacred and secular literature, they attracted a large number of students, into whose minds they poured the waters of wholesome knowledge day by day. In addition to instructing them in the holy Scriptures, they also taught their pupils poetry, astronomy, and the calculation of the church calendar. In proof of this, some of their students still alive today [731] are as proficient in Latin and Greek as in their native tongue. Never had there been such happy times as these since the English settled in Britain, for the Christian kings were so strong that they daunted all the barbarous tribes. The people eagerly sought the new-found joys of the kingdom of heaven, and all who wished for instruction in the reading of the Scriptures found teachers ready at hand.
>
> (*HE*, IV, 2; p.201)

Theodore's first task was to organize the English episcopacy, for the plague which was raging in Europe (and which had precipitated the apostasy of the East Saxons) had claimed the lives of several bishops as well as of Archbishops Deusdedit and Wighard. Indeed, the English episcopacy had reached an all-time low, morally as well as numerically. Only three bishops remained: Wine of London, who had purchased his position, and two virtually rival bishops in Northumbria, Ceadda (Chad) at York and Wilfrid at Ripon.

The situation in Northumbria was complicated. After the Synod of Whitby in 663/664 and the withdrawal of the Celtic party, Lindisfarne had ceased to be an episcopal see. Alhfrith, the sub-king who ruled Deira (the southern part of Northumbria), chose his friend Wilfrid as bishop and sent him to Gaul for consecration. The brilliant Englishman Wilfrid was opposed to the Celtic party in Northumbria, preferring the ceremonies, liturgy and architecture he had seen on the continent. He had already travelled to Rome with Benedict Biscop and had spent several years in Gaul, where he received the Roman tonsure. On his return to England he had become abbot of a monastery at Ripon, bestowed by Alhfrith, and he was consecrated priest by the Gaulish Agilbert, Bishop of Wessex, for whom Wilfrid spoke at the Synod of Whitby. When appointed bishop, Wilfrid took Ripon as his see. His consecration included twelve bishops and splendid ceremonial. His biographer, Eddius Stephanus, describes it:

[The kings] prepared him a ship and a force of men as well as a large sum of money, so as to enable him to enter Gaul in great state. Here at once there took place a large meeting consisting of no less than twelve catholic bishops, one of whom was Bishop Agilbert. When they heard the testimony to his faith they all joyfully consecrated him publicly before all the people with great state, and raising him aloft in accordance with their custom as he sat in the golden chair, the bishops unaided and alone carried him with their own hands into the oratory, chanting hymns and songs in chorus.

(*Vita Wilfridi*, XIII; Colgrave (ed. and trans.), p.27)

Wilfrid lingered in Gaul and returned to find that his patron's father, King Oswiu, himself educated in Celtic ways, had chosen Ceadda, a monk of Celtic training, to be Bishop of York. Ceadda (or Chad) was a modest, studious man, the brother of Cedd who was missionary to Mercia and Bishop of the East Saxons. Oswiu sent him to Canterbury for consecration, but as Archbishop Deusdedit had recently died he travelled to Wessex to be consecrated by Wine (the last remaining properly consecrated bishop) in association with two British (that is, Celtic) bishops. For a while both Ceadda and Wilfrid ruled as bishops in Northumbria. Ceadda's personal qualities were undisputed, but Wilfrid objected to the manner of his consecration. Archbishop Theodore had the same objection and recognized that Ceadda had been appointed to a see which was not vacant. He placed Wilfrid as Bishop of all Northumbria. Ceadda retired to the monastery of Lastingham which his brother had founded, without any bitterness. Theodore admired his attitude and provided him with full consecration according to Roman rites. When King Wulfhere of Mercia requested a bishop for Mercia and Lindsey, Theodore sent Ceadda, with the instruction that he was to adopt Roman ways. Bede tells us that the unpretentious Ceadda preferred to undertake preaching missions on foot (as Aidan had done) but that Theodore ordered him to ride, personally helping the reluctant horseman on to his steed (*HE*, IV, 3). Ceadda established Lichfield as the permanent see for Mercia. He died in 672 and was succeeded by his deacon Winfrid.

Theodore filled other vacant sees. Putta, an unworldly man, but skilled in Gregorian chant and a willing teacher of it, was appointed to Rochester, in Kent. Bisi was appointed to Dunwich, in East Anglia; and in 670 Wessex received Leuthere, nephew of the deposed Agilbert (whom Theodore knew well) as Bishop of Winchester. The Archbishop also created two new sees in the west, Worcester and Hereford, and established Leicester as a religious centre for the Middle Angles, reducing the size of the Lichfield see. When the elderly Bishop Bisi died, his see of East Anglia was split into the two bishoprics of Dunwich and Elmham. This policy of dividing sees into smaller units was, however, to prove contentious in Northumbria.

Northumbria had been governed by Wilfrid alone since the expulsion of Ceadda, but he had incurred the wrath of King Ecgfrith of Northumbria by encouraging the king's wife Æthelthryth in her desire to forsake secular life. (She was one of the religiously inclined daughters of King Anna of East Anglia. She later founded the convent at Ely and was venerated as a saint.) Ecgfrith took a second wife who resented Wilfrid's wealth and power and the bishop was driven out in 677. Theodore visited Northumbria and divided Wilfrid's see into three. The division reflected the historical composition of Northumbria, which had originally been two separate kingdoms, Bernicia and Deira. The new Bishop of Bernicia was given a choice of Lindisfarne or Hexham for his see, and York became the seat of the Bishop of Deira. The third see was Lindsey, a territory which had passed from Mercian control to Northumbrian in 674.

Wilfrid was not the kind of man to retire meekly into a monastery. He spent much of his remaining thirty-two years trying to regain the territory he had lost. He travelled twice to Rome for judgement, and towards the end of his life was restored to Ripon and Hexham, but never to his full claim, although the Pope judged his expulsion to be wrong. In the intervening years he preached to the Frisians and was responsible for converting the last Anglo-Saxon territories to remain heathen. He converted Sussex himself, establishing a seat at Selsey; and he entrusted the conversion of the Isle of Wight to his nephew. He spent many years in Mercia and founded a number of monasteries there. He is one of the outstanding personalities of Anglo-Saxon history, but his actions did not, ultimately, deflect the English Church from the direction on which Theodore had set it.

In 672 Theodore had summoned a council of the whole English Church at Hertford, at which the Archbishop proposed, and the bishops agreed, certain canons. (They were chiefly concerned with Church administration and with marriage.) Although not all the bishops attended the Council of Hertford, historians consider it important as the first occasion on which the English Church was publicly united. The impetus for the conversion had come, as we have seen, variously from Rome, Ireland and Gaul, while Theodore himself trained in the east; yet in 672 the descendants of these various missions had coalesced into one Church acknowledging the Archbishop of Canterbury. At this first formal gathering it was decreed that annual synods should be held at *Clofeshoh* (a place which has not been identified). Theodore died in 690 and is remembered as the unifier and organizer of the early Anglo-Saxon Church.

The eighth century saw Theodore's work consolidated. The diocese of Leicester, which he had founded in Middle Anglia, was formally established in 737. His policy of dividing large, unwieldy dioceses was continued by the creation of a new bishopric for Wessex, at Sherborne, in 705. Its first bishop was the scholar Aldhelm. Selsey, which had been Wilfrid's headquarters in Sussex, became a diocese in 709.

Lichfield, the Mercian episcopal see, became an archbishopric in 788.

This was not part of Theodore's policy, nor had it been Gregory's plan to create a third archiepiscopal see for England. The elevation of Lichfield was a result of the political supremacy of Mercia, and in particular of Offa, its most famous king. It did not long survive him. A later king of Mercia, Cenwulf, wrote to the Pope in 798 apparently with the intention of seeing Lichfield and Canterbury both demoted for the expansion of London, which was Gregory's original choice of see, and which was, by this time, Mercian; but the Pope upheld the primacy of Canterbury and as a result Lichfield was reduced to a bishopric in 803.

By the end of the eighth century the Church was firmly established under the control of bishops whose duties had been laid down by Theodore at the Council of Hertford, and reasserted at the Synod held in 747 at *Clofeshoh*. It is significant that, while in Roman Britain Christianity had begun as a religion of the lower classes, in Anglo-Saxon England it enjoyed royal patronage from the first; indeed in some kingdoms, such as East Anglia and Wessex, the baptism of kings preceded by some years the conversion of the population as a whole. Bishops enjoyed the closest friendships with kings. We find the unworldly Aidan sitting down to an Easter feast side-by-side with King Oswald (*HE*, III, 6); Wilfrid enjoyed the friendship of Alhfrith, sub-king of Deira, and later of Æthelred of Mercia.

Many Anglo-Saxon rulers appear to have been extremely pious. Outstanding examples include Oswald of Northumbria, who was venerated as a saint after his death, and Aldfrith, who ruled Northumbria from 685 to 704, a king successful in war and famous for his scholarship.

Several kings and royal ladies were sufficiently moved by the example of their Christian teachers to reject worldly pomp and join monasteries. Well-known examples include Sigeberht of East Anglia (see p.144), Sebbi and Offa of Essex, and Æthelred and Cenred of Mercia. Offa and Cenred travelled to Rome to receive the tonsure and entered monastic life there. Royal ladies frequently founded or entered convents on widowhood, following the example of Edwin's widow Æthelburg (see pp.131, 138). Seaxburg, daughter of King Anna of East Anglia and widow of Eorcenberht of Kent, founded a convent in the Isle of Sheppey before succeeding her sister Æthelthryth at Ely. Seaxburg's daughter Ermenhild married a Mercian king before serving under her mother at Sheppey and following her as abbess at Ely.

Æthelthryth (St Etheldreda or Audrey) offers one of the most extreme examples of Christian renunciation in the early Anglo-Saxon Church (plate 30). She was widowed after a brief marriage to Tonberht, 'a prince of the South Gyrwas', then became the wife of King Ecgfrith of Northumbria. She refused to consummate the marriage, and after twelve years, encouraged by Bishop Wilfrid, she persuaded her husband to release her and entered the Northumbrian nunnery of Coldingham. She later founded a convent at Ely where she lived in conditions of extreme asceticism:

It is said that from the time of her entry into the convent, she never wore linen but only woollen garments, and that she washed in hot water only before the greater festivals such as Easter, Pentecost, and the Epiphany, and then only after she and her assistants had helped the other servants of Christ to wash. She seldom had more than one meal a day except at the greater festivals or under urgent necessity, and she always remained at prayer in the church from the hour of Matins until dawn unless prevented by serious illness.

(HE, IV, 19; pp.233–4)

A tumour which afflicted her during her last illness was borne with fortitude:

It is said that when she was affected by this tumour and pain in her jaw and neck, she welcomed pain of this kind, and used to say: 'I realize very well that I deserve this wearisome disease in my neck, because I remember that when I was a girl, I used to wear the needless burden of jewellery. And I believe that God in His goodness wishes me to endure this pain in my neck so that I may be absolved from the guilt of my needless vanity. So now I wear a burning red tumour on my neck instead of gold and pearls.'

(HE, IV, 19; p.235)

The tumour was lanced, but she died three days later, with the wound still open. When, after seventeen years, her body was exhumed to be translated from the convent cemetery to the church, her flesh was found to be incorrupt and the scar healed, a typical miracle as recorded by Bede.

The Anglo-Saxon converts accepted miracles with simple faith. In particular the preservation of the flesh after death was understood to indicate sanctity. Famous examples of this sort of wonder include the right arm of King Oswald (which, while the king was alive, had given generously to the poor, HE, III, 6). The arm was severed on the orders of Penda of Mercia when Oswald died in battle and it became a celebrated relic. Bede tells us that the bodies of the monk Fursey and the saints Cuthbert and Æthelthryth (Etheldreda) remained incorrupt after death. However much monks and nuns may have venerated their dead leaders, it strikes the twentieth-century reader as extremely morbid to exhume and wash a body after several years, even if the reason was that it was to be moved to a more honourable resting-place. It was on such occasions that bodies were found to be incorrupt. Perhaps the Anglo-Saxons half-expected miracles at such times. Is it cynical to suppose that the bodies of potential saints were embalmed in some way?

incor-
rupt
flesh

Bede recorded several miracles of healing through places or objects associated with saints: the grave-clothes and coffin of Æthelthryth drove out devils and healed those who touched them. Earth from the place where King Oswald was killed cured a sick horse and a paralytic girl. Other people took soil from the place and made a medicinal drink from it, eventually removing so much earth that a pit was left. The body of St Cuthbert, his grave-clothes and even soil watered with the slops in which his bones had been washed cured the sick; and the wooden beam against which Aidan leaned as he died was twice preserved from fires which destroyed the rest of the church.

Anglo-Saxon miracles were, on the whole, posthumous wonders of this kind. St Cuthbert's prayers made water spring from the ground and crops grow when the seed was planted out of season (*HE*, IV, 28), but his miraculous cures of the sick were brought about by his relics, after he died. The only personality who seems to have been a healer after the example of Christ is John of Beverley, Bishop of Hexham and Archbishop of York. Bede, who knew him personally, having received ordination from him, describes his undramatic cures of dumbness, sickness and injury (*HE*, V, 2–6).

The Anglo-Saxons seem to have accepted the stories of saints and venerated the British saint, Alban, who had lived in their country. They themselves lacked martyrs, but they honoured as saints many of the outstandingly pious figures of their time, including several people of royal birth.

The greatest innovation which the new religion brought to life in Anglo-Saxon England was monasticism. Many men and women of high station chose to enter religious houses but monastic life was open also to those of humble birth. St Cuthbert had tended sheep as a boy and the poet Cædmon was a cowherd until middle-age, when he became a monk. He was illiterate all his life. The lesser-known Owini had risen to the rank of chief thane, but he joined Ceadda at Lastingham with axe and trowel in his hands and found fulfilment working with his tools for his brethren (*HE*, IV, 3).

Monasticism also gave women the opportunity for a life of prayer and study. Several widows as well as single women of royal birth (such as Hild and Ælfflæd) became abbesses, holding positions of power and respect. All the early Anglo-Saxon convents were 'double' establishments of a type introduced from France in the seventh century. Each convent comprised a community of nuns, plus a group of monks, who both served the sisters as priests and performed the heavier manual work. The double house was ruled by an abbess. There is no hint of any impropriety between the sexes in these double communities. We know that at Barking and at Wimborne the nuns and monks lived in separate houses and were strictly segregated but this was not always the practice. At Whitby, for instance, Abbess Hild was able to bring together learned men to hear the poet Cædmon recite and apparently was herself present at the performance. Eddius Stephanus refers to Abbess Ælfflæd as 'always the comforter and best counsellor of the whole province [of Northumbria]', and depicts her as taking part in the debate about the restoration of Wilfrid's power at the Synod held by the River Nidd in 706 (*Viva Wilfridi*, LX; Colgrave (ed. and trans.), pp.128–32). Ælfflæd's pedigree links her to many of the important characters in the history of the conversion; she was the daughter of Oswiu of Northumbria, thus the niece of King Oswald and kinswoman of Hild. Her mother was Eanflæd, daughter of Edwin and Æthelburg. Ælfflæd was thus the great-granddaughter of Æthelberht of Kent. She was vowed to God in infancy by her father Oswiu in thanks for his defeat of the heathen Penda of Mercia. She entered the convent at Whitby under Hild and later succeeded as abbess there.

The monasteries were from the beginning centres of learning. In the monastic *scriptoria* were copied the books essential for the growing Church—gospels, psalters and occasionally, complete Bibles. Other books too were being brought into England. They included the works of the Church Fathers such as Ambrose, Augustine of Hippo, Isidore of Seville and Jerome, and some classical literature, particularly Latin Christian poetry. The libraries which were built up and the willing teachers of both Celtic and continental origin produced fine scholars from the Anglo-Saxon people.

Bede (*c*.673–735), a monk of Jarrow, whose *Ecclesiastical History* is the source of much of this chapter, was himself a translator from, and commentator upon, the Bible. He also wrote upon such diverse subjects as chronology, poetry, orthography and science, and he compiled a martyrology and biographies of saints and abbots.

Alcuin of York (*c*.730–804) was taught by one of Bede's former pupils, Egbert, Archbishop of York. Alcuin was a biblical commentator, biographer and poet, but his chief claim to fame is as a teacher. He was master of the school at York before accepting the invitation of the Frankish Emperor Charlemagne to teach at the palace school in Aachen. He was influential in the Carolingian renaissance which was to be a source of inspiration to later generations of Anglo-Saxons.

Another outstanding literary figure of the early days of Anglo-Saxon Christianity was Aldhelm, Abbot of Malmesbury and Bishop of Sherborne (*c*.640–*c*.709). He was probably a West Saxon, possibly of noble birth. He may have had some Irish training and studied in the school at Canterbury under Hadrian. He wrote prose and poetry including riddles, and his best-known work is a treatise on virginity, composed for the nuns of Barking, which exists in prose and poetic versions, and which was an extremely popular work in Anglo-Saxon times. He wrote in fluent but tortuous Latin. According to tradition he was an accomplished minstrel and would attract an audience for his preaching by first singing secular songs.

Poetry, chanted to the accompaniment of music, had traditionally been part of Germanic life, and secular poems continued to be recited in the age-old way after the arrival of Christianity. These poems were not written down, but performed spontaneously, the minstrel drawing on the stock of poetic 'formulas' he held in his memory, rearranging them as appropriate to his subject matter and probably never giving exactly the same performance twice. It seems that, at first, church music was entirely divorced from secular. As far as we know, secular Anglo-Saxon minstrels were solo performers, but the Christian Church introduced choral music. Its notes and words

155

were taught, and had to be learned by heart, to be reproduced repeatedly. We know of several teachers: James at Catterick, Putta in Rochester, Maban in York and John who came from Rome to instruct the Wearmouth monks. Wilfrid boasted that he had introduced the system of two choirs chanting antiphonally and one of Aldhelm's poems suggests that choirs of monks and nuns could be used for this alternating chant.[9]

According to Bede, it was the cowherd Cædmon who was first inspired to praise the Christian God in English. His poem is in the traditional, alliterative metre of Germanic secular verse:

Nu sculon herigean   heofonrices weard,
meotodes meahte   and his modgeþanc,
weorc wuldorfæder,   swa he wundra gehwæs,
ece drihten,   or onstealde.
He ærest sceop   eorðan bearnum
heofon to hrofe,   halig scyppend;
þa middangeard   moncynnes weard,
ece drihten,   æfter teode
firum foldan   frea ælmihtig.

(*ASPR*, VI, p.106)

Now we must praise the Guardian of the heavenly kingdom, the power of the Creator and His conception; the work of the Father of glory: in that He, Eternal Lord, first created the beginning of every wonder. He, Holy Creator, first made Heaven as a roof for the children on earth. Then the Guardian of mankind, the Eternal Lord, the Lord Almighty, after made the world for men on earth.

Middangeard, the 'middle earth' of pagan belief, has become one of several synonyms for the world under God's heaven. God himself is praised as a lord, father and guardian of a kingdom, just as earthly kings were praised in secular poetry.

This adaptation of the Germanic idea of the *comitatus* with its protective lord and loyal retainers, was found to have lasting appeal and occurs in most religious poetry later composed in Old English. Cædmon himself became a monk at Whitby, where his more literary brethren told him biblical stories, which he versified. His invention gave traditional Anglo-Saxon poetry a legitimate place within the monastery, and it must have helped to bring the Christian God out of the latinate ivory tower and into the English-speaking countryside.

Christianity brought a new dimension to visual art in this country. We know that the walls of churches were adorned with paintings, but unfortunately none of these survive. We do, however, have a number of religious books which were illuminated for the glory of God. In the south of England,

9.   See J. Godfrey, *The Church in Anglo-Saxon England*, p.158.

illuminators of the Canterbury School copied the Late Antique style of the paintings in the books brought by the Roman missionaries; we find in them naturalistic, but stiff, figures of the Evangelists and the creatures which symbolized them.[10] At Lindisfarne illumination was strongly influenced by Celtic tradition: letters of the text were elaborated by the addition of red dots, and were extended into spirals, crosses and animal heads; whole pages were given over to 'carpets' of ornament. In the Book of Durrow we find that where human or animal figures are depicted naturalism is sacrificed to pattern (plate 29). Traditions of Germanic art may be detected in these Northumbrian manuscripts in the serpentine animals which decorate the 'carpet' pages, and the influence of Mediterranean culture is unmistakable in the Lindisfarne Gospels (plate 31) where stylized figures of the Evangelists sit in formal poses beneath their symbols, among the riot of patterns and animals on other pages of the Codex. The lovely Lichfield Gospels resemble the Lindisfarne Gospels in many respects, but the two surviving 'portraits' of the Evangelists depict SS Luke and Mark in stylized, ribbon-like garments and rigid attitudes. In contrast, Jarrow, always consciously imitating the continent, produced the *Codex Amiatinus*, a complete Bible decorated almost entirely in Italian style.

The Mercian Church produced the Vespasian Psalter, which is closer to the Canterbury School of art. Its frontispiece depicts King David composing (plate 32). He has the hairstyle of Christ, the shoes of a bishop, the cloak and throne of a Roman emperor, but he plays an Anglo-Saxon lyre.

The art of sculpting in stone seems to burst fully fledged onto the Anglo-Saxon scene—the earliest examples we have are the finest. The Ruthwell Cross (plate 33), at Ruthwell in Dumfriesshire, 15ft (4·6m) high, of sandstone, was probably erected as a preaching cross, a centre for a large congregation in a place where the church was too small to hold them, or where there was no church. The front and back of the cross depict scenes from Christian history, chosen to emphasize the ascetic way of life, in particular the desert, which was the cradle of monasticism. The scenes include John the Baptist, the Desert Fathers (SS Paul and Antony), the Flight into Egypt, Christ in Majesty dominating the Beasts of the Desert and Mary Magdalen washing the feet of Christ. All this reflects the contemplative character of Celtic Christianity. The vine scroll which decorates the sides of the cross, the costumes worn by the figures and the execution of the carving are of the Mediterranean; but, reminding us that the cross belonged to the Anglo-Saxon world, Mary's hand and arm are carved with barbaric crudeness, and

---

10. St Matthew was traditionally symbolized by a man, Mark by a lion, Luke by a calf or ox, John by an eagle. The symbols were sometimes depicted as winged and with haloes, carrying books and trumpets.

Germanic runes spell out lines from an Old English poem in which Christ is depicted as the young hero of Germanic tradition:

Ondgeredæ hinæ God almehttig,
þa he walde on galgu gistiga,
modig fore allæ men ...
Ahof ic riicnæ Kyniŋc,
heafunæs Hlafard ...

(*The Dream of the Rood*, Swanton (ed.), p. 90, lines 39–41, 44–5)

God Almighty stripped himself when he wished to ascend the gallows, proud in front of all men ... I lifted up the powerful King, the Lord of Heaven ...

The Bewcastle Cross, which stands in the churchyard at Bewcastle (Cumb.), bears fewer, but similar, carvings. It was erected as a memorial cross as its runic inscription tells us. Some scholars believe it was raised in memory of Wilfrid's royal friend Alhfrith and his wife, but the inscription is far from clear and we cannot be certain.

Many other sculptured stones survive, whole or in fragments, from this Golden Age. It is ironic that the Christians, who had frowned upon pagan funeral ceremonies, should erect stones as posthumous memorials for their own people. This was not a practice confined to wealthy seculars. We know that crosses were raised at the head and feet of Bishop Acca at Hexham, while flat stones, engraved with the names of the dead, were provided for the nuns of the convent at Hartlepool.

Since the historians who recorded this era for us were monks, our available information is chiefly about people in holy orders and the religious monarchs who were their patrons; but what of the seculars who were not of royal birth? How were their lives affected by a change in the national religion?

Paganism was evidently still rife, since heathen practices are mentioned in Theodore's *Poenitentiale*, a text compiled after the archbishop's death, from the answers to questions about various offences. People must have still enjoyed the old legends since the Northumbrian carver who made the whalebone box now known as the Franks Casket saw nothing ludicrous in depicting Welund the Smith beside the Adoration of the Magi (see plate 10).

Yet by the eighth century Christianity must have imbued almost all aspects of life. Most seculars would be baptized and confirmed. If a priest were available he might bless a marriage, but was not an essential part of the proceedings. Similarly, he would officiate at burials if he were in the area (but in the absence of a priest many half-heathen communities seem to have taken the opportunity to place a few grave-goods with their dead). Yet the general abandonment of the old graveyards in the seventh century shows that Christian rituals were taking over.

Secular people certainly contributed to the maintenance of the Church, although tithes were not so strictly enforced as they were to be later. Layfolk were expected to attend mass on Sundays and feast days. If they lived near a monastery they would worship at the monastery church. Since contemporary records concentrate upon the famous monasteries which were centres of learning, we know little about the establishment of the less prestigious parish churches in this country; but it is likely that the beginnings of a parochial system were laid down by Theodore. There were probably district churches or missionary centres, as on the continent, staffed by clergy who lived communally. Godfrey (p.317) suggests that many modern place-names containing the element '-minster' derive from such churches (for example Axminster and Warminster). Where there was no such centre, a village or estate might have a great cross, like the one at Ruthwell, where people would gather to hear preaching and take part in religious ceremonies such as baptism and confirmation; but quite soon landowners began to erect and endow churches on their estates and in their villages. Most of these churches were wooden, but some were built in stone. Many, like the church at Escomb (see p.142), must have been of modest proportions, but there were also more splendid edifices such as the churches built by Wilfrid at Hexham, Ripon and York in Northumbria and the still-existing church at Brixworth (Northants.), which has the architectural features of the early Kentish monastery churches, but is of more imposing size.

The organization of the Church was the responsibility of the bishops (although where a church was founded by a secular the priest tended to be the landlord's retainer, which somewhat threatened the bishop's authority). A bishop was expected to travel his diocese, confirming the faithful, preaching and generally exercising his authority. Many bishops, particularly those of Celtic training, did travel extensively, but dioceses were large, transport slow and bishops few. Bede, in a letter written in 734 to his former pupil Egbert, then Bishop of York, complained of a lowering of standards in the Church and spoke of villages which had not seen a bishop for years. In his *Ecclesiastical History* he wistfully compared the life of the missionary Aidan with 'the apathy of our own times' (*HE*, III, 5).

The Anglo-Saxons were used to a hierarchical society and the new professional clergy were slotted into the hierarchy with appropriate rights. Until the missionaries arrived with their civilizing influence the Anglo-Saxons could not read or write, and their laws (presumably) were a matter of memory and recitation. In a blending of secular and ecclesiastical interests written laws were formulated for King Æthelberht of Kent and for later Kentish kings, for Ine of Wessex and for Offa of Mercia, all of which were later utilized by Alfred the Great in making his own important law-code.

Loyalty to one's lord and kin was traditional among the Anglo-Saxons. The new Christian relationship of a godparent to his godchild was taken seriously and may be compared with the bond between uncle and nephew which traditionally had been considered almost sacred: in the *Anglo-Saxon Chronicle* entry for the date 755, which describes a fight to the death by rival factions claiming the throne of Wessex, we find a godfather sparing the life of his godson, although the two had fought on opposite sides.

The new faith brought its own taboos—in particular relationships between the sexes were subject to a new morality. Incest, as we have seen (see p.136), was an early source of concern to the missionaries, although Christian ethics were ignored as late as 858 by King Æthelbald of Wessex when he married his (teenage) step-mother. Theodore took an early opportunity to discuss Christian marriage at the Hertford Council in 672, where he condemned incest, the abandonment of a wife (except for adultery) and subsequent remarriage. Yet, like Gregory before him, Theodore showed understanding for the seculars in his flock. In his *Poenitentiale* he permits remarriage after five years' desertion, the captivity or enslavement of a spouse, or on the retirement of one partner into a monastery or convent.

The Anglo-Saxons seem to have been inherently tolerant of male promiscuity and to have acknowledged and honoured illegitimate children. Aldfrith, illegitimate son of Oswiu, trained for the priesthood and became a successful king of Northumbria (685–704), although both were contrary to the morality preached by the Church. In canons issued in 786 it was laid down that illegitimate children could not inherit property, succeed to kingship or be ordained as priests.

It is interesting to find that the new religion was soon brought to bear on the authority of kings, in that the practice of anointing (which had been used in the ordination of clerics) came to be part of the ceremony vesting power in a secular leader. The first English instance of this was apparently in 787 when King Offa of Mercia had his son Ecgfrith anointed, in his own lifetime. Offa was no doubt copying his powerful neighbour Charlemagne, whose sons had been anointed by the Pope in 781.

At the other end of the social scale individual slaves may have felt the effect of the conversion since owners sometimes released them for the good of their own souls; but slavery was not yet abolished so the social order as a whole was not affected.

The Church was soon well endowed with land and no doubt people previously employed on royal estates found themselves employees of the Church. This may or may not have influenced their lives. Bede was born on the Jarrow/Wearmouth estates and was given into the keeping of the abbot at the age of seven; yet Cædmon, who worked on or near the Whitby estates, was in the habit of attending a secular *gebeorscip* (beer-drinking party) quite undeterred by the proximity of the convent.

Conversely, several monasteries were founded and owned by laymen and could be bequeathed by them to their descendants. The religious communities in such houses, although they were nominally monks and nuns, were

160

in effect retainers of the monastery owner.

Perhaps the greatest change in day-to-day living brought by Christianity was in the calendar. Obviously the pattern of the seasons, with their significance for agriculture, continued unchanged; but the Church took over the major celebrations and augmented them. The great spring celebration was now associated with the crucifixion and resurrection, and was preceded by the strictly enforced fasting of Lent. Other festivals had holy days associated with them. Peculiarly Christian festivals were added and holy days associated with saints, both local and remote, became annual events. With the adoption of the Roman calendar the pagan names of the seasons were dropped and the months with which we are now familiar were substituted.

The Christian Church had inherited from the Jewish religion the practice of keeping holy a sabbath day in every week. The seven-day week, with its weekly religious ritual and abstention from work was, as far as we know, new to the Anglo-Saxons. Christianity also meant that the time of day was of ritual importance. Whereas previously the Anglo-Saxons had probably related time to daylight and darkness, the need to eat and rest, the Christian had to be aware of the canonical hours. Although the singing of the daily offices was the province of monks and other clerics, this sense of time was undoubtedly transmitted to the laity at an early date, since the *Beowulf* poet says *Ða com non dæges* (line 1600; *ASPR*, IV, p.49) meaning 'Then three o'clock came'. The context is secular, but the poet quite unselfconsciously uses the Christian name for the canonical service held at 3p.m.

Furthermore, in his *Ecclesiastical History* Bede popularized the method of calculating years from the incarnation of Christ. The Anglo-Saxons, whose sense of chronology before had probably been dependent on such factors as the number of seasons their king had reigned, were now introduced to the concept of date, *anno domini*.

The great figures who made the English Church in the seventh century must have thought that they had built a firm foundation; but the great wave of enthusiasm began to lose its impetus. Our earliest intimation of a decline in monastic development is Bede's account of behaviour at the convent of Coldingham, where the monks and nuns neglected prayers and used their cells for 'eating, drinking, gossip or other amusements'. Nuns wore fine clothes 'either to adorn themselves like brides, or to attract attention from strange men' (*HE*, IV, 25). When the convent was burnt down in the 680s, righteous people knew it was God's punishment. Bede complained to Egbert that bishops were neglecting their duties and that some clerics were ignorant of Latin, not even knowing the Creed and Lord's Prayer in that language. King Alfred of Wessex confirmed this decline in the knowledge of Latin when he wrote that, even before the Vikings destroyed the libraries, there were books which could no longer be read because the teaching of Latin had been neglected.

The eighth century produced some ardent Christians, but many of them journeyed to the continent, taking the Gospel to the Germanic peoples who remained heathen. Indeed, Godfrey suggests that the decline in standards in the English Church was largely due to the creaming-off of the best talent in favour of the continental missions.[11] Numerous men and women felt called to work among the continental Germans from whose stock they themselves sprang. Some of the most important figures were Willibrord, who continued Wilfrid's work in Frisia, and Boniface, who spent some years with him before moving on to missionary work and martyrdom among the Old Saxons. Like his comrade Lull, who succeeded him as Bishop of Mainz, Boniface corresponded with friends and colleagues in England. In 746 or 747 he wrote to King Æthelbald of Mercia complaining of moral deterioration in the English.

The 747 Synod at *Clofeshoh* was called in response to a demand from the Pope that the English Church reform. The thirty canons issued on this occasion attempted to improve the behaviour of clerics from bishop to monk and suggest that secular amusements had begun to drive out study and prayer. Certainly the secular ownership of monasteries was a factor in this debate. The visitation of two papal legates in 786 reflects the anxieties of Rome about the Church in England. The canons adopted at both northern and southern synods on this occasion emphasized again the responsibilities of the clergy.

Perhaps the English Church, with help from Rome, would have recovered from its decline—but in 793 Viking raiders sacked Lindisfarne, and a new, pagan horror threatened England.

---

11. *The Church in Anglo-Saxon England*, p.260.

31 Illuminated pages from the Lindisfarne Gospels, BL MS Cotton Nero Div, fols. 209v, 210v and 211. The richly coloured folios mark the opening of St John's Gospel: a 'portrait' of the Evangelist with his symbol, the eagle, a 'carpet page' of cruciform design and the opening words of the gospel: *In principio erat verbum*, 'In the beginning was the word . . .' (*British Museum, British Library*)

32 King David from the Vespasian Psalter, BL MS Cotton Vespasian Ai, fol. 30. The king composes to an Anglo-Saxon lyre. Scribes take down his words on a scroll (left) and wax tablet (right). Musicians play and figures below the king dance (*British Museum, British Library*)

6

The Viking Age and the
Benedictine Reform

A king's reeve and his men were brutally murdered near Dorchester, in Wessex, in what was probably the first Viking attack on England. The reeve was evidently taken completely by surprise, since he had approached the three boatloads of raiders in the mistaken assumption that they were peaceful traders. We do not know the exact date of this incident, but it was sometime after 786. It was, however, with the attack on Lindisfarne of 793 and on Jarrow/Wearmouth in 794 that the Vikings became a terrifying threat to England and to English Christianity.

The aggressors were Norwegians, heathens, who had no respect for the sanctity of religious houses and the pacifism of their inmates. The Vikings' ships were swift and of shallow draught, enabling them to negotiate coastal waters and rivers, then to escape with the booty they eagerly sought. A gravestone, carved at Lindisfarne some time after the island monastery was attacked, depicts a terrifying procession of men armed with swords and battle axes. Church treasures, such as altar crosses and metal book covers, were among the loot seized, to be melted down or re-used as ornaments in pagan Scandinavia. The unarmed monks could offer little defence. Their monasteries, often deliberately isolated from the secular settlements where fighting men could be found, were easy targets.

To the Christians, such destruction of God's property by heathens could be explained in only one way: God must be angry with them. (Gildas the Briton had come to the same conclusion when heathen Anglo-Saxons drove out his people four-and-a-half centuries earlier.) This explanation is all the more understandable in view of the fact that for some time pious men had been deploring a decline in standards (see p. 161). Alcuin wrote from abroad in a moralizing tone to King Æthelred of Northumbria and his advisers after the sack of Lindisfarne:

Consider carefully, brothers, and examine diligently, lest perchance this unaccustomed and unheard-of evil was merited by some unheard-of evil practice. I do not say that formerly there were no sins of fornication among the people. But from the days of King Ælfwold fornications, adulteries and incest have poured over the land, so that these sins have been committed without any shame and even against the handmaids dedicated to God. What may I say about avarice, robbery, violent judgments?—when it is clearer than day how much these crimes have increased everywhere, and a despoiled people testifies to it. Whoever reads Holy Scriptures and ponders ancient histories and considers the fortune of the world will find that for sins of this kind kings lost kingdoms and peoples their country; and while the strong unjustly seized the goods of others, they justly lost their own.

(*EHD*, p.776)

He expressed sympathy but equal firmness to the stricken monks:

Let your company be of decent behaviour, an example to others unto life, not unto perdition. Let your banquets be in soberness, not in drunkenness. Let your garments be suitable to your order. Do not adapt yourself to the men of the world in any vain thing. Empty adornment of clothing, and useless elegance, is to you a reproach before men and a sin before God. It is better to adorn with good habits the soul which will live for ever, than to deck in choice garments the body which will soon decay in the dust.

(*op. cit.*, p.779)

The island monastery of Iona, mother-house of Northumbrian monasticism, was under attack in 795, 802 and 806, together with other targets around the Irish, Welsh and Scottish coasts. England seems to have enjoyed a respite although Vikings were active on the continent.

Then there came a new threat to England. In 835 a band of Danish Vikings

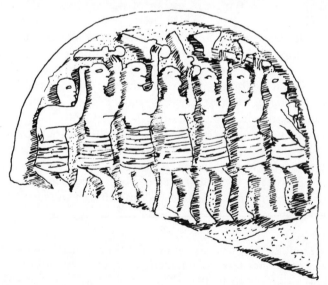

Fig 31   Grave-stone from Lindisfarne, Northumberland

raided the island of Sheppey in the Thames, the first of numerous attacks. Kent suffered particularly during the following years. The *Anglo-Saxon Chronicle* records a menacing change of policy in 850, when the Danes, instead of withdrawing at the end of the campaigning season as they were accustomed to do, encamped for the winter on the island of Thanet. This tactic was repeated in 854, when the Vikings wintered on Sheppey.

They were not unopposed. King Æthelwulf of Wessex inflicted a defeat on them in 851, but the effects were short term. The four sons of Æthelwulf, who, in turn, ruled Wessex—Æthelbald, Æthelberht, Æthelred and Alfred—all faced the Viking threat. Wessex was, by this time, the predominant kingdom of England. Æthelwulf's father Egbert had absorbed Essex, Kent, Surrey and Sussex; Mercia, although still an independent kingdom, seems to have been bound to Wessex in an amicable but subservient position.

In 865, when Æthelred I was king of Wessex, there was another new development in Viking policy. A mighty invading army descended on East Anglia. The sons of the famous Ragnar Lothbrok were among the commanders, and many others of royal and noble birth were among this Viking force determined to despoil England. They demanded horses from the people of East Anglia, where they remained for a year before conquering Northumbria and setting up a puppet king there. In the course of this war the historic monastery at Whitby was sacked and York, seat of the northern archbishopric, was captured. The city was destined to become the heart of a Viking kingdom.

Mercia was attacked in 867, and although King Burgred was supported by his brothers-in-law Æthelred and Alfred of Wessex, the Vikings avoided battle and forced Burgred to buy them off. This practice of demanding money in return for peace seems to have begun during the raids on Kent and was to drain England's resources in the Viking wars which followed.

The Danes' return to East Anglia in 869 was followed by the death of the East Anglian king, Edmund. He was almost certainly killed as a captive in Viking hands since his death was seen as martyrdom and he was being honoured as a saint within about twenty-five years.

In 870 the Viking army moved into Wessex. In January 871 King Æthelred and his brother Alfred won a battle at Ashdown; the *Chronicle* proudly enumerates the Viking dead, but we recognize that this was only one of several such encounters, and that the Vikings were victorious on most occasions. Æthelred I died after Easter and the young King Alfred succeeded to a kingdom dangerously threatened. He bought off the Vikings that year and they wintered in London.

The Vikings temporarily lost control of Northumbria in 872 but in 874 a section of their army, under Halfdan, moved into the region and began to divide up the land, transforming themselves from raiders to colonizers. York, a fundamental part of the structure of the English Church, now became the centre of a settlement of people who, initially at least, were pagans. In 875 the Lindisfarne monks finally left their island monastery, carrying with them the bones of their saints, Aidan, Cuthbert and King Oswald, and the Lindisfarne Gospels.

Mercia too became an area of Viking settlement. A Viking nominee, Ceolwulf, had succeeded King Burgred who, after a heavy defeat, retired to Rome in 874. In 877 the kingdom was divided between Ceolwulf and Viking colonists.

Meanwhile Alfred's Wessex was under attack from the rest of the great Viking army. By 876 the West Saxons were holding their own, so much so that the pagans gave hostages and swore oaths on their holy ring, a gesture which, the chronicler tells us, they had never stooped to before. The Vikings are often depicted as enemies of Christianity but such evidence of their own religious practices is rare. Professor Whitelock has pointed out that the Icelandic sagas refer to a holy ring which was kept in the heathen temple and worn by the chief at assemblies.[1] The Danish Vikings must have had a similar custom.

In January 878 the tide turned against the English again. A Viking army under the leadership of Guthrum took the West Saxons by surprise with an out-of-season attack, inflicting defeat and forcing some of the population into exile. Alfred himself took refuge in the swamps of the Isle of Athelney. He and his men ventured out at first only in raiding parties, but when Alfred emerged after seven weeks men flocked to him and he defeated the Vikings decisively at Edington. Three weeks later, as part of the Vikings' peace agreement, their leader Guthrum received baptism at Aller, near Athelney, taking the Christian name of Athelstan. King Alfred stood as godfather to him and gifts exchanged hands. The ceremonial removal of Guthrum's baptismal fillet took place at Wedmore, which has given its name to the treaty. Guthrum's army later withdrew to East Anglia and began to settle the area. There was some reverting to their old war-like ways—the East Anglian Vikings lent their weight to another Viking army in the mid-880s—but Wedmore marked the beginning of more settled co-existence.

In 886 Alfred recaptured London and established himself as leader of all the English people not under Danish occupation. English Mercia, while independent, was ruled no longer by a king, but by an ealdorman, and, after his death, by the ealdorman's widow, Æthelflæd, who was Alfred's daughter. The rest of Mercia, East Anglia and part of Deira were by this time settled by Viking colonists. This area has since come to be called 'the Danelaw'. Viking kings ruled in York. Beyond, the remains of Northumbria retained independence but was ruled by ealdormen, not kings.

Alfred's kingdom was strong enough to withstand the attacks of another

---

1. *English Historical Documents*, I, p.179, n.4.

Viking army in the last years of his reign. His son Edward the Elder succeeded him in 899, and working in conjunction with his sister in Mercia, strengthened the English defences and eventually pushed back the Vikings' frontier to the Humber. (He also expanded the influence of Wessex in other directions. Wessex absorbed Mercia after Æthelflæd's death and Edward was also acknowledged overlord by kings in western Wales.)

While the kings of Wessex had been fighting off Danish Vikings, Norwegian Vikings had established themselves in Ireland. The Viking trading centre of Dublin had regular commercial links with the Viking mercantile capital of York. In the early tenth century, Norwegian Vikings from Ireland came as settlers to north-west England in regions equivalent to parts of modern Cumbria, Lancashire and Cheshire.

Athelstan, son of Edward the Elder, continued his father's expansion in Wales and also brought the North temporarily into subjection. He first tried the age-old alliance of dynastic marriage between his sister and the Viking king, but, on the death of his brother-in-law, military conquest was necessary. Athelstan was opposed in the latter venture by an alliance of Scots, of Britons from the kingdom of Strathclyde and of Irish Vikings. His victory in 937 against these enemies at an unidentified place, *Brunanburh*, is celebrated poetically in the *Anglo-Saxon Chronicle*. During the reign of his brother Edmund, control of the North alternated between Wessex and rival Vikings from Norway and Dublin. The Norwegian contender, Eric Bloodaxe, was killed in 954 and power over the North passed to Eadred, a subsequent king of Wessex. The ceremonial celebration of this victory was left to King Edgar. In 973, following his long-delayed coronation at Bath, the king sailed to Chester where six, or possibly eight, northern kings (of Viking origin) paid homage to him; according to tradition they rowed him along the River Dee. This must have seemed a triumph for the English and for Christendom. Edgar's reign marked a new Golden Age. It was a time of peace, the era when, under the king's patronage, the Benedictine Reform brought renewed enthusiasm for Christianity. The English people could not have foreseen that seven years later Viking raids would begin again and that in 1016 a heathen-born Dane would rule their land.

Whatever the shortcomings of the clergy in the years before and during the Viking Age, there seems to have been no diminution in the piety of the English leaders. Indeed some seem to have been more inclined to the spiritual life than the fighting of a war. Burgred of Mercia retired to Rome leaving his kingdom in the hands of a Viking nominee. Æthelwulf of Wessex too journeyed to Rome in 855 when the Vikings had wintered in his country, and remained in Rome for a year with the infant Alfred. Æthelred I, Æthelwulf's son, remained in his tent to hear mass when the Battle of Ashdown had already begun. Even the practical Alfred was occupied by Æthelred's funeral ceremony at a time when the Danes were routing an English army.

169

Alfred himself combined firm generalship with his piety. Nevertheless, religious idealism manifested itself in the Treaty of Wedmore, where rejoicing at Guthrum's conversion undoubtedly tempered the attitude of the English.

The Vikings' lack of respect for the Christian way of life had, since the raid on Lindisfarne, caused the northerners to be regarded with horror by the English. Missionaries had entered Scandinavia from the Frankish Empire as early as the ninth century, but it was not until the eleventh and twelfth centuries that Christianity was to become firmly established there. The Vikings who attacked and settled England were pagans, exhibiting a polytheism similar to that of their Anglo-Saxon predecessors, although no doubt the myths associated with their gods and heroes were still evolving and continued to develop up to the time when they were written down. The name of the northern war-god Odin (OE Woden) is perpetuated in the name of a hill in North Yorkshire now known as Roseberry Topping. Until the twelfth century the place was known as *Othenesberg* (Odin's Hill). This seems to be the only place-name in the area of Scandinavian settlement to commemorate a god, but there are others which suggest that the Vikings shared with the Anglo-Saxons a belief in monsters or demons: Thirlspot (Cumb.), Thrushgill (Lancs.) as well as obsolete place-names in Yorkshire (*Thruslane, Thursegilmos, Thursmare*) may all derive from the Scandinavian word *þurs*, the equivalent of Old English *þyrs*.

Rather more evidence of the legends and heathen beliefs brought by Viking settlers may be derived from stone sculptures. The Danes and Norwegians who formed the Scandinavian population of England had not been accustomed to the art of carving stone (although their neighbours, the Swedes of Gotland, had produced carved and painted picture-stones); but Anglian sculpture had flourished in pre-Viking days and the newcomers to Anglian regions eagerly adopted and developed the tradition. Both the well-established cross and the new medium of the house-shaped tombstone, or 'hog-back', were, under Scandinavian patronage, carved with designs which combined traditional motifs with inspiration from secular life and from pagan mythology.[2]

The outstanding example of Viking mythology in sculpture is the ring-headed cross 14ft 6in (4·4m) high, which still stands in the churchyard at Gosforth (Cumb.). All four sides of the tapering shaft are decorated. At the foot of the west side Loki, the villain of the northern pantheon, lies bound beneath a serpent from which poison drips. This was the gods' punishment for Loki's successful plot to kill Balder the Beautiful (see pp.25–6). Loki's wife Sigyn catches in a bowl as much of the poison as she can. Figures on horseback with down-pointed spears probably belong also to northern mythology. On all four faces of the cross, geometric patterns terminate in fierce animal

---

2. The material is discussed in detail in R. N. Bailey, *Viking Age Sculpture in Northern England.*

Fig 32   The Gosforth, Cumbria, cross. Reproduced from W. G. Collingwood, *Northumbrian Crosses of the Pre-Norman Age*, Fig 184 (*by permission of Faber and Faber Ltd*)

heads, opposed on the western face by a figure with spear and horn, and on the eastern by a spearman who thrusts hand and foot into the jaws of a monster. These scenes belong to the northern legend of *Ragnarok* (the Last Day) when the gods and their world would be destroyed. According to a late version of the story (probably influenced by Christianity) Balder would then return. The sculptor of the Gosforth Cross may have exploited deliberately the parallels between Balder's story and Christ's, for at the bottom of the east face a figure is depicted, outstretched in the position of crucifixion. Below him stand Longinus, the spearman of Christian tradition, and an ambiguous female figure. (Suggested interpretations of the woman include Mary Magdalene and *Ecclesia*.)[3] Christ and the figures beneath him wear the costume of northern art, like the pagan figures on the cross.

Another stone at Gosforth proves that the Vikings brought with them legends about Thor (OE Thunor). It shows the god fishing from a boat, accompanied by the giant Heimir. According to a story well known in the Scandinavian world, Thor baited his hook with the head of one of Heimir's oxen and caught the world-serpent, a monster which encircled the earth.

The hammer emblem of Thor now reappeared in England. The god's devotees probably wore hammer amulets like the example found in a hoard of Viking silver at Goldsborough (Yorks.). The Thor's hammer device appears on a few surviving tenth-century coins minted at York.

Tyr (OE Tiw) is almost certainly depicted in a well-known situation on

---

3.   See Bailey, *Viking Age Sculpture*, pp.130–1.

Fig 33　Anglo-Saxon penny in Leeds City Museum with sword and Thor's hammer motifs

Fig 34　The Halton, Lancashire, cross. Reproduced from W. G. Collingwood, *Northumbrian Crosses of the Pre-Norman Age*, Fig 191 (*by permission of Faber and Faber Ltd*)

a hog-back at Sockburn (Co. Durham): Fenrir the wolf is biting off his hand.

Several Viking carvings represent Sigurd. This character was a hero rather than a god, although his adventure with the dragon Fafnir was provoked by the gods. Urged on by his foster-father Regin, who was a smith, Sigurd killed the dragon and cooked its heart, burning his fingers. He instinctively put them in his mouth, thus tasting the dragon, which gave him the ability to understand the language of birds. Birds warned him of Regin's treachery, so Sigurd killed his foster-father. The Anglo-Saxons had known some version of the killing of Fafnir, for the exploit is mentioned in *Beowulf* (lines 874–97; *ASPR*, IV, pp.28–9), although the victory is there attributed to Sigemund, who according to Germanic legend, was Sigurd's father. The Viking settlement evidently gave this tale renewed popularity in England for there are several surviving carvings which unmistakably depict the story. At Halton (Lancs.) a cross shaft is carved with birds above the figure of Sigurd, who roasts meat on a spit and sucks his burnt thumb. Beneath, there is a smithy filled with tools. A smith is at work and a headless body appears among the tools. There are obvious parallels here with the legend of Welund (see pp.37–9 and 173), but the juxtaposition with birds and a figure roasting meat points rather to the Sigurd story. The smithy scene, according to Bailey (p.120), 'shows Regin twice, once at work and once beheaded'. Bailey lists other Sigurd scenes on sculptures from York, Ripon and Kirby Hill (Yorks.) as well as several other Anglo-Viking carvings which might possibly illustrate the story. It is also well represented in Viking Age carvings on the Isle of Man.

172

Leeds
Parish Church

Leeds
Museum

Sherburn

Bedale

Fig 35 Reconstruction of Welund's flying mechanism. (*Drawn and reproduced by permission of Dr J. T. Lang*)

Welund the smith, like Sigurd a legendary hero and well known to the Anglo-Saxons (see pp.37–9), was also famous in the Scandinavian world. On one of the picture-stones from Gotland, Sweden, a bird-like figure flies, with a woman, from a chamber containing smith's tools and from two headless bodies. This can be readily identified as Welund making his escape by flight, having killed his enemy's sons and raped his daughter. Four Anglo-Viking carvings from Yorkshire (two from Leeds, one from Bedale, one from Sherburn) depict Welund in flight. Modern reconstructions may seem, at first glance, fanciful, but the resemblance in iconography to the Gotland stones and the fact that there are so many similar Yorkshire carvings help to clinch the identification. Welund is strapped into a flying machine which, mechanically, is based upon the structure of a bird. His legs are looped into attachments leading to a blunt, wedge-shaped tail, wings are fastened to his body, and above his own head there rises the beaked head of a bird. On the Leeds crosses the parts of the mechanical bird seem to be strapped together as well as to Welund. We should perhaps not be surprised at the bird-like nature of Welund's machine if we recall that the hero had been married to a swan-maiden, who, in one version of his story, returned to help in his escape. The Anglo-Viking sculptors seem to have depicted Welund clasping in his hands and beak the hair, body and gown of a woman—probably his victim Beaduhild.

As well as their gods and legends, the Scandinavian settlers must have brought with them some of the rituals of paganism. Viking burials with

173

grave-goods have been found in the British Isles, including ship burials in the Isle of Man. The number of inhumations recovered from England is, however, extremely small. A sculpted cross from Middleton (Yorks.), clearly of the Viking Age since it bears on one side a contorted beast depicted in the Scandinavian-inspired Jellinge Style, shows a warrior with a pointed cap or helmet, a knife at his belt, surrounded by his weapons: spear, shield, sword and axe. Some scholars have thought that a pagan funeral is depicted here; but others argue that the warrior is seated on a throne, surrounded by the emblems of his power.[4]

In a famous sermon composed in 1016, Wulfstan, the second Archbishop of York to bear this name, writes of paganism as if it were an institution organized similarly to the Church: he mentions sanctuaries and sacrifices to false gods. Just as Christian priests were called *Godes þeowas* (servants of God) so Wulfstan refers to *gedwolgoda þenan* (servants of false gods); and he refers indirectly to payment made to pagan gods (D. Bethurum (ed.), *The Homilies of Wulfstan*, p.268). His sermon was, however, designed to shake up backsliders among the Christian community, who failed to offer proper respect to priests and to pay their tithes and other church dues. To rebuke the Christians by a parallel with the heathens is typical of Wulfstan's rhetorical style. We have no evidence that the paganism of the English Scandinavians was so formalized. Certainly an individual might swear by the old gods,[5] but we have no proof of purpose-built temples or professional priests among the Viking settlers.

Whatever form the Vikings' paganism may have taken, it does not seem to have caused the English to revert to worship of the northern gods. Admittedly, Wulfstan II wrote of *apostatan abroþene* (degenerate apostates) but he seems to have been criticizing those who ignored Christian laws and morality rather than testifying to a renewal of pagan rituals.

In their raiding days, the Vikings had made so many violent attacks on religious foundations that their antipathy to Christianity was well publicized. 'Heathen' became virtually a synonym for 'Dane' and 'Viking'. Certainly monastic life, already in decline before the Viking Age, was destroyed by the Scandinavian incursions. The libraries and schools which had existed in the Golden Age were wiped out during the years of violence. The episcopal structure was shaken in the areas occupied by Viking settlers—in East Anglia the see of Dunwich ended its existence, and there was a century's hiatus at Elmham. The Leicester see was removed to the safer Dorchester-on-Thames. The see of Lindsey, weakened in the ninth century, came to an end in the tenth, and in the North, the sees of Hexham, Lindisfarne and

---

4. The arguments are summarized in Bailey, p.212.
5. An anonymous eleventh-century *History of St Cuthbert* tells of a notorious pagan named Olaf Ball who swore to Thor and Odin in church. Whitelock (ed.), *English Historical Documents*, I, p. 262.

Fig 36   The Middleton Cross, Lancashire

Whithorn[6] ceased to exist in the ninth century. The political struggles of the ninth century even briefly interrupted the northern archbishopric: Archbishop Wulfhere spent some time in exile.

There is not a great deal of documentary evidence from this period; often we are forced to reconstruct events in retrospect. Yet it is clear that Christian life continued in England, to some degree even in the Danelaw. Probably some unpretentious parish churches had been unmolested by the Vikings. Quietly, without the help of a systematic mission, Christianity infiltrated the new population. In East Anglia the Scandinavian settlers enthusiastically promoted the cult of St Edmund, the king who had (presumably) died at the hands of their people. In Northumbria the threat of domination by Wessex from the reign of Athelstan onwards may have been a greater cause of anxiety to the Christian Northumbrians than the heathen background of the Scandinavian settlers:[7] Archbishop Wulfhere seems to have cooperated with the Scandinavians when he was reinstated in York, and in the mid-tenth century Archbishop Wulfstan I seems to have allied himself with the northern kings against the southern, although he owed his position and a generous endowment of land to Athelstan. As early as 883, after the death of the Viking leader Halfdan, a Christian was chosen as king of York, apparently under the influence of the Abbot of Carlisle (see p.176). This

(see p.176)

---

6.   A Christian centre in Roman times, Whithorn was a diocese from 681 to 686 and again from c.730. Bede refers to this Galloway see as *Candida Casa*.
7.   See D. Whitelock, 'The dealings of the kings of England with Northumbria in the tenth and eleventh centuries', *The Anglo-Saxons, Studies in some Aspects of their History and Culture presented to Bruce Dickins* (ed. P. Clemoes), pp.70–88.

king, Guthfrith, was buried in York Minster when he died in 895. As early as the second decade of the tenth century the symbol of a cross appeared on the coins minted in the name of King Sihtric of York. He had become a Christian on his marriage to one of King Athelstan's sisters.

Just as Gregory had instructed the Roman missionaries to England to show tact in dealing with Anglo-Saxon paganism, so it seems the Viking Age Church tolerated Scandinavian customs when they were not directly offensive. This compromise is demonstrated in the mid-eleventh-century *History of St Cuthbert*, which describes the accession of King Guthfrith. The holy relics of Christian tradition and the holy ring of Viking heathenism together ratified his election. The Abbot of Carlisle had been directed by St Cuthbert, in a vision, to choose Guthfrith. The saint instructed him:

'... at the ninth hour lead him with the whole army on to the hill which is called "Oswiu's down", and there place on his right arm a gold armlet, and thus they all may appoint him as king.' ... Then Bishop Eardwulf brought to the army and to the hill the body of St Cuthbert, and over it the king himself and the whole army swore peace and fidelity, for as long as they lived; and they kept this oath well.

(*EHD*, p.261)

The peculiar blend of northern taste with Christian tradition, which we have seen in the sculptures of the Viking North, exhibits the same kind of compromise. There is no doubt that the Scandinavians, under the influence of Christian teachers, were able to interpret their northern legends in a way that was relevant to Christianity, just as the ancient stories of the Old Testament were made to prefigure the New.

Clearly the Danelaw population remained culturally distinct. Even after the Wessex kings had permanently established their military authority over them, the Scandinavians remained to some extent a law unto themselves, a fact acknowledged in the law-codes of the southern kings (IV Edgar and VI Æthelred). It is probable that the strict enforcement of ecclesiastical law was as difficult as secular. The Scandinavians were powerful and confident enough to take Christianity on their own terms. They would accept baptism, Christian funerals and religious art; but where ecclesiastical law forbade them to marry a kinswoman or demanded dues they were unwilling to pay, some doubtless ignored it. Wulfstan II inveighed against adultery, incest and fornication; breaking of oaths and failure to observe fasts; neglect of Church dues and lack of respect for those in holy orders.[8] He was almost certainly drawing upon his experience of the Scandinavian population, gathered while he was Archbishop of York.

---

8.   The full text of the sermon may be found in Bethurum, pp.267–75, and is translated by Whitelock, *English Historical Documents*, I, pp.855–9.

Against this negative evidence we must weigh the strong indications of Christianity among the Scandinavians. The Viking leader Guthrum took an English name when he was baptized. Perhaps this practice explains why Wistan, a warrior mentioned in the Old English poem *The Battle of Maldon* is said to be both *Þurstanes sunu* (Thurstan's son) and *Wigelines bearn* (Wigelin's son) (lines 297–300; *ASPR*, VI, p. 15). The father was probably a Scandinavian who had changed his name on baptism, but had named his son with a syllable from each name.[9] Wistan is fighting, in the poem, on the side of the English Christians, against a band of heathen Vikings. Prosperous Scandinavian settlers might become patrons of churches. One of them, Orm, Gamal's son, rebuilt St Gregory's minster, Kirkdale (Yorks.), in the mid-eleventh century. This fact is commemorated on a sundial in the church.

The outstanding example of Vikings-turned-Christian may be seen in one Danish family who had probably settled in East Anglia. In the second generation Oda became Archbishop of Canterbury (in 941); Oda's nephew (St) Oswald, Bishop of Worcester and Archbishop of York, was one of the architects of the Benedictine Reform in England.

In the south efforts were being made to re-establish cultural life. King Alfred deplored the fact that the learning of the Golden Age had been allowed to decline:

Swæ clæne hio wæs oðfeallenu on Angelcynne ðæt swiðe feawa wæron behionan Humbre ðe hiora ðeninga cuðen understondan on Englisc, oððe furðum an ærendgewrit of Lædene on Englisc areccean; and ic wene ðætte noht monige begiondan Humbre næren.

(Sweet (ed.), *King Alfred's West-Saxon Version of Gregory's Pastoral Care*, EETS, 45, 50, p.3, lines 13–16)

It was declined so much in England that there were very few on this side of the Humber who knew how to understand their divine services in English or even translate an epistle from Latin into English; and I think that there were not many beyond the Humber.

Having made peace with Guthrum, Alfred had the opportunity to concentrate upon restoring literacy and education. He imported scholars into the culturally impoverished Wessex. They came from those parts of Britain where the Vikings had not destroyed the traditions of learning and from the continent, to where, in more prosperous days, the English Church had sent missionaries. Asser, from Wales, became Bishop of Sherborne, and Alfred's biographer; from Mercia came Plegmund, who was to become Archbishop of Canterbury in 890, also Werferth, Bishop of Worcester and the lesser known Athelstan and Werwulf; from the continent came two

---

9. I am grateful to Professor B. M. H. Strang for this suggestion.

monks, Grimbald, who eventually became Abbot of the New Minster at Winchester, and John, who became Abbot of the monastery which Alfred founded at Athelney. Accepting that Latin was, for the time being, lost to his people, Alfred and his team of scholars began translating a series of Christian 'classics' into English. The texts chosen were Pope Gregory's *Dialogues* and his *Pastoral Care*, a manual about the duties of bishops; Bede's *Ecclesiastical History*, Orosius's *History*, Boethius's *Consolation of Philosophy* and Augustine's *Soliloquies*. The *Anglo-Saxon Chronicle* was probably compiled in Alfred's reign. Beginning at 60 BC, it listed historical events year by year until the date of compilation (probably 891); copies were distributed to various monasteries where the *Chronicle* was kept up to date with annual entries. We have no evidence to associate the *Chronicle* with Alfred personally, but as a historical work, written in the vernacular, it exhibits a similar spirit to the king's own projects.

Alfred made some attempt to restore monasticism. Those religious houses which had survived were apparently no longer observing monastic discipline and it seems that the time was not yet ripe for a renewal of fervour for the ascetic way of life. The monastery Alfred founded in the swamps of Athelney had a stormy history. Built by foreign craftsmen, it also had to be filled with foreign monks and foreign children. The religious house he founded for women at Shaftesbury, under the abbacy of his second daughter Æthelgifu, was more successful and had a long life. The king was not, however, prepared to allow education to be limited to those in holy orders. His intention, stated in the preface to his translation of the *Pastoral Care*, was that all free-born boys who had the means and could be spared from other employment should be taught to read English. Latin learning was to follow for those destined to hold ecclesiastical office. The king's own children were educated, in particular the youngest, his son Æthelweard, who studied English and Latin books at the court school in company with noblemen's sons. Alfred, who regretted his own lack of early education, was himself an eager student, and he learned from his reading, applying in his later campaigns against the Vikings strategies suggested to him by Orosius's *History*.

As a small child, Alfred had been sent to Rome, where the Pope invested him with the regalia of a Roman consul. A few years later he had accompanied his father Æthelwulf to Rome. The pious foundation thus laid remained with him. He sent alms to the Pope and received gifts, including, in 885, a fragment of the True Cross. The king was devout in his personal life. Asser tells us that as a child he had

> learnt the daily course, that is, the services of the hours, and then certain psalms and many prayers. He collected these into one book and carried it about with him everywhere in his bosom (as I have myself seen) day and night, for the sake of prayer, through all the changes of this present life, and was never parted from it.

As an adult, in addition to the pursuits of warfare, the arts, hunting, building and learning Anglo-Saxon poetry

> He also was in the habit of hearing daily the divine office, the Mass, and certain prayers and psalms, and of observing both the day and the night hours, and of visiting churches at night-time, as we have said, in order to pray without his followers knowing. Moreover, he showed zeal for almsgiving, and generosity both to his countrymen and to strangers from all nations, and very great and matchless kindness and pleasantness towards all men, and skill in searching into things unknown.
>
> (Asser's *Life of King Alfred*, XXIV, LXXVI; *EHD*, pp. 266, 267-8)

There were further developments in Church organization in the reign of Edward the Elder. He founded the New Minster, a house of clerks (not, significantly, of monks) in Winchester, the chief city of Wessex. The Nun's Minster was shortly after founded in the same city by Ealhswith, Alfred's widow. The nunnery at Wilton may have been founded about this time. The two Wessex dioceses of Winchester and Sherborne, which were too large and unwieldy, were divided following the deaths of both bishops (in 908 and 909). The new arrangement was influenced by the geographical shires: three new dioceses were created at this time, Crediton, Ramsbury and Wells; St Germans was added in the reign of Athelstan.

Athelstan was a generous benefactor to the Church, including the religious foundations in the conquered north. He is believed to have presented to the community of St Cuthbert (then at Chester-le-Street) the silken embroidered stole and maniple which still survive among the saint's relics. In Wessex, he founded a religious house at Milton Abbas. It was in the reign of Athelstan that a monk named Ælfheah became Bishop of Winchester and that Oda, also a monk, first came to prominence as Bishop of Ramsey. These appointments heralded the revival of monasticism which eventually brought monks to every English bishopric.

Athelstan was not insular in his interests. His court received many foreign visitors, including suitors for his sisters' hands and refugees. Ecclesiastical and political matters also took Englishmen abroad at this time. It is certain then, that England received news of the monastic reform that was beginning on the continent in Burgundy and Lotharingia. There were two parallel movements. In Burgundy the monastery of Cluny, founded in 910, was becoming famous; the older monastery of Fleury was reformed by Cluny in the 930s. In Lotharingia ruined churches and abbeys were rebuilt, and monasteries which had fallen into lay hands were restored to the mode of life outlined in the Rule of St Benedict. Among the other foundations restored under Lotharingian influence were two abbeys at Ghent, in Flanders. It was at Fleury and at Ghent that English clerics observed the reform.

179

Dunstan, the man most readily associated with the monastic reform in England, seems to have felt the need for a revival of monastic strictness even before he visited the continent. Dunstan was born near Glastonbury. He was related to the West Saxon monarchy and to Ælfheah, monk and bishop. His uncle, Athelm, first Bishop of Wells, later Archbishop of Canterbury, introduced him to Athelstan's court where his asceticism made him unpopular. He also spent much time in study at Glastonbury, where he became a monk. King Edmund first favoured Dunstan, then banished him, then recalled him and made him Abbot of Glastonbury, where, under his influence, the Benedictine Rule came to be strictly observed. Dunstan was a trusted friend of the next king, Eadred, but incurred the dislike of his successor Eadwig and went into exile in Ghent. Eadwig's brother Edgar was chosen as king by the Mercians and Northumbrians in 957, and he recalled Dunstan, making him Bishop of Worcester and London. Edgar succeeded to Wessex when Eadwig died in 959. Archbishop Oda and his designated successor had recently died. Edgar, with a courteous excuse, rejected Eadwig's chosen successor and appointed Dunstan Archbishop of Canterbury.

Since the days of Oswald and Aidan there had not been such a conjunction of aims between a king and his chief ecclesiastic. Edgar enthusiastically gave royal patronage to Dunstan's idealistic policy; Dunstan moulded an unprecedented union of Church and state. It was he who engineered Edgar's coronation, uniting in him, for the first time in England, the functions of secular monarch and Lord's anointed.

The reform period brought a new strictness to monasticism and ensured that men of the calibre to choose this disciplined life filled influential positions. Monasteries and convents became important again. Dunstan, even as Archbishop, visited the monasteries in his care. He founded a monastery at Westminster, reformed one at Malmesbury and seems to have introduced Glastonbury monks as abbots of St Augustine's, Canterbury. At the Cathedral of Christ Church, Canterbury, he seems to have added monks to the secular clergy.

Clerks, who were not monks, but who lived communally, had been a recognized part of English Christianity in earlier times. By the tenth century, however, it seems that clerks, or canons, no longer lived communally and that many were married. In these circumstances Church property might easily become dispersed through inheritance. The replacement of such secular clergy by monks sworn to chastity, who held no property individually, represented a practical safeguarding of Church interests as well as an idealistic return to a stricter life-style.

Dunstan's associate Æthelwold took dramatic measures against the clerks. Æthelwold, like Dunstan, had been at Athelstan's court and was a Glastonbury monk. In the reign of King Eadred, he had wished to go to Fleury,

33 The Ruthwell Cross. A sandstone preaching cross carved with figure-sculpture front and back and with vine scroll on the sides. Photographed in its present location, at Ruthwell Church, Dumfries (*The Minister, Ruthwell Manse*)

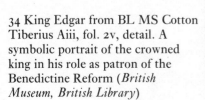

34 King Edgar from BL MS Cotton Tiberius Aiii, fol. 2v, detail. A symbolic portrait of the crowned king in his role as patron of the Benedictine Reform (*British Museum, British Library*)

replen · ut cum af caeleftif fpon
fi thalamum ualeatf ingre
di · q̄uod ipf̄e ·

35 A bishop celebrating mass from The Benedictional of St Æthelwold, BL MS Additional 49598, fol. 118v. The bishop, altar and arch are richly painted. The congregation and church are lightly depicted in ink (*British Museum, British Library*)

36 Chalice from Trewhiddle, Cornwall. Part of a ninth-century hoard of silver (*Trustees of the British Museum*)

but the king was reluctant to lose his services and instead appointed him Abbot of Abingdon, a declined monastery. Taking five chosen men with him (three from Glastonbury), Æthelwold set about reforming the monastery. He sent Osgar to Fleury to observe the Benedictine Rule, and received a group of monks skilled in Gregorian chant from Corbie. In 963, under Edgar, Æthelwold was made Bishop of Winchester. The Old Minster (the Cathedral) was at that time occupied by secular clergy of lax behaviour. Æthelwold ejected them, and, when they appealed to the king, was supported by Edgar and by Dunstan. The New Minster and the Nun's Minster at Winchester were subsequently reformed. Æthelwold purchased and restored the ruined religious houses at *Medeshamstede* (Peterborough), Ely, Thorney and, probably, Evesham. At Chertsey and Milton Abbas secular clerics were replaced by monks, probably at Æthelwold's instigation. It was Æthelwold also, who probably translated the Rule of St Benedict into English and who compiled the *Regularis Concordia*, a guide for English monks and nuns, based upon the Benedictine Rule.

The third important reformer of these years was the Anglo-Danish Oswald. His career began in an unreformed monastery at Winchester, but he studied for six years at Fleury, following in the footsteps of Oda, his uncle, Bishop of Ramsey and Archbishop of Canterbury. When Dunstan succeeded Oda at Canterbury in 961, Oswald became Bishop of Worcester and in 972, in addition, Archbishop of York. (Since the disloyalty of Archbishop Wulfstan I, the English kings seem to have taken the precaution of arranging that York was held in plurality with a richer, southern see. Oswald, and other archbishops, had the added qualification that their connections with the eastern Danelaw regions gave them advantage in handling Scandinavian settlers.)[10] Oswald's methods were not so drastic as Æthelwold's. Rather than turn out the secular clergy at Worcester and replace them with monks, he set up new monasteries at Westbury-on-Trym and Ramsey. He made a gradual transformation in the community at Worcester Cathedral, from clerks to monks, and later re-established monasticism at Ripon. Deerhurst, Pershore and Winchcombe owed their restoration to Oswald.

Apart from the Nun's Minster at Winchester, other religious houses for women were restored at this time, including establishments at Berkeley, Exeter, Horton, Ramsey, Shaftesbury, Thanet, Wareham, Wherwell and Wilton.[11]

At first there seems to have been a lack of uniformity in the practices of the new, and reformed, foundations. Some time in the decade 965 to 975 a Council was held at Winchester to draw up a common code which English

---

10. See Whitelock, 'The dealing of the kings of England with Northumbria', pp.73–6.
11. T. Symons, *Regularis Concordia*, xxiii.

monks and nuns agreed to abide by. The proem to the final agreement gives the king the credit for calling the Council:

> When therefore the Rule of the holy Father Benedict had been accepted with the greatest goodwill, very many of the abbots and abbesses with their communities of monks and nuns vied with one another in following in the footsteps of the saints; for they were united in one faith, though not in one manner of monastic usage. Exceedingly delighted with such great zeal the aforesaid king, after deep and careful study of the matter, commanded a Synodal Council to be held at Winchester.
>
> (*Regularis Concordia*, 4; Symons (trans.), p.2)

The Council was attended by Archbishop Dunstan, together with bishops, abbots and abbesses and invited monks from the continent. Together they drew up a code of practice which combined the austerity of the original Benedictine Rule with the elaborations introduced by the ninth-century reformer Benedict of Aniane, with the result that more time was spent in prayer and far less given over to manual work than in St Benedict's original plan.

The version of the *Regularis Concordia* in BL MS Cotton Tiberius Aiii contains a symbolic picture (plate 34): King Edgar, in the square crown which Dunstan made for his coronation, sits flanked by two nimbed figures, one a bishop (probably Æthelwold), the other, wearing the pallium in its developed form, an archbishop (Dunstan). The three hold a scroll, representing the Rule. Below them (not illustrated) a monk kneels, 'under the yoke of the Rule' (*Regularis Concordia*, 14; Symons, p.11).

The text of the *Regularis Concordia* gives us a full picture of monastic life, as it was (ideally) lived in the tenth and eleventh centuries. A formidable routine of prayer, beginning at 2.30 a.m. in winter and 1.30 a.m. in summer occupied the monks for most of the day, punctuated by two meals in summer, one in winter, one drink, work, reading, intervals for washing and changing shoes, and, in summer, a siesta. The day's programme ended at 6.30 p.m. in winter, later in summer when the day was longer. The account of the duties of the *circa*, the brother responsible for discipline, shows us that monks were often sleepy:

> the *circa* shall have a lantern so that he may look about him in the night hours, when it is proper so to do; and when the lessons are read at Nocturns, at the third or fourth lesson, as seems good to him, he shall go about the choir; and if he finds a brother drowsy with sleep he shall put the lantern before him and return to his place. Whereupon this brother, shaking off sleep, shall do penance on his knees and, taking up the lantern, shall himself go round the choir, and if he finds another overcome by the disorder of sleep, he shall do to him as was done to himself and so return to his own place.
>
> (*Regularis Concordia*, 57; p.56)

The monk's day was regulated by religious ritual from the moment he woke:

> when a brother arises from bed in the night hours for the work of God, he shall first of all sign himself with the sign of the Holy Cross, invoking the Holy Trinity. Next, he shall say the verse, *Domine labia mea aperies*, and then the whole of the psalm *Deus auditorium meum intende* with the *Gloria*. After this, having provided for the necessity of nature, if at that time he must, he shall hasten to the oratory saying the psalm *Ad te Domine levavi animam meam*, entering with the most profound reverence and taking the greatest care lest he disturb others at their prayers ...
>
> For his first prayer, then, he shall recite the first three Penitential psalms with the *Pater noster*—which shall be repeated in the following prayers—for his own intentions. He shall then say this collect: *I give thanks to Thee, Almighty Father, Who has deigned to protect me this night: I beseech Thy clemency, merciful Lord, to grant me this day so to bear myself with humility and discretion in Thy holy service that our worship may please Thee. Through our Lord.* He shall now go on to the second prayer in which he shall recite the next two Penitential psalms for the King, Queen and benefactors with this collect: *O God Who hast poured forth the gifts of love into the hearts of thy faithful through the grace of the Holy Ghost, grant to Thy servants, for whom we beseech Thy clemency, health of mind and body that they may love Thee with all their strength, and with all their love do those things which are pleasing to Thee. Through our Lord.* Passing thence to the third prayer he shall say the last two Penitential psalms, for the faithful departed, with this collect: *We beseech Thee O Lord that the souls of Thy servants may attain to the fellowship of eternal light who in the light of this life have followed after holiness. Through our Lord.*
>
> (*Regularis Concordia*, 15, 16; pp.11-12, 12-13)

Monks were expected to keep the canonical hours even if travelling, when they were to dismount and kneel in prayer (*Regularis Concordia*, 11).

It is evident that in the reformed monasteries great emphasis was placed upon humility: at the daily meetings of the Chapter monks were expected to confess their faults publicly or to accept humbly the accusations of others. The Saturday Maundy ceremony, in which those monks appointed to read and serve for the week washed the feet of their brethren, also demonstrated humility and brotherhood.

Despite the continental influence upon the reform movement in England, some of the practices outlined in the *Regularis Concordia* seem to have been peculiar to the English Church. In particular, the repeated psalms and collects for the King and Queen probably reflect the close association of King Edgar with the monastic reform.

Among the liturgical elaborations of the *Regularis Concordia* we find the earliest known description of religious drama. This consisted of a re-enactment of the events at Christ's sepulchre and took place in church on Easter Sunday. The scene had already been set on Good Friday:

on that part of the altar where there is space for it there shall be a representation as it were of a sepulchre, hung about with a curtain, in which the holy Cross, when it has been venerated, shall be placed in the following manner: the deacons who carried the Cross before shall come forward and, having wrapped the Cross in a napkin there where it was venerated, they shall bear it thence, singing the antiphons *In pace in idipsum, Habitabit* and *Caro mea requiescet in spe*, to the place of the sepulchre. When they have laid the cross therein, in imitation as it were of the burial of the Body of our Lord Jesus Christ, they shall sing the antiphon *Sepulto Domino, signatum est monumentum, ponentes milites qui custodirent eum*. In that same place the holy Cross shall be guarded with all reverence until the night of the Lord's Resurrection.

(*Regularis Concordia*, 46; pp. 44–5)

On Easter Day the cross was removed to its 'proper place' and during the reading of the third lesson the action of the play began:

four of the brethren shall vest, one of whom, wearing an alb as though for some different purpose, shall enter and go stealthily to the place of the 'sepulchre' and sit there quietly, holding a palm in his hand. Then, while the third respond is being sung, the other three brethren, vested in copes and holding thuribles in their hands, shall enter in their turn and go to the place of the 'sepulchre', step by step, as though searching for something. Now these things are done in imitation of the angel seated on the tomb and of the women coming with perfumes to anoint the body of Jesus. When, therefore, he that is seated shall see these three draw nigh, wandering about as it were and seeking something, he shall begin to sing softly and sweetly, *Quem quaeritis*. As soon as this has been sung right through, the three shall answer together, *Ihesum Nazarenum*. Then he that is seated shall say *Non est hic. Surrexit sicut praedixerat. Ite, nuntiate quia surrexit a mortuis*. At this command the three shall turn to the choir saying *Alleluia. Resurrexit Dominus*. When this has been sung he that is seated, as though calling them back, shall say the antiphon *Venite et videte locum*, and then, rising and lifting up the veil, he shall show them the place void of the Cross and with only the linen in which the Cross had been wrapped. Seeing this the three shall lay down their thuribles in that same 'sepulchre' and, taking the linen, shall hold it up before the clergy; and, as though showing that the Lord was risen and was no longer wrapped in it, they shall sing this antiphon: *Surrexit Dominus de sepulchro*. They shall then lay the linen on the altar.

(*Regularis Concordia*, 51; pp. 49–50)

The *Quem quaeritis in sepulchro* sequence ('Whom are you seeking in the sepulchre?') was a trope, a musical ornamentation of the Gregorian chant. The art of troping had become popular in the ninth century and seems to have been much used in England after the Benedictine Reform began. There are two extant tropers (manuscript collections of tropes) believed to be of the Anglo-Saxon period. The singing of antiphons also elaborated the performance of the psalms. These antiphons were also recorded in books at this time. The brethren, we know, would be divided into choirs. For comparison, we may consider St Riquier, a famous, early medieval church in the Frankish Empire, where, as Dr Taylor has pointed out, there were three choirs of adults and one of boys; the latter might sing as a unit or be divided among the other three choirs. Each choir consisted of one hundred singers.[12] The author of the *Regularis Concordia* describes antiphonal singing of the *Kyrie eleison* which the English monasteries might adopt if they wished:

> We have also heard that, in churches of certain religious men, a practice has grown up whereby compunction of soul is aroused by means of the outward representation of that which is spiritual, namely, that when the singing for the night is over, the antiphon of the gospel finished and all the lights put out, two children should be appointed who shall stand on the right hand side of the choir and shall sing *Kyrie eleison* with clear voice; two more on the left hand side who shall answer *Christe eleison*; and, to the west of the choir, another two who shall say *Domine miserere nobis*; after which the whole choir shall respond together *Christus Dominus factus est oboediens usque ad mortem*. The children of the right-hand choir shall then repeat what they sang above exactly as before and, the choir having finished their response, they shall repeat the same thing once again in the same way. When this has been sung the third time the brethren shall say the *preces* on their knees and in silence as usual. The same order of singing shall be observed for three nights by the brethren.
>
> (*Regularis Concordia*, 37; pp.36–7)

Polyphonic singing, more than one voice chanting in harmony, had been introduced by the end of the Anglo-Saxon period. Organ music was also known, but the instrument was used as an accompaniment to procession rather than to song.[13]

Processions, from church to church and within the church, were important in religious ritual. Dr Taylor has suggested that some of the sculptures which have been found in English churches were processional stations.

The more elaborate rituals of the tenth and eleventh centuries were certainly paralleled by an increased sophistication in church architecture. Unfortunately the more important Anglo-Saxon churches were replaced by Norman structures after the Conquest and the Anglo-Saxon stone buildings which remain standing are relatively minor ones. Among the best examples are the churches at Deerhurst (Glos.), which contains an Anglo-Saxon font, and Earls Barton (Northants.), its tower elegantly ornamented with pilaster strips. The numerous remains of late Anglo-Saxon churches throughout the country demonstrate that a square bell-tower was a characteristic feature in most areas.

---

12. H. M. Taylor, 'Tenth-century church building in England and on the continent', *Tenth-Century Studies* (ed. D. Parsons), pp.141–68.
13. Godfrey, *The Church in Anglo-Saxon England*, p.380.

Fig 37   The tower of the church at Earls
Barton, Northamptonshire

We know that elaborate churches were built or rebuilt towards the end
of the tenth century. They include Augustine's original cathedral, Christ
Church at Canterbury, rebuilt by Oda with a western oratory, two towers,
an enclosed choir, a sanctuary and, below it, a crypt. An illustration in the
Benedictional of St Æthelwold shows the Bishop celebrating mass, at (presumably) Winchester (plate 35). The clergy are before him, the seculars
apparently in a gallery. Above him elaborate roofs and a tower are visible.
In the North, the new cathedral of Durham, built in 999, provided a final
home for the community of St Cuthbert, driven from Lindisfarne in 875.

Documentary evidence tells that churches were lavishly equipped, but
little Anglo-Saxon church furniture survives. We have a censer cover from
Canterbury, and two chalices, from Hexham (Northumb.) and Trewhiddle
(Cornwall) (plate 36), both far less elaborate than the famous Irish Ardagh
Chalice, a bejewelled specimen dating to the eighth century. A metal cross
of insular workmanship, possibly Northumbrian, dating to about the eighth
century, survives in Austria (plate 37). It is elaborately decorated and inlaid,
and measures 5ft 2in by 3ft 1in (1·58m by 94cm). Several book covers exist,
decorated with elaborate ivory carvings (plate 38), and some ivory crozier
heads, which may date to the Anglo-Saxon period, are extant. The
vestments which were presented at various times to the shrine of St Cuthbert, and which have survived in the reliquary coffin of the saint, give us
some idea of the elaborate textiles available for mass vestments and church

188

hangings. They include silk fabrics imported into England, some with exotic motifs upon them. The stole and maniple made for Bishop Frithestan in the early tenth century and presented to St Cuthbert's shrine by King Athelstan, demonstrate the skill of English embroideresses, famous in later years.

The Benedictine Reform rekindled interest in learning and many books were copied in the tenth and eleventh centuries. Some of the Latin service books in use at this time have survived. They are based upon the Gregorian sacramentary, a Roman massbook sent to Charlemagne at his own request in the late-eighth century, and augmented, according to generally accepted tradition, by the English scholar Alcuin.[14] One of the augmented manuscripts, the Leofric Missal (BL MS Additional 15419) also includes the older Gelasian sacramentary. The missal contains services for the Church year and for special occasions, including a coronation. It was written (by a foreign hand) *c*.900. A calendar of saints was appended to it about eighty years later, which included, apart from continental figures, a number of men important in the history of English Christianity: Augustine of Canterbury, Aidan, Ceolfrith, Cuthbert and the seventh-century hermit, Guthlac.[15]

Some of the books were lavishly illuminated. Famous examples associated with well-known figures include the *Benedictional of St Æthelwold* (see plate 35) and the Bosworth Psalter compiled for Archbishop Dunstan. In these it can be seen that the geometric and zoomorphic motifs beloved by earlier illuminators in Northumbria and Mercia have given way to the humanistic art of the Winchester School. Under the influence of Carolingian art (and ultimately the traditions of Byzantium) the English artists now created rounded human figures with fluttering garments. They are best displayed in the formal, lavishly coloured portraits of biblical and saintly figures in the *Benedictional*. The Winchester Style artists also adopted from Carolingian sources the motif of the acanthus leaf. We find this fleshy plant clinging round the trellis forming the frames to some of the pictures in the *Benedictional* and illuminating an initial in the Bosworth Psalter. The new style of art was transmitted to the stone carver, who thus produced works very different from the contemporary sculptures of Viking-influenced Northumbria. A fine example of late Anglo-Saxon sculpture is the pair of flying angels, still to be seen on the wall of the little church at Bradford-on-Avon (Wilts.). They were almost certainly part of a large crucifixion (a motif found only rarely in earlier Anglo-Saxon art but now popular). Small ivory carvings from this period, with animated figures in fluttering drapery, also reflect the Winchester Style.

Despite this rebirth of culture, which permeated so many branches of the arts, it seems that few Englishmen of the reform period were first-class

---

14. According to a recent scholar, the Supplement was not written by Alcuin but by Benedict of Aniane. See J. Deshusses, *Le Sacramentaire Grégorien*, pp.64–7.
15. C. E. Hohler, 'Some service-books of the later Saxon church', *Tenth-Century Studies*, p.69.

Fig 38   Censer cover from Canterbury

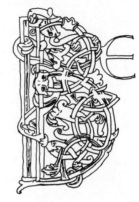

Fig 39   Initial from The Bosworth Psalter
          MS BL Additional 37517 fol. 4

Latin scholars. Mr Hohler has pointed out the significance of the facts that the compilers of some service books got incredibly muddled, and that, although there exist from this period some biographies of English saints written in Latin, most works of this kind were the product of foreign scholars.[16] King Alfred had already legitimized translation from Latin into English. Now Æthelwold translated the Benedictine Rule, the Gospels were translated into West Saxon, and the hexateuch was rendered into English. Ælfric, the famous abbot, schoolmaster and homilist, was responsible for parts of this translation. (This text survives in BL MS Cotton Claudius Biv, where it is lavishly illustrated with coloured drawings inserted into the text (plate 39). The instructive method of illustrating—a step-by-step depiction of the material described in the text—represents a very different attitude to book decoration from that in the *Benedictional* and is very unlike the patterns and stark symbols of the Book of Durrow and other manuscripts of the earlier Hiberno-Saxon school.) At this time some Latin books were provided with interlinear glosses in English, among them the Lindisfarne Gospels, which was glossed in the Northumbrian dialect, by, according to a colophon in the manuscript, a priest named Aldred. The glossing was done while the community of St Cuthbert was at Chester-le-Street, before its move to Durham. Glosses like these were collected at various times and put into subject or alphabetical order as an aid to reading Latin. Ælfric produced a *Grammar* and *Glossary* to help students of Latin, as well as the *Colloquium*, a simple form of play in Latin for the boys in a monastic school.

Many English sermons survive from this period, often exhibiting a polished and rhetorical prose style. Ælfric wrote the *Catholic Homilies*, two

---

16.   'Some service-books', pp. 72–3.

Fig 40   Carved angel from Bradford-on-Avon, Wiltshire

series of forty and forty-five sermons designed for priests to use on the Sundays and festivals of the Church year; also the *Lives of the Saints*, designed for a monastic audience. This work consists of thirty-seven homilies on saints particularly reverenced by monks, such as King Oswald of Northumbria and Æthelthryth, as well as the later English King, Edmund, and foreign saints. Wulfstan II, Archbishop of York, wrote a number of sermons, of which the most famous is the 'fire and brimstone' *Sermo Lupi ad Anglos*, in which the homilist recognized the possibility that the end of the world was near (expected by many in the year 1000) and urged his audience to repent. Another author of this period known to us by name is Bryhtferth, a monk of Ramsey. His best-known work is the *Handboc* or *Manual*, a text in Latin and English on the calculation of time and the calendar (always an important consideration for the clergy) and he may have been responsible for compiling the translation of the hexateuch.

The period of the Benedictine Reform also brought a stimulus to the collecting and copying of vernacular poetry. Most of the Old English poems which survive have come down to us in tenth- or eleventh-century manuscripts, although some of the material may be much older. *The Dream of the Rood*, for example, a poem in the *Vercelli Book*, a late tenth-century manuscript, had existed in some form in the seventh or eighth century, since it was carved upon the Ruthwell Cross. Two poems in the *Vercelli Book* bear the cryptic signature of the poet Cynewulf, who is believed to have flourished in the ninth century. This Christian author signed his poems by means of runes, ironically taking a scholarly interest in the ancient symbols which may once have been associated with paganism.

Some of our surviving poems are scriptural, deriving from both the Old Testament (for example *Genesis A, Exodus, Judith*) and the New (*Christ, The Fates of the Apostles*); some material is apocryphal (*Genesis B*) and some based on well-established Christian legend (*Elene*). Several poems draw heavily on the writings of the Church Fathers to demonstrate moral themes, such as the worthlessness of life on this earth (*The Wanderer, The Seafarer*). Anglo-Saxon poets also versified in English the Lord's Prayer, the Creed and certain psalms, not being content with prose translations.

Cædmon (see p.156), in composing his first Christian hymn in the English

191

language, had used the traditional vocabulary of heroic poetry. *The Dream of the Rood* poet made a Germanic hero of the suffering Christ. This fusion of heroic and Christian continued in later Old English poetry and was a two-way process: thus *Judith*, a late Anglo-Saxon poem on the subject of the Old Testament heroine's defeat of Holofernes and his army, contains a feast scene which is a parody of a Germanic banquet, as well as a heroic battle in which the traditional Beasts appear (see p.15); while in *The Battle of Maldon*, a poem commemorating a historical battle fought in 991, the hero dies with a prayer on his lips and the heathenism of the enemy (Vikings) is never forgotten. Modern scholars agree that *Beowulf*, our longest extant poem, which contains some very old Germanic legends, was deliberately structured by a Christian scholar; some would even interpret it as a religious allegory.

On the death of King Edgar in 975, there seems to have been some reaction against monasticism in Mercia, as a result of which some lands which had been given to monasteries were reclaimed; but the general tendencies of the reform movement continued. New monasteries were established and monks replaced secular clergy at the cathedrals of Canterbury and Sherborne. The cultural renaissance lasted into the reign of Æthelred II.

Meanwhile the English Church had gained another royal saint. Edward ('the Martyr'), Edgar's elder son, had succeeded to the throne on his father's death, but was murdered in 978. His body was hastily disposed of, but on its translation to Shaftesbury a year later, miracles were associated with his relics and he became honoured as a saint during the reign of his half-brother Æthelred II. The murder clouded the accession of the young king. It may well have been committed by one of Æthelred's own household; suspicion fell on his mother, Edward's step-mother.

Æthelred's reign continued to be troubled. Viking raids began again in the 980s. Although Christianity had begun to penetrate Scandinavia it was not yet universally accepted there, and the plunderers who attacked the English were again violent heathens. The English probably feared for their own back-door—that the Danelaw settlers might join forces with the enemy. We find a Northumbrian hostage in Essex on the occasion of the Battle of Maldon, no doubt as a safeguard against this. The constant demands of the Vikings for Danegeld—money payment—threatened to impoverish England, and no doubt much English metalwork was melted down or handed over as bullion at this time.

Æthelred seems to have precipitated the Viking conquest by ordering the massacre of Danes living in England on St Brice's Day (13 November) 1002. According to later tradition, Gunnhild, a Danish hostage and sister of King Swein of Denmark, was among the victims. If so, it was probably in a proper Germanic spirit of revenge that Swein invaded England in 1003 and continued to attack it until ten years later Æthelred was driven into exile. Æthelred regained his throne briefly when Swein died in 1014, but he soon faced the opposition of his own son, Edmund Ironside, and of Cnut, Swein's son. Æthelred died in 1016 and in the same year the surviving contenders divided England between them; but Edmund died within a year of his father and Cnut, a Viking, took control of all England.

Cnut's father had been a heathen in his early life, and it could have happened that the accession of a Danish king struck a blow against English Christianity; but the opposite happened. Cnut became a zealous Christian king. This certainly does not mean that he became meek or even totally submissive to ecclesiastical law. In the early years of his reign he was ruthless towards his enemies and throughout his time in power he kept an army of retainers, his 'housecarls', whose upkeep was paid for by public taxation. In 1017 he married Emma (Ælfgifu) of Normandy, widow of Æthelred and mother of Æthelred's surviving children, so avoiding any defensive action by Normandy on behalf of those children. They remained in Normandy, and Emma had other children by Cnut and was acknowledged as his queen. However, Cnut had already what is best described as a 'common-law wife', Ælfgifu of Northampton. Apparently he never repudiated her and in 1030 appointed her regent of Norway on behalf of Swein, his son by her.

Despite these drawbacks Cnut was anxious to be seen as a Christian monarch. A well-known miniature in the *Liber Vitae* (BL MS Stowe 944) shows him beside the altar cross at the New Minster at Winchester (plate 40). Surmounted by God, the Virgin and St Peter, crowned by an angel and with his hand touching the cross, Cnut is depicted as king by God's grace; but the cynic might observe the flanking figure of the wife who gave him security in his kingdom, and that the king's left hand rests upon his conquering sword.

Cnut was certainly a benefactor to the Church, although he did not make a practice of founding new houses. The recent emphasis on monasticism continued as monks were appointed to bishoprics. In 1027 Cnut visited Rome in order to attend the coronation of the Holy Roman Emperor Conrad. He seems to have treated the journey as a pilgrimage and while in Rome took the opportunity to negotiate the relief of tolls imposed on English merchants and travellers and the charges on archbishops visiting Rome. On his return he issued a proclamation explaining this.

Archbishop Wulfstan II seems to have been a strong influence upon Cnut. Wulfstan had composed law-codes for Æthelred and he composed them for Cnut, so continuing the English legal tradition despite the change of dynasty. The laws reflect Wulfstan's obsession with order and with the protection of those in holy orders. Repeatedly, reference is made to religion among the 'secular' legislation:

6 Homicides and perjurers, injurers of the clergy and adulterers, are to submit and make amends or to depart from their native land with their sins.
7 Hypocrites and liars, robbers and plunderers, shall incur God's anger, unless they desist and atone very deeply.
7.1 And he who wishes to purify the country rightly and to put down wrong-doing and to love righteousness, must diligently correct and shun such things ...

38 Wrong-doing is not permitted at any time; and yet it should be especially guarded against at festival seasons and in sacred places.
38.1 And ever as a man is mightier or of higher rank, he must atone the deeper for wrong-doing both to God and to men.
38.2 And ecclesiastical amends are always to be diligently demanded according to the instruction in books [of penance] and secular amends according to the secular law ...

45 And if it can be arranged, no condemned man should ever be put to death during the Sunday festival, unless he flees or resists; but he is to be seized and kept until the feast-day is over.
45.1 If a freeman work on a feast-day, he is to pay his *healsfang* in compensation and indeed to atone for it deeply to God, as he is directed.
45.2 A slave, if he work, is to suffer a flogging or redeem himself from one, in proportion to the deed.
45.3 If a master compels his slave to work on a feast-day, he is to forfeit the slave, who is afterwards to be a free man; and the master is to pay *lahslit* among the Danes, a fine among the English, in proportion to the deed; or to clear himself ...

47 If anyone openly commits a breach of the Lenten fast by fighting or intercourse with women or by robbery or by any other grave crime, double compensations are to be paid, as in a high festival, in proportion to the deed.
47.1 And if anyone denies it, he is to clear himself with the three-fold process of exculpation.

(II Cnut; *EHD*, pp.420, 424, 425, 426)

When Cnut died in 1035, Harthacnut, his son by Emma, was living in Denmark and unable to claim his English throne for fear of losing Denmark to King Magnus of Norway. Harold Harefoot, Cnut's son by Ælfgifu of Northampton, became regent. When he was declared king in 1037, his illegitimacy must surely have disturbed some members of the Church, but the problem was solved by Harold's death and Harthacnut's succession in 1040. When Harthacnut himself died, still a young man, his half-brother Edward succeeded to the throne. Edward was the son of Æthelred and Emma and had come from Normandy the previous year at Harthacnut's request.

Having spent most of his life in exile in Normandy, Edward, naturally enough, appointed Normans to high office, including the sees of Dorchester and London and the archbishopric of Canterbury. The last two offices were held, in succession, by Robert of Jumièges. He and another of Edward's nominees were expelled by a nationalist reaction in 1051, and Stigand, Bishop of Winchester, succeeded as Archbishop of Canterbury, in the life-time of his predecessor, and holding Winchester and Canterbury in plurality. He was excommunicated by three popes, but continued to hold office, despite dissatisfaction with his position at home. (Pope Alexander II supported the Norman Conquest in the hope that William of Normandy would depose Stigand, which he did in 1070.) Secular clergy were now being appointed to bishoprics once more and the zealous monasticism of the reform era seems to have declined. It did not, of course, decay to the same extent as during the Viking Age and remained a potent force for several centuries more.

During Edward's reign there began a development that was to accelerate after the Norman Conquest, with the removal in 1050 of Leofric's see from Crediton to Exeter. Within thirty years of the Conquest the distribution of cathedrals in England would be far more urbanized than before; the see of Dorchester moved to Lincoln; Lichfield to Chester, then to Coventry; North Elmham to Thetford, then to Norwich; Selsey to Chichester; and Sherborne to Salisbury.

If the English Church in Edward's day was less zealous about asceticism and monasticism than before, the king himself was particularly noted for his holiness. He was a benefactor of religious houses and was responsible for the rebuilding and endowment of the monastery on Thorney Island; but he was too ill to attend the dedication of its great church, Westminster Abbey, and when he died eight days later (on 5 January 1066) he was buried there.

The asceticism of his life had given rise to a belief in his sanctity, which was supported by the fact that his marriage was childless. He was the first English monarch believed to have the power to cure scrofula—'the king's evil'—by his touch. Edward was canonized a confessor[17] by papal bull in 1161.

Edward the Confessor was the last ruler of the old Anglo-Saxon line. At the time he died England was triply threatened: by Tostig, the rebellious Earl of Northumbria, by Harold Hardrada, King of Norway, and by William of Normandy. The English immediately elected as king Harold, son of Earl Godwine and of Gytha of Denmark. Harold's sister Edith had been Edward's queen, and he himself was the country's leading nobleman. He was hastily consecrated king in Westminster Abbey, on the day of Edward's burial there.

---

17. Originally the title was applied to one who suffered for confessing the faith, but was not martyred. Later, it was given to one who resisted the temptations of the world. See F. Barlow, *Edward the Confessor*, p.xix and note.

Harold successfully fought off Tostig and Harold Hardrada, but was killed fighting Duke William in October 1066. On the following Christmas Day William was crowned at Westminster. In his reign the government of the English Church passed largely into foreign hands. The excommunicated Stigand was replaced as Archbishop of Canterbury by Lanfranc, previously Abbot of Caen. Several bishops were replaced by foreigners: Æthelmær of North Elmham, Stigand's brother; Leofwine of Lichfield, a married man; and Æthelric of Selsey. The only Anglo-Saxon bishops to retain their offices were Wulfstan at Worcester and Siward at the relatively unimportant see of Rochester. (Leofric, first Bishop of Exeter, may have been of English birth, but had received a foreign education.) Under Lanfranc, abbots of English monasteries were gradually displaced by Normans, and the customs of the English Church gradually changed. The practice of writing in the vernacular, for example, long accepted in England, decreased considerably in favour of Latin scholarship; while the rebuilding of cathedral and abbey churches swept away many Saxon buildings in favour of grand Norman structures, some of which still stand today.

Despite the elaborate organization of the Church in late Anglo-Saxon times, even as late as the reign of Cnut there were still distinctly unchristian elements in the kingdom. The remains of a stone frieze, contemporary with Cnut, found in the Old Minster, Winchester, apparently depicts a northern legend, probably one of Sigemund's exploits. Cnut himself legislated against heathen practices:

> It is heathen practice if one worships idols, namely if one worships heathen gods and the sun or the moon, fire or flood, wells or stones or any kind of forest trees, or if one practises witchcraft or encompasses death by any means, either by sacrifice or divination, or takes any part in such delusions.
>
> (II Cnut, 5.1; *EHD*, p.420)

Possibly the Danelaw population, more recently converted than the Anglo-Saxons, were the chief offenders, since in a text of Cnut's reign which deals with religious matters in the North, there are more explicit references to the offences:

> 48   If, then, any man is discovered who henceforth carries on any heathen practice, either by sacrifice or divination, or practises witchcraft by any means, or worship of idols, he is to pay, if he is a king's thegn, 10 half-marks, half to Christ, half to the king.
>
> 54   If there is on anyone's land a sanctuary round a stone or a tree or a well or any such nonsense, he who made it is then to pay *lahslit*, half to Christ and half to the lord of the estate.
>
> 54.1   And if the lord of the estate will not help in the punishment, then Christ and the king are to have the compensation.
>
> (The law of the Northumbrian priests; *EHD*, pp.437, 438)

When the northern archbishop Wulfstan II railed against the evils of his day he included sorcerers, calling them *wiccan and wælcyrian* (witches and valkyries; Bethurum, p.273, lines 164–5). The second term, which Cnut also used in a proclamation of 1030, literally means 'choosers of the slain' and owes its origin to northern mythology, in which supernatural creatures selected warriors, on behalf of Woden, to dwell in Valhalla. The precise meaning of the term had no doubt been forgotten, but it remained a convenient name for people whose practices gave rise to suspicion of heathenism. It is clear though, that the old gods had been banished. The 'heathenism' remaining took the form of a primitive nature worship, superstition and attempts at magic. Superstitious rituals were still, apparently, employed against sickness, for difficult childbirth and to ensure the well-being of fields and stock. The following example of a charm, from an eleventh-century manuscript, designed to ensure the safe capture of a swarm of bees, employs both ritual actions and incantation:

Nim eorþan, oferweorp mid þinre swiþran handa under þinum swiþran fet and cweð:
    Fo ic under fot, funde ic hit.
    Hwæt, eorðe mæg wið ealra wihta gehwilce,
    and wið andan and wið æminde,
    and wið þa micelan mannes tungan.
And siððon forweorp ofer greot þonne hi swirman, and cweð:
    Sitte ge, sigewif, sigaþ to eorþan.
    Næfre ge wilde to wuda fleogan.
    Beo ge swa gemindige mines godes,
    swa bið manna gehwilc metes and eþeles.
                           (Storms, *Anglo-Saxon Magic*, p.132)

Take earth, throw it down with your right hand under your right foot and say: 'I catch it under my foot, I have found it. Lo, earth has power against all creatures, and against hatred and against jealousy and against the great tongue of man.' And afterwards throw earth over them when they swarm, and say: 'Stay, victory-women, descend to earth. Never fly wild to the wood. Be as mindful of my good, as every man is of food and dwelling.'

Many charms relied upon mumbo-jumbo derived from Latin prayers. The following charm, *wiþ ylfa gescotum*, is against sickness in a horse. The disease itself is attributed to hostile elves, the cure involves a prayer and a ritual bleeding involving the sign of the cross:

Gif hors ofscoten sie, nim þonne þæt seax þe þæt hæfte sie fealo hryþeres horn and sien III ærene næglas on.
    Writ þonne þam horse on þam heafde foran Cristes mæl þæt hit blede; writ þonne on þam hricge Cristes mæl and on leoþa gehwilcum þe þu ætfeolan mæge. Nim þonne þæt winestre eare, þurhsting swigende.

Þis þu scealt don: genim ane girde, sleah on þæt bæc, þonne biþ þæt hors
hal.
And awrit on þæs seaxes horne þas word:
Benedicite omnia opera domini dominum
Sy þæt ylfa þe him sie, þis him mæg to bote.

(Storms, *Anglo-Saxon Magic*, p.248)

If a horse is diseased from an elf's shot, then take the knife of which the handle
is made from the yellow horn of an ox and on which there are three brass nails.
Then write Christ's sign on the horse's forehead, so that it bleeds; then write
Christ's sign on the back and on each of the limbs which you can hang on to.
Then take the left ear, pierce it, being silent. This you must do: take a rod,
strike it on the back, then the horse will be well. And write these words on
the knife's horn: *Benedicite omnia opera domini dominum*. Whatever the elf in
him is, this can bring about a remedy for him.

The medieval Christian Church was not ready to recognize or condemn
cruelty to beast or man. In fact, although God was accepted as the meter-
out of justice, God's will was sometimes found out by submitting a suspect
villain to the ordeal. This, which might involve hot water or a hot iron, was
carried out in church. There even exist prayers for the blessing of the iron,
to be spoken by the bishop who anointed the instrument with holy oil, before
it was applied to the suspect in the hope that it would not harm him if he
were innocent.

According to the laws of Cnut, the 'three-fold ordeal' was not the end
of the matter for someone proved guilty:

30.3*b*   And if he is then convicted, on the first occasion he is to pay two-fold
compensation to the accuser and his wergild to the lord who is entitled to his
fine, and to appoint trustworthy sureties that he will afterwards cease from all
evil-doing.
30.4   And on the second occasion there is to be no other compensation, if he
is convicted, but that his hands, or feet, or both, in proportion to the deed,
are to be cut off.
30.5   And if, however, he has committed still further crimes, his eyes are to
be put out and his nose and ears and upper lip cut off, or his scalp removed,
whichever of these is then decreed by those with whom the decision rests; thus
one can punish and at the same time preserve the soul.

(II Cnut; *EHD*, p.423)

By late Anglo-Saxon times the Church was regularly sharing in the important ceremonies of secular life. Marriage had been a mercenary arrangement
in early Germanic society, but in late Anglo-Saxon times the woman's agreement was required:

37 The so-called Rupert Cross, which survives in the presbytery at Bischofshofen, Austria. Probably Anglo-Saxon work of about the eighth century, the cross is of gilded copper, decorated with vine-scroll and animal ornament and set with enamel discs (*Bayerisches Nationalmuseum, Munich*)

38 Ivory book cover, upper side, Paris *Bibliothèque Nationale MS latin* 323. The ivory plate is set into the leather binding. It shows Christ in Majesty. A Virgin and Child plaque ornaments the back of the book (*Bib. Nat., Paris*)

39 The sacrifice of Isaac from the Ælfric Hexateuch, BL MS Cotton Claudius Biv, fol. 38. The late-Anglo-Saxon artist was familiar with traditional painting and drawing, but his figures and scenes have a lively originality (*British Museum, British Library*)

40 King Cnut and Queen Emma (Ælfgyfu) from BL MS Stowe 944, fol. 6. The Viking king is pictured as benefactor of the Church, surmounted by Christ, the Virgin, St Peter and angels (*British Museum, British Library*)

And neither a widow nor a maiden is ever to be forced to marry a man whom she herself dislikes, nor to be given for money, unless he chooses to give anything of his own freewill.

(II Cnut, 74; *EHD*, p.429)

It was now usual, and correct, for a priest to officiate at a wedding:

At the marriage there should by rights be a priest, who shall unite them together with God's blessing in all prosperity.

(Concerning the betrothal of a woman, 8; *EHD*, p.431)

The custom that a royal bridegroom would woo his chosen queen with precious gifts was so firmly established that we find it stated among the *Maxims* of the *Exeter Book*, among such obvious truths as 'Frost must freeze':

Cyning sceal mid ceape   cwene gebicgan,
bunum ond beagum

(*ASPR*, III, p.159, lines 81–2)

'A king must buy a queen with property, with cups and with rings.'

Even this practical, secular transaction now became influenced by Christianity as one may judge from William of Malmesbury's account of the treasures which Hugh, Duke of the Franks, sent to the devout King Athelstan when requesting the hand of one of Athelstan's sisters:

perfumes such as never before had been seen in England; jewellery, especially of emeralds, in whose greenness the reflected sun lit up the eyes of the bystanders with a pleasing light; many fleet horses, with trappings, 'champing', as Maro says, 'on bits of ruddy gold'; a vase of onyx, carved with such subtle engravers' art that the cornfields seemed really to wave, the vines really to bud, the forms of the men really to move, and so clear and polished that it reflected like a mirror the faces of the onlookers; the sword of Constantine the Great, on which could be read the name of the ancient owner in letters of gold; on the pommel also above thick plates of gold you could see an iron nail fixed, one of the four which the Jewish faction prepared for the crucifixion of our Lord's body; the spear of Charles the Great, which, whenever that most invincible emperor, leading an army against the Saracens, hurled it against the enemy, never let him depart without the victory; it was said to be the same which, driven by the hand of the centurion into our Lord's side, opened by the gash of that precious wound Paradise for wretched mortals; the standard of Maurice, the most blessed martyr and prince of the Theban legion, by which the same king was wont in the Spanish war to break asunder the battalions of the enemies, however fierce and dense, and to force them to flight; a diadem, precious certainly for its quantity of gold, but more for its gems, whose splendour so threw flashes of light on the onlookers that the more anyone strove to fix his gaze on it, the more was he driven back

201

and forced to give in; a piece of the holy and adorable Cross enclosed in crystal, where the eye, penetrating the substance of the stone, could discern what was the colour of the wood and what the quantity; a portion also of the crown of thorns, similarly enclosed, which the madness of the soldiers placed on Christ's sacred head in mockery of his kingship.

(*De Gestis Regis Anglorum*, 135; *EHD*, p.282)

Obviously the most elaborate ceremonies of Anglo-Saxon times were connected with the court, and one royal occasion stands out above all others: the coronation of King Edgar.[18] This ceremony is unusually well documented. A monk of Ramsey who witnessed the coronation described the occasion in his biography of Archbishop Oswald,[19] and the *ordo*, the formal account of the prayers for the ceremony, is extant. There are two earlier drafts (in the Leofric Missal and the so-called Egbert Pontifical) as well as what was apparently the final version in Paris, *Bibliothèque Nationale MS latin* 943. A comparison between the versions shows that Dunstan, the architect of the coronation, had carefully revised his plans, rejecting some and selecting other details from other *ordines*.

Some of Edgar's coronation regalia had ancient precedent—the king buried at Sutton Hoo had owned a sceptre, a sword and a helmet which may have been a *cynehelm*, the symbolic headgear of royalty; but Edgar's ceremony was not the climax of a slow evolution from early Anglo-Saxon times. It was deliberately created for him by Dunstan. It demonstrates Edgar's unique position among English kings and marked the beginning of a tradition in which the coronation of the English monarch was a sacred as well as a secular ceremony.

The involvement of the clergy in the accession of kings had been established at the beginning of the ninth century when popes began to crown Holy Roman Emperors. Carolingian kings copied the ceremony, and chose to be crowned and invested with royal regalia by priests. The use of a crown in England seems to have been always associated with a religious coronation and the crown seems to have been the symbol *par excellence* of kingship in late Anglo-Saxon times.[20] Anglo-Saxon kings almost certainly wore their crowns on the great feast-days, Christmas, Easter and Whitsuntide. We have pictures of Athelstan, Edgar, Cnut, Edward the Confessor and Harold II wearing crowns. Eadwig, Edgar's brother (branded irresponsible by history), had a jewelled crown which he carelessly placed on the floor while he disported himself with women. Cnut made the dramatic (if not original) gesture of offering his crown to the Church, laying it upon the altar of Christ

---

18. P. E. Schramm, *A History of the English Coronation* (trans. L. G. Wickham Legg), pp.18–23.
19. J. Raine, *The Historians of the Church of York and its Archbishops*, I, pp.436–8.
20. The Anglo-Saxons continued to use the Old English word *cynehelm* to mean crown.

Church Cathedral in Canterbury. It was later placed on top of a cross, above the image of Christ.[21] Edward the Confessor's crown was buried with him. Edgar's crown, according to tradition, was made for him by his mentor Archbishop Dunstan, who was a skilled goldsmith.

The coronation ceremony as conceived by Dunstan had, as its climax, the act of consecration. The anointing of a king with oil was a custom descended from Jewish practice as documented in the Old Testament, but in medieval times anointing had been chiefly associated with the consecration of bishops. Offa of Mercia had had his son consecrated (see p.160) but this did not become a regular practice. The Anglo-Saxons came into contact with elaborate coronation ceremonies in 856 when Æthelwulf of Wessex married the child Judith, daughter of the Frankish King Charles the Bald. Judith was anointed, as was the custom of her people, according to the *ordo* for her marriage and coronation drawn up by the influential Archbishop Hincmar of Reims. This anointing did not at the time set a precedent in England, but Dunstan drew upon Judith's ceremony when he composed the *ordo* for Edgar's.

King Edgar's coronation took place at Bath, contrary to tradition, which had established Kingston (Surrey) as the coronation site. The ceremony was held on Whit Sunday, 973, although Edgar had taken Mercia and Northumbria in 957 and succeeded to Wessex in 959. The delay in his coronation meant that at the time of the ceremony Edgar was thirty years old, the canonical age for ordination to the priesthood. It also had the effect that by the time the coronation took place Edgar was well established. Although he was no saint (he had an illegitimate daughter), he could be contrasted favourably with his predecessor Eadwig. His reign was free from war. It was a period of prosperity, of cultural revival and of a reassertion of Christian standards. The coronation stressed Edgar's role as a King of Peace, wielding secular power by the right of divine coronation.

At the beginning of the ceremony Edgar removed his crown and prostrated himself at the altar while the *Te Deum* was sung. He then made a formal promise to keep peace and justice. After prayers and an anthem he was acclaimed by the people, then the chrism was placed on his head. He was subsequently invested with sword, ring and sceptre, and was crowned. A statement was made about the meaning of Christian kingship, and Edgar's wife Ælfthryth was anointed, crowned and invested with a ring. Mass was celebrated, after which Edgar feasted with the archbishops and other guests while his queen entertained the abbots and abbesses in a nearby room.

Shortly after, the king sailed to Chester where subordinate kings did

---

21. W. A. Chaney, *The Cult of Kingship in Anglo-Saxon England*, p.139. The gift is recorded in a contemporary charter (A. J. Robertson, *Anglo-Saxon Charters*, p.158). Its placing on the cross is a later tradition.

homage to him, and according to later tradition, rowed him on the River Dee (see p.169).

The coronation banquets of late Anglo-Saxon kings united secular and ecclesiastical interests in that the feast itself was a long-established Germanic tradition, but on these occasions the chief ecclesiastics of the land were the most honoured guests. Indeed, the sanctity of the occasion was impressed upon the seculars, even upon the king himself, as we know from an anecdote about King Eadwig. He had succeeded in 955 at the age of about fifteen, when he discourteously absented himself from his coronation banquet with its company of archbishops and bishops, in order to amuse himself in an undignified way with his future wife and her mother. Archbishop Oda despatched Dunstan, then Abbot of Glastonbury, together with the Bishop of Lichfield, to fetch the king back. He was literally dragged from the women, an ignominy which Eadwig probably never forgot, or forgave.

Since banqueting was so much a part of Germanic life and the Anglo-Saxons were never happier than when in company, feasting at the table of a generous lord, it is hardly surprising that one Anglo-Saxon poet conceived heaven in these terms:

>   ... ic wene me
> daga gehwylce   hwænne me dryhtnes rod,
> þe ic her on eorðan   ær sceawode,
> on þysson lænan   life gefetige
> ond me þonne gebringe   þær is blis mycel,
> dream on heofonum,   þær is dryhtnes folc
> geseted to symle,   þær is singal blis,
> ond me þonne asette   þær ic syþþan mot
> wunian on wuldre,   well mid þam halgum
> dreames brucan.
>   (*The Dream of the Rood*, lines 135–44; *ASPR*, II, p.65)

I hope every day for the time when the Lord's cross which I formerly looked on here on earth will fetch me from this transitory life and then bring me to where there is great happiness, joy in the heavens, where the Lord's family is seated at the banquet, where is continuous happiness; and shall then set me where I afterwards may dwell in glory, to enjoy gladness well with the saints.

Homilists and vernacular poets constantly urged the 'loaned' or transitory nature of earthly life and the need to seek salvation:

> Her bið feoh læne,   her bið freond læne,
> her bið mon læne,   her bið mæg læne ...
>   ... Wel bið þam þe him are seceð,
> frofre to fæder on heofonum,   þær us eal seo fæstnung stondeð.
>   (*The Wanderer*, lines 108–9, 114–15; *ASPR*, III, p.137)

Here money is transitory, here friend is transitory, here servant is transitory, here kinsman is transitory. . . . It is well for him who seeks grace, comfort from the Father in the heavens, where all security stands for us.

In retrospect it seems that the Anglo-Saxons did indeed live pious lives. The homilist Wulfstan may have condemned the wickedness of the times he lived in, but to counter this we have many documents recording gifts to the Church of lands and of treasures such as books, vessels and hangings. Many people included bequests to the Church in their wills. Some, absorbing humanitarian principles, formally released their slaves.

The monasteries, with their extremes of asceticism, may have been enclosed; but this did not prevent the diffusion of monastic ideals among the secular population. The monastery schools educated young people, some of whom returned to secular life, and the appointment of monastic bishops brought the idealism of the Benedictines before the people. The door to the religious life was never closed and some pious seculars chose to end their days attached to a religious house, or on pilgrimage.

By the tenth century every village had its priest, and churches abounded in towns. Landowners endowed their own churches, and groups of freemen sometimes co-operated together to found churches. Parish priests were often married, which may have offended purists but was certainly taken for granted by most people. If this was decadence, it was a minor fault compared with the corruption of the English Church later in the Middle Ages, as we find it, for instance, in Chaucer's *Canterbury Tales* or Langland's *Piers Plowman*, when pardoners, friars, 'hermits' and other supernumeraries crowded England and took advantage of her more gullible inhabitants.

In late Anglo-Saxon times the Church saw that a child was baptized within nine days of birth, and it was close beside him all through his life. It provided the last rites and it received his body. Monks and nuns were interred in their convents, seculars in churchyards. Important people who had been patrons of the Church might find a resting-place in a foundation they had taken an interest in. For example, Ealdorman Byrhtnoth, hero of the Battle of Maldon, was interred at Ely. The great kings found their resting-places in churches particularly associated with their work. Thus Edgar was buried at Glastonbury, the first monastery to feel the effects of the Benedictine Reform and the home of his friend, Archbishop Dunstan; Cnut, like Alfred before him, was buried in Winchester. Edward, the last of the old dynasty, was buried in Westminster Abbey, which he had created, and which remains an important symbol of English Christianity up to the present day.

Bibliography

Alexander, J. G. G., 1976 *see* Temple, E.

Apel, W., *Gregorian Chant*, London, 1958

Bailey, R. N., *Viking Age Sculpture in Northern England*, London, 1980

Barlow, F., *Edward the Confessor*, London, 1970

Battiscombe, C. F. (ed.), *The Relics of St. Cuthbert*, Oxford, 1956

Beckwith, J., *Early Medieval English Ivories*, London, 1972

Bede, *De Temporum Ratione see* Jones, C. W.

——, *Historia Ecclesiastica see* Colgrave, B. and Mynors, R. A. B.; Sherley-Price, L.

Berg, K., 'The Gosforth Cross', *Journal of the Warburg and Courtauld Institute*, XXI, 1958, pp.27–43

Bethurum, D. (ed.), *The Homilies of Wulfstan*, Oxford, 1957

Bosworth, J. and Toller, T. N. (eds.), *An Anglo-Saxon Dictionary* and *Supplement* with enlarged Corrigenda and Addenda by A. Campbell, 2 vols., London, 1972

Brøgger, A. W., Falk, H. and Schetelig, H. (eds.), *Osbergfundet*, 2 vols., Kristiania and Oslo, 1917–28

Brown, D., 1979 *see* Hawkes, S. C., Brown, D. and Campbell, J.

Bruce-Mitford, R. L. S., *Aspects of Anglo-Saxon Archaeology*, London, 1974

——, *The Sutton Hoo Ship Burial*, 2 vols., London, 1975–8

——, *The Sutton Hoo Ship Burial: A Handbook*, 3rd ed., London, 1979

——, *The Sutton Hoo Ship Burial: Reflections after Thirty Years*, University of York Medieval Monograph Series, II, 1979

—— and Luscombe, M. R., 'The Benty Grange helmet and some other supposed Anglo-Saxon helmets', *Aspects of Anglo-Saxon Archaeology* (ed. R. Bruce-Mitford), London, 1974, pp.223–52

Caesar *see* Edwards, H. J.

Campbell, A., 1972 *see* Bosworth, J. and Toller, T. N.

Campbell, J., 1979 *see* Hawkes, S. C., Brown, D. and Campbell, J.

Caspar, E. (ed.), '*Fragmenta registri Johannes VIII, papae*', *Monumenta Germaniae Historica, Epistolae*, l, VII, Berlin, 1928, pp.293–4

Chaney, W. A., *The Cult of Kingship in Anglo-Saxon England*, Manchester, 1970

Clemoes, P. (ed.), *The Anglo-Saxons, Studies in some Aspects of their History and Culture presented to Bruce Dickins*, London, 1959

——, 1974 *see* Dodwell, C. R. and Clemoes, P.

Colgrave, B. (ed. and trans.), *The Life of Bishop Wilfrid by Eddius Stephanus*, Cambridge, 1927

Colgrave, B. (ed. and trans.), *Two Lives of St Cuthbert*, Cambridge, 1940
—— and Mynors, R. A. B. (eds.), *Bede's Ecclesiastical History of the English People*, Oxford, 1969
Collingwood, R. G. and Myres, J. N. L., *Roman Britain and the English Settlements*, 2nd ed., Oxford, 1937
Collingwood, W. G., *Northumbrian Crosses of the Pre-Norman Age*, London, 1927
Copley, G. J., *An Archaeology of South-East England*, London, 1958
Cramp, R. J. and Lang, J. T., *A Century of Anglo-Saxon Sculpture*, Newcastle upon Tyne, 1977
Davidson, H. R. E. *see* Ellis Davidson, H. R.
Deanesly, M., *Sidelights on the Anglo-Saxon Church*, London, 1962
——, *The Pre-Conquest Church in England*, 2nd ed., London, 1963
——, *A History of the Medieval Church 590–1500*, 9th ed., London, 1969
Deshusses, J., *Le Sacramentaire Grégorien*, Fribourg, 1971
Dickins, B., 'English names and Old English heathenism', *Essays and Studies*, XIX, 1933, pp.148–60
——, 'Place-names formed from animal-head names', *Place-Names of Surrey*, English Place-Name Society, XI, 1934, pp.403–6
Dobbie, E. V. K, 1931–53 *see* Krapp, G. P. and Dobbie, E. V. K.
Dodwell, C. R. and Clemoes, P. (eds.), *The Old English Illustrated Hexateuch*, Early English Manuscripts in Facsimile, XVIII, Copenhagen, 1974
Dumville, D. N., 'The Anglian collection of royal genealogies and regnal lists', *Anglo-Saxon England*, V, 1976, pp.23–50
——, 'Kingship, genealogies and regnal lists', *Early Medieval Kingship* (eds. P. H. Sawyer and I. N. Wood), Leeds, 1977, pp.72–104
Earle, J., 1892–9 *see* Plummer, C. and Earle, J.
Eddius *see* Colgrave, B.
Edwards, H. J. (trans.), *Caesar The Gallic War*, Loeb Classical Library, London, 1917
Ekwall, B. O. E., *The Concise Oxford Dictionary of English Place-Names*, Oxford, 1936
Elliott, R. W. V., 'Runes, yews, and magic', *Speculum*, XXXII, 1957, pp.250–61
——, *Runes*, Manchester, 1959
Ellis Davidson, H. R., 'The sword at the wedding', *Folklore*, LXXI, 1960, pp.1–18
——, *The Sword in Anglo-Saxon England*, Oxford, 1962
——, *Gods and Myths of Northern Europe*, Harmondsworth, 1964
——, 'Thor's hammer', *Folklore*, LXXVI, 1965, pp.1–15
——, 1965 *see* Hawkes, S. C., Ellis Davidson, H. R. and Hawkes, C.
——, *The Battle God of the Vikings*, University of York Medieval Monograph Series, I, 1972
Evison, V. I., 'The Dover, Breach Downs and Birka men', *Antiquity*, XXXIX, 1965, pp.214–17
——, 'The body in the ship at Sutton Hoo', *Anglo-Saxon Studies in Archaeology and History* (eds. S. C. Hawkes, D. Brown and J. Campbell), I, *British Archaeological Reports*, LXXII, 1979, pp.121–38

Falk, H., 1917–28 *see* Brogger, A. W., Falk, H. and Schetelig, H.

Garmonsway, G. N. and Simpson, J. (trans.), *Beowulf and its Analogues*, London, 1968

Gildas *see* Winterbottom, M.

Glob, P. V., *The Bog People* (trans. R. Bruce-Mitford), London, 1969

Godfrey, J., *The Church in Anglo-Saxon England*, Cambridge, 1962

Green, B., 1973 *see* Myres, J. N. L. and Green, B.

Grimm, J. L. C., *Teutonic Mythology* (trans. J. S. Stallybrass), 4 vols., London, 1882–8

Grinsell, L. V., 'The breaking of objects as a funerary rite', *Folklore*, LXXII, 1961, pp.475–91

Harden, D. B. (ed.), *Dark Age Britain, Studies presented to E. T. Leeds*, London, 1956

Hawkes, C., 1965 *see* Hawkes, S. C., Ellis Davidson, H. R. and Hawkes, C.

Hawkes, S. C., Brown, D. and Campbell, J. (eds.), *Anglo-Saxon Studies in Archaeology and History*, I, *British Archaeological Reports*, LXXII, 1979

——, Ellis Davidson, H. R. and Hawkes, C., 'The Finglesham man', *Antiquity*, XXXIX, 1965, pp.17–32

—— and Page, R. I., 'Swords and runes in south-east England', *Antiquaries Journal*, XLVII, 1967, pp.1–26

——, 1970 *see* Meaney, A. L. and Hawkes, S. C.

Hinton, D. A., *A Catalogue of the Anglo-Saxon Ornamental Metalwork 700–1100 in the Department of Antiquities, Ashmolean Museum*, Oxford, 1974

Hohler, C. E., 'Some service-books of the later Saxon church', *Tenth-Century Studies* (ed. D. Parsons), London and Chichester, 1975, pp.60–83

Hope-Taylor, B., *Yeavering*, London, 1977

Irwin, K. G., *The 365 Days*, London, 1965

Jones, C. W. (ed.), *Bedae Opera de Temporibus*, Cambridge, Mass., 1943

Kemble, J. M. (ed.), *The Dialogue of Salomon and Saturnus*, London, 1848

Kendrick, T. D., 'The Sutton Hoo finds', *British Museum Quarterly*, XIII, 1939, pp.111–36

—— et al. (eds.), *Evangeliorum quattuor Codex Lindisfarnensis*, 2 vols., London, 1956–60

Kirk, J. R., 'Anglo-Saxon cremation and inhumation in the Upper Thames Valley in pagan times', *Dark Age Britain, Studies presented to E. T. Leeds* (ed. D. B. Harden), London, 1956, pp.123–31

Klindt-Jensen, O., 1966 *see* Wilson, D. M. and Klindt-Jensen, O.

Krapp, G. P. and Dobbie, E. V. K. (eds.), *The Anglo-Saxon Poetic Records, A Collective Edition*, 6 vols., London and New York, 1931–53

Lang, J. T., 1977 *see* Cramp, R. J. and Lang, J. T.

Leeds, E. T., 'A Saxon village at Sutton Courtenay, Berkshire (second report)', *Archaeologia*, LXXVI, 1927, pp.59–80

Lethbridge, T. C., *Recent Excavations in Anglo-Saxon Cemeteries in Cambridgeshire and Suffolk, Cambridge Antiquarian Society Quarto Publications*, 2nd series III, Cambridge, 1931

Levison, W., *England and the Continent in the Eighth Century*, Oxford, 1946

Luce, A. A. *et al.* (eds.), *Evangeliorum quattuor Codex Durmachensis*, 2 vols., Olten, Lausanne and Freiburg, 1960

Luscombe, M. R., 1974 *see* Bruce-Mitford, R. [L. S.] and Luscombe, M. R.

Macalister, R. A. S., *Ecclesiastical Vestments*, London, 1896

Magnusson, M. (ed.), *Viking Expansion Westwards*, London, 1973

Mason, O., *The Gazetteer of England*, Newton Abbot, 1972

Mattingly, H. (trans.), *Tacitus On Britain and Germany*, Harmondsworth, 1948

Meaney, A. L., *A Gazetteer of Early Anglo-Saxon Burial Sites*, London, 1964

—— and Hawkes, S. C., *Two Anglo-Saxon Cemeteries at Winnall, Winchester, Hampshire, The Society for Medieval Archaeology Monograph Series*, IV, London, 1970

Mearns, J., *The Canticles of the Christian Church, Eastern and Western, in Early and Medieval Times*, Cambridge, 1914

Mynors, R. A. B., 1969 *see* Colgrave, B. and Mynors, R. A. B.

Myres, J. N. L., *A Corpus of Anglo-Saxon Pottery of the Pagan Period*, 2 vols., Cambridge, 1977

—— and Green, B., *The Anglo-Saxon Cemeteries of Caistor-by-Norwich and Markshall, Norfolk, Reports of the Research Committee of the Society of Antiquaries of London*, XXX, Oxford, 1973

——, 1937 *see* Collingwood, R. G. and Myres, J. N. L.

Neckel, G. (ed.), *Edda. Die Lieder des Codex Regius*, 2 vols., Heidelberg, 1914–27

Page, R. I., 'The Old English rune *ear*', *medium Ævum*, XXX, 1961, pp.65–79

——, 1967 *see* Hawkes, S. C. and Page, R. I.

——, *An Introduction to English Runes*, London, 1973

Parsons, D. (ed.), *Tenth-Century Studies*, London and Chichester, 1975

Pirie, E. J. E., *Coins in Yorkshire Collections, Sylloge of Coins of the British Isles*, XXI, London, 1975

Plummer, C. and Earle, J. (eds.), *Two of the Saxon Chronicles Parallel*, 2 vols., Oxford, 1892–9

Raine, J. (ed.), *The Historians of the Church of York and its Archbishops*, I, *Rolls Series*, London, 1879

Reaney, P. H., *The Origin of English Place-Names*, London, 1961

Robertson, A. J. (ed. and trans.), *Anglo-Saxon Charters*, Cambridge, 1939

Ryan, J. S., 'Othin in England', *Folklore*, LXXIV, 1963, pp.460–80

Sawyer, P. H. and Wood, I. N. (eds.), *Early Medieval Kingship*, Leeds, 1977

Schetelig, H., 1917–28 *see* Brøgger, A. W., Falk, H. and Schetelig, H.

Schipper, J. M. (ed.), *König Alfreds Übersetzung von Bedas Kirchengeschichte, Bibliothek der angelsächsischen Prosa*, IV, Leipzig, 1899

Schramm, P. E., *A History of the English Coronation* (trans. L. G. Wickham Legg), Oxford, 1937

Sedgefield, W. J. (trans.), *King Alfred's Old English Version of Boethius 'De Consolatione Philosophiae'*, Oxford, 1899

Sherley-Price, L. (trans.), *Bede A History of the English Church and People*, Harmondsworth, 1955

Simpson, J., 1968 *see* Garmonsway, G. N. and Simpson, J.

Sisam, K., 'Anglo-Saxon royal genealogies', *Proceedings of the British Academy*, XXXIX, 1953, pp.287–348

Smith, A. W., 'The luck in the head: a problem in English folklore', *Folklore*, LXXIII, 1962, pp. 13–24

Smith, R. A., *British Museum. A Guide to the Anglo-Saxon and Foreign Teutonic Antiquities*, London, 1923

Stanley, E. G., 'The search for Anglo-Saxon paganism', *Notes and Queries*, CCIX, 1964, pp.204–9, 242–50, 282–7, 324–31, 455–63; CCX, 1965, pp.9–17, 203–7, 285–93, 322–7

Stenton, F. [M.], *Anglo-Saxon England*, 2nd ed., Oxford, 1947

Stevenson, W. H. (ed.), *Asser's Life of King Alfred*, with article ... by D. Whitelock, Oxford, 1959

Storms, G., *Anglo-Saxon Magic*, The Hague, 1948

Stubbs, W. (ed.), *Memorials of Saint Dunstan, Rolls Series*, London, 1874

—— (ed.), *Willelmi Malmesbiriensis monachi de gestis regum Anglorum*, 2 vols., *Rolls Series*, London, 1887–9

Swanton, M. J. (ed.), *The Dream of the Rood*, Manchester, 1970

Sweet, H. (ed.), *The Oldest English Texts, Early English Text Society*, Original Series LXXXIII, Oxford, 1885

—— (ed.), *King Alfred's West-Saxon Version of Gregory's Pastoral Care*, *Early English Text Society*, Original Series XLV, L, reprinted in one volume, London, 1958

Symons, T. (ed. and trans.), *Regularis Concordia, Nelson's Medieval Classics*, London, etc., 1953

Tacitus *see* Mattingly, H.

Taylor, H. M., 'Tenth-century church building in England and on the continent', *Tenth-Century Studies* (ed. D. Parsons), London and Chichester, 1975, pp. 141–68

—— and J., *Anglo-Saxon Architecture*, 2 vols., Cambridge, 1965

Temple, E., *Anglo-Saxon Manuscripts 900–1066, A Survey of Manuscripts Illuminated in the British Isles* (ed. J. G. G. Alexander), II, London, 1976

Thorpe, B. (ed.), *Ancient Laws and Institutes of England*, London, 1840

Toller, T. N., 1972 *see* Bosworth, J. and Toller, T. N.

Weinberger, G. [W.], *Anicii Mantii Severini Boethii Philosophiae Consolationis, Corpus Scriptorum Ecclesiasticorum Latinorum*, LXVII, Part 4, Vienna and Leipzig, 1934

Wells, C., 'A study of cremation', *Antiquity*, XXXIV, 1960, pp.29–37

Whitelock, D. (ed.), *English Historical Documents*, I, London, 1955

——, 'The dealings of the kings of England with Northumbria in the tenth and eleventh centuries', *The Anglo-Saxons, Studies in some Aspects of their History and Culture presented to Bruce Dickins*, (ed. P. Clemoes), London, 1959, pp.70–88

William of Malmesbury *see* Stubbs, W.

Wilson, H. A., *The Gelasian Sacramentary*, Oxford, 1894

Wilson, D. M., *Anglo-Saxon Ornamental Metalwork, 700–1100 in the British Museum, Catalogue of Antiquities of the later Saxon period*, I, London, 1964

—— and Klindt-Jensen, O., *Viking Art*, London, 1966

Winterbottom, M. (ed. and trans.), *Gildas The Ruin of Britain and Other Works*, London and Chichester, 1978

Wood, I. N., 1977 *see* Sawyer, P. H. and Wood, I. N.

Wormald, F., *The Benedictional of St Ethelwold*, London, 1959

Wright, D. H. (ed.), *The Vespasian Psalter, Early English Manuscripts in Facsimile*, XIV, Copenhagen, 1967

The principal sources for quotations are abbreviated as follows:

ASPR	*The Anglo-Saxon Poetic Records*, 6 vols., eds. G. P. Krapp and E. V. K. Dobbie
Beowulf and its Analogues	trans. G. N. Garmonsway and J. Simpson (some spelling has been altered for the sake of consistency)
De Excidio	Gildas *De Excidio* in *Gildas The Ruin of Britain and Other Works*, ed. and trans. M. Winterbottom
EHD	*English Historical Documents*, I, ed. D. Whitelock
Germania	Tacitus *Germania* in *Tacitus on Britain and Germany*, trans. H. Mattingly
HE	Bede *Historia Ecclesiastica* in *Bede A History of the English Church and People*, trans. L. Sherley-Price
Regularis Concordia	ed. and trans. T. Symons

The spelling of Anglo-Saxon personal names can vary. They have been standardized here according to the usage in Stenton's *Anglo-Saxon England*.

Titles of OE poems are those given by modern editors. There are no titles in the manuscripts. All translations from OE are the author's unless otherwise specified.

Index